LITERARY HISTORY

AN

MLQ

READER

DURHAM & LONDON 1999

T

10021927 1 0

Typeset in New Baskerville by Running Feet Books
Library of Congress Cataloging-in-Publication Data appear
on the last printed page of this book.

These essays originally were published in the following issues of *Modern Language Quarterly*: Nancy Armstrong and Leonard Tennenhouse, "A Novel Nation; or, How to Rethink Modern England as an Emergent Culture," 54:3 (September 1993); Catherine Gallagher, "Nobody's Story: Gender, Property, and the Rise of the Novel," 53:3 (September 1992); Jonathan Brody Kramnick, "Reading Shakespeare's Novels: Literary History and Cultural Politics in the Lennox-Johnson Debate," 55:4 (December 1994); Jon Klancher, "Godwin and the Republican Romance: Genre, Politics, and Contingency in Cultural History," 56:2 (June 1995); Jill Anne Kowalik, "Feminine Identity Formation in *Wilhelm Meisters Lehrjahre*," 53:2 (June 1992); Jerome McGann, "Mary Robinson and the Myth of Sappho," 56:1 (March 1995); Thomas M. Kavanagh, "Reading the Moment and the Moment of Reading in Graffigny's *Lettres d'une péruvienne*," 55:2 (June 1994); Ruth Perry, "De-familiarizing the Family; or, Writing Family History from Literary Sources," 55:4 (December 1994); Christie McDonald, "The Anxiety of Change: Reconfiguring Family Relations in Beaumarchais's Trilogy," 55:1 (March 1994); Michael B. Prince, "The Eighteenth-Century Beauty Contest," 55:3 (September 1994); Sanford Budick, "Descartes's Cogito, Kant's Sublime, and Rembrandt's Philosophers: Cultural Transmission as Occasion for Freedom," 58:1 (March 1997).

CONTENTS

A journal is made by its authors. My greatest debt is to the writers of these essays—all freely submitted and evaluated (mostly anonymously) by readers—who were willing to share their work with *MLQ* and to await the results. The journal and the book would not appear without the devoted labors of the assistant editors: Caroline Klumpar, who had the lion's share; James McNelis, Graham Shutt, and Michael Magoolaghan, each responsible for some of the essays in the collection; and Marguerite Finnigan, who is finishing the process. The exacting copy editors, Chris Mazzara and Paula Dragosh, polished and filed tirelessly and kept the office (and sometimes the authors) amused as they did so. The index was Tedra Osell's first; I can only wish her equal good fortune in finding assistants to index her books. Finally, the decision to publish this collection was made by a consensus of three wise men at the press: Reynolds Smith, the voice of truth, Steve Cohn, the voice of hope, and Ken Wissoker, the voice of good sense. What a team!

Marshall Brown

Introduction:

Provocations

Roger Chartier will be the exemplary villain of my piece. In a scrupulously argued chapter of his book on the cultural origins of the French Revolution, Chartier has asked just the right question, "Do Books Make Revolutions?" and has given just the wrong answer.[1] They did not make the French Revolution, as he deduces by studying the diffusion of radical philosophical literature in the late eighteenth century. Philosophy was never very clearly distinguished from licentious ephemera, and its public consisted as much of wealthy aristocrats as of protorevolutionaries. Voltaire and the others were sufficiently diverse and even evasive that they could be grist for anyone's mill. It is "impossible to conclude . . . that their interpretation could be reduced to any one simple ideological statement" (87); consequently, "the crux of the matter is not the content of 'philosophical' books" (91). Rather than books making the Revolution, the exact opposite happened: "It was the Revolution that 'made' the books" (89), in the sense that it both selected its precursors and determined how they were subsequently understood. Paving the way, he argues, was a breakdown of "a communitarian and respectful relation to the book" in favor of "a freer, more

---

1 Chartier, *The Cultural Origins of the French Revolution*, trans. Lydia G. Cochrane (Durham, N.C.: Duke University Press, 1991), 67–91.

1

casual, and more critical way of reading" (90) that encouraged thinking readers to doubt what they read. Chartier's Revolution was made
by liberated subjects whose heightened literacy emancipated them
from their books.

The essays in the present collection, all originally published in *Modern Language Quarterly: A Journal of Literary History*, amount to a collective response to arguments like Chartier's.[2] When John Coldewey and
I added the subtitle to the journal's masthead, we envisioned a home
for essays motivated by a belief in the effective power of imaginative
texts. As the introduction to the redesigned *MLQ* declares, "Human
expressions do not make history, but they do make history human; it is
our texts that shape events, turning them, for better and for worse,
into the ongoing equipment of our experience."[3]

There is no doubt that in Chartier's terms "books" did not in any
sense "make" the "Revolution." But that is because each of the terms I
have highlighted acquires in his usage a meaning different from,
indeed almost antithetical to, the meaning that an *MLQ* essay posits.
For as texts of literary history, books are not reducible to their content
or their ideological statements, simple or otherwise. The debate content of books never "makes" history, because it is always in dispute, and
readers have always been free to choose the books they read or at a
minimum—even in regimes of the most extreme censorship—to read
with eyes averted. Nor could books "make" a revolution if a revolution
is understood as a thing made. That would be what philosophers call a
category error. No one imagines that books met in the Tennis Court or
guillotined the King. But even the grandest local events are in themselves merely rebellions or revolts. They only become revolutions when
they are known as such. To the extent that we allow ideas, sentiments,
and states of feeling to have a history, books surely make revolutions;
nothing else quite could. The making, however, then manifests itself in

---

2 Two of the essays actually appeared prior to the refocusing and redesign of the
journal (nominally in 1992, actually in 1994), but were published with its imminent definition of mission in mind and hence can be considered part of its current
project.

3 "Prelude, Chorale, and Fugue," *Modern Language Quarterly* 54 (1993): 2.
Repeated in the first *MLQ* anthology, *The Uses of Literary History*, ed. Marshall Brown
(Durham, N.C.: Duke University Press, 1995), vii.

intangibles. In denying that books make revolutions Chartier, consciously or not, materializes all the essential terms. Chartier—and he
stands for many others—does it brilliantly, with all his facts and figures in place, but it's a Gradgrindish endeavor.

The underlying term at issue—much fought over in today's academy—is culture.[4] Writing in extended response to Daniel Mornet's
Intellectual Origins of the French Revolution (1933), Chartier wants to
recover the cultural sphere as a domain for historical investigation. But
culture, for Chartier, means "practices" and "social mechanisms" (18).
In endeavoring "to move from the 'intellectual' to the 'cultural'" (18),
he appears to divorce the cultural from the intellectual altogether.
Between "social and intellectual positions . . . there is neither continuity nor necessity" (18). Such a reduction of the cultural to the social,
and within the social to the realm of practice, is a general trend in
what today is often, perversely, termed cultural studies. The aim of
Modern Language Quarterly is to reverse that trend.

MLQ is devoted to the ghosts in the cultural machine. The occult
force in "Do Books Make Revolutions" is "the reader." Citing a German
theory of a *Leserevolution*, Chartier endorses what he cannot explain yet
somehow cannot do without: "Debatable and much debated, this hypothesis nonetheless accounts adequately for the transformation of reading
practices in eighteenth-century France" (90). Featureless and agentless,
reading "became" different ("a silent and individual act") when an
older form "gave way to" a newer "way of reading," which "became widespread" and "a new relationship between reader and text was forged"
(90–91). That something distinctive had to forge these readers—that
they had to read particular works—and that in fact (on Chartier's evidence) the new-style texts of the *philosophes* with their new, pluralist
characteristics were what made the new reading possible or even
inevitable—none of this quite gets said, in his book. It does get said in
this book, not in direct critique of Chartier, but in implicit response to
the presuppositions of his entire mode. In place of his unreadable
books and bookless readers, read what Nancy Armstrong and Leonard

4 For representative—strong and consequently polemical—presentations of
debates about "culture" see Alain Finkielkraut, *The Defeat of the Mind*, trans. Judith
Friedlander (New York: Columbia University Press, 1995), and Geoffrey Hartman, *The
Fateful Question of Culture* (New York: Columbia University Press, 1997), 27–60.

Tennenhouse have to say about the force of books in transforming, indeed revolutionizing, our cultures: "We believe that texts addressing a community of readers had to precede the self-definition of the literate sectors of the population as readers first and foremost" (21). Chartier's last chapter, "Do Revolutions Have Cultural Origins?" (169–92), builds on a thesis of Lawrence Stone's; read Ruth Perry's sharp critique of Stone's tone-deaf conflation of texts with their contents. And while Chartier's social-material knife surreptitiously undercuts what Stone takes to be "intellectual and ideological" (169) elements of culture, Perry shows how apt it is that he suborns Stone to his purposes. For both historians read literally what must be read literarily, imaginatively. The essays in this book reinstate the imagination without which culture is, finally, just nature.

Some of these essays trace origins. Catherine Gallagher describes an "almost inevitable" evolution in fictional narrative that "played a very real role in the creation of the modern self" (42). Michael Prince locates the moment when "the beauty contest takes its modern form" (207). And while Jonathan Brody Kramnick appears to reverse the priority in arguing for "the social origins of literary history" (67), he edges the social toward imaginative culture almost as much as Chartier and Stone edge the cultural toward the materially social: "The particular conjuncture of 'novels and romances' *brings about and informs* the language of Johnson's formation of the vernacular canon" (66; my emphasis). In a conjuncture of disputed words and ideas, writers and readers become the engines transforming the societies in which they are housed.

Not all the essays concern evolutions in this fashion, but all encounter history as a problem: they confront both the pastness of the past and the mystery of its presence to us. Coming to the eighteenth century as a Victorianist, Gallagher finds the earlier novels unfamiliar, disorienting, even alienating.[5] Literary evidence "has the potential to

---

5 It is interesting to confront Gallagher's discussion of "nobody" with chapter 2 ("Nobody's Power") of Patricia M. Spacks's *The Adolescent Idea: Myths of Youth and the Adult Imagination* (New York, Basic Books, 1981), 19–52, where the same text from Burney's diary is quoted in connection with an argument that the topic has remained constant while the situation of Nobody (the adolescent girl) has deteriorated. See

de-familiarize our unthinking assumptions" and hence to bring "to life attitudes . . . that are very different from our own" (Perry 164–71). Thus, Jerome McGann's reconstruction of the "cultural value" of senti- mental poetry (115) works to recover what he has elsewhere called a "somewhat lost world."[6] Conversely, Jill Kowalik undertakes to legiti- mate a retrospective psychoanalysis by thematizing "the function of the past in the present" (90). Better to lay the wager of anachronism con- sciously, with a theory of incorporation and individuation, than to ignore the dilemmas of the historian.

The essays, then, engage a "dialogue with th[e] past" (McDonald 203). However, their dialogue is neither a New Historicist agon nor a Gadamerian accommodation. Rather, because literary history is always surprising us with the freshness of its texts, dialogue should be thought of as dramatic repartee, in which the past is never quite seized yet never altogether escapes. Hence the element of freedom, spontaneity, or unpredictability that colors several of the contributions. Contin- gency is Thomas Kavanagh's presiding deity; in Jon Klancher's account "the unheard-of" becomes the opening into the future of "potential conjunctures of thought and action yet to be made" (86, 82); and San- ford Budick speculatively localizes the dialectic of freedom and cul- tural transmission in Kant's encounters with Descartes and Rembrandt. As McDonald rightly suggests, teleology teeters in the balance; it lies as much in the past's appeal to us as in its resistance to being comman- deered by the now.

McGann enjoins us to read closely, but not in order to fall into the embrace of a hermeneutic circle. Rather, as he has said in many books, the shock is in recognizing the incommensurability of the objects that remain vitally historical. The history in these essays lies in the fascination with what Budick calls "resistance in freedom" (266). The past is not transparent (Perry 168); that is why it forces us to pause and look.

---

also what a distinguished eighteenth-century scholar has written in *MLQ*, apropos of Foucault and the "nonlegibility of the past": Eric Rothstein, "Foucault, Discursive History, and the Auto-Affection of God," *Modern Language Quarterly* 55 (1994): 414.

6 Jerome McGann, *The Poetics of Sensibility: A Revolution in Literary Style* (Oxford: Clarendon, 1996), 1.

These essays represent a broad cross-section of eighteenth-century literary history. They focus on different parts of the century; on the classical triad of novel, drama, and lyric poetry as well as on aesthetic and philosophical essays; on Britain, France, and Germany; on the intersection of literary studies with history, philosophy, psychology, and visual arts; on feminism, nationalism, and domestic ideology; on precursors and consequences, determinations and evasions. Part of this collection's aim is to present possibilities for studying the ever-new eighteenth century. And part, extending beyond the particular period focus, is to project a spirit of inquiry in literary history generally.

In rereading the essays and pondering what this collection and *Modern Language Quarterly* stand for, I am struck by a consistency of spirit that had previously escaped my awareness. The fascinating yet resistant past that they all evoke is not an archive, nor is it an echo chamber resonating the interests of our day. When Kramnick says that history has "imaginary authority" (58), he is signaling its claims toward us: it is a *provocation*, compelling because never entirely surrendering its secrets. The essays all register unheard voices; Perry's *cri du sang* is a metaphor for the uncanny appeal of our beloved and estranged relation, the past.

The beauty contest is another metaphor. In one way or another, all the essays concern self-realization. Literary history records change as make-up or make-over, not as spectacle or progress. Utterance is the very identity of texts, so in making themselves heard, the voices first become what they are. As Kavanagh's essay preeminently argues, texts become beautiful and historical at the same moment, and only for the (longer or shorter) moment when they are heard. He might well have cited that great lover of chance, Stendhal: the essays are crystallizations constituting texts from the past as agents in history, partners in our own identity romances but not part of us. The interpreter as literary historian brings texts out, and into movement.

Such metaphors will do for a time, but not without meanings. In historicizing their provocative texts, the critics in this collection employ three closely related strategies: the lost are found, the subordinate authorized, the private published. Recovery in the most literal sense is practiced by Klancher and Budick: reading an unread text or unearthing an unsuspected source unlocks the door to "cultural realization" (Budick 236). Following Walter Benjamin, Prince generalizes from the unknown to the overlooked or minor as "at once marginal and representative" (220). But, really, any essay aiming to bring a text to life by bringing out its nature must seek some respect in which it has been minor, kept from itself, stalled in its unfolding. Thus Kowalik finds what no one has found in *Wilhelm Meisters Lehrjahre*, and McDonald reads Beaumarchais's masterpieces of premarital desire in the light of his minorpieces of postmarital exhaustion, helping them to grow up in the process.

Although there are many kinds of literary subordination, those instituted by gender hierarchies have been the most studied in recent years, and are so here as well. For those from the English or French academic spheres, the degree of subordination in Germany may come as a shock. Kowalik's essay is the most contemporary in the volume, precisely because German women's lives were so insignificant hitherto. Goethe buries them because their real counterparts had nothing to show. That, at least, is the message of Silvia Bovenschen's depressing, and by now classic, study of "imagined femininity." Framing her book (in the absence of any usable German figure) with evocations of Virginia Woolf, Bovenschen demonstrates how woman was a mere appendage—a reduced or supplemental existence, object, or idea but not agent. There is no history of women, she concludes, except as the "history of feminine ahistoricity."[7] Women were allowed as little substance then as in Bovenschen's own day and culture. As Kowalik demonstrates, literary history then becomes a recovery of the history *in* literature rather than the history *of* literature. In England the situation was less grim, though that appears only to involve greater resources of non-personhood or more techniques of "presence-by-absence" (McGann 135). As the subordinate, the feminine exercises occult virtue in all the different senses of the phrase. "Special in their extreme typicality," as Gallagher has phrased it in the book that grew from the essay reprinted here, women become keys to historical discovery or emergence.[8] Kavanagh slyly exposes the subreption that takes woman as the

7 *Die imaginierte Weiblichkeit: Exemplarische Untersuchungen zu kulturgeschichtlichen und literarischen Präsentationsformen des Weiblichen* (Frankfurt: Suhrkamp, 1971), 265.

8 Gallagher, *Nobody's Story: The Vanishing Acts of Women Writers in the Marketplace, 1670–1820* (Berkeley: University of California Press, 1994), xv. The book does not include the kernel essay from *MLQ*.

answer rather than the question, and hence reaffirms the provocative, antidogmatic character that (to my mind) the other essays here reprinted presuppose.

The final modality I would highlight in these essays is generalization. Private and (in the privative senses of the terms) merely formal or psychological in their appearance, literary works become historical when they spread their wings. A contingency becomes a norm (Prince 234), the local calls out the universal (McDonald 174), fiction universalizes privacy, and the separation from community "becomes the basis for [renewed] community existence" (Armstrong and Tennenhouse 26). As these examples show, generalization is the trickiest of these resources of the literary historian. Wedding "the longest philosophical view . . . with full, intense, and immediate awareness" (McGann 135) runs risks of divorce on all sides. Time reclaims a role as mediator, notably when the nation, as the horizon of individual destinies, becomes an imagined past (Armstrong and Tennenhouse) or else an unrealized future able to "refute the necessity of British history" (Klancher 82).

Kant's term for an imagined past or future is a regulative ideal. In contradistinction to a merely external history of literature or a merely pragmatic history of reading, the literary history practiced in these essays interrogates determinations by fact or by law and regulates the existent in terms of the possible. The "return to formal analysis and close reading" that McGann explicitly advocates (117) is critical, again in a Kantian sense. It engages with history as the resistance to positive truth, in a spirit of unlimited discovery and renewal.

A Novel Nation; or, How to Rethink Modern England as an Emergent Culture

Nancy Armstrong &

Leonard Tennenhouse

In a note to *Discipline and Punish*, Foucault declares his intention to "study the birth of the prison only in the French penal system. Differences in historical developments and institutions would make a detailed comparative examination too burdensome and any attempt to describe the phenomenon as a whole too schematic."[1] By giving Jeremy Bentham's panopticon the status of the "after" in his "before-and-after" scenes of punishment, however, Foucault invites his readers to regard characteristically modern institutional practices as pan-European. What he discusses is not only the kind of writing peculiar to the late seventeenth and eighteenth centuries in France but also the cultural apparatus for which an Englishman's architectural drawings can supply the most effective explanatory metaphor. Neither in practice, then, nor in theory can he stay within the boundaries of a national history and still describe the process by which knowledge gained ascendancy over other forms of power and consolidated a national culture.

In *The History of Sexuality*, Foucault argues that the migration of discipline to the center of a field of symbolic practices coincided with the rise of writing to dominance over the field, accompanied by a funda-

---

1 Foucault, *Discipline and Punish: The Birth of the Prison*, trans. Alan Sheridan (New York: Vintage, 1979), 309.

9

mental change in the nature of the individual. Writing began to represent speech, which in turn presupposed someone thinking those thoughts and putting them into words. The inversion of what had been a rather loose relationship between speech and writing relocated the source of language within the body of a modern individual; writing became one's self-objectification. The rather sudden appearance of the "self-in-writing" established a bond between text and writing subject that made writing not only capable of regulating subjects but also responsible for ruptures that distinguish the modern period from all earlier moments in Western history. Foucault's genealogies provide us with marvelous accounts of how such cultural institutions as the family and the police joined forces with the new national educational system and medical profession to produce the very kind of individuated subjects that constitute a modern nation-state. By healing their bodies, educating their minds, or socializing their behavior, modern institutions sought to make individuals healthy, literate, and normal. They also saw to it that they would be English, French, Dutch, Spanish, or Portuguese.

Yet, in describing the interiorized and interiorizing power of the new disciplinary practices, or what in the first volume of *The History of Sexuality* he calls "discourse," Foucault does not say how the newly individuated and sexualized person acquired the collective identity that constituted nationality. He does suggest that those who occupied the centers of particular institutions produced the various discourses we associate with modern culture and so formulated the conditions for belonging to the nation. He also declares that they were already subject to the gaze, to discourse, and therefore to the state. However, Foucault allows decidedly traditional concepts of individual and nation to linger in his genealogies precisely where he wants to identify the ruptures into which old categories vanished and out of which entirely new ones emerged.[2] He cannot tell us how the idea of the nation came to serve

2 Foucault writes, "If genealogy in its own right gives rise to questions concerning our native land, native language, or the laws that govern us, its intention is to reveal the heterogenous systems which, masked by the self, inhibit the formation of any form of identity" ("Nietzsche, Genealogy, History," in *Language, Counter-memory, Practice: Selected Essays and Interviews*, ed. Donald F. Bouchard, trans. Donald F. Bouchard and Sherry Simon [Ithaca, N.Y.: Cornell University Press, 1977], 162).

interests implicitly hostile to those of monarchy. Nor can he tell us much about the relationship between the emergent nations and mass culture.

The double omission in Foucault's thought is symptomatic. For all the new work in minority discourse and postcolonial culture, we have yet to understand our own peculiar situation as a nation that was both a colony and a colonial power. What ideological work does written English perform for such a nation? And for all the revisionism in historiography, literary history, and cultural studies, we have yet to confront the problem of mass mediation squarely. How was it put in place? How did it affect its consumers? By positioning individuals in relation to themselves and to each other, how did mass culture redefine their collective identity? Here we offer the theoretical justification for addressing such questions and sketch the contours of an argument for the next generation of scholars to substantiate, correct, appropriate, or simply toss out. Rather than make statements provable within any single essay, however, we outline a sequence of moves that adapts Foucault's notion of discourse to the task at hand.[3]

Being English in British North America

Marxism attacks poststructuralism, especially Foucault, for representing entire cultures in terms of elite texts, as if their textualizing procedures possessed some innate capacity to displace people, things, and all the other ways in which they have been and perhaps still are represented.[4] Indeed, Foucault never does explain why certain kinds of writing, technologies of reproduction, and methods of distributing information suddenly migrated to the center of the Western cultural-historical stage. Instead, he concentrates on the moments when they underwent change and explains how they did so. For him, the only true history is the history of textualizing practices. In search of a cause

3 This essay recapitulates the argument underlying *The Imaginary Puritan: Literature, Intellectual Labor, and the History of Personal Life* (Berkeley: University of California Press, 1992), in which we rethink the so-called rise of the English middle class as the beginning of mass-mediated culture.

4 See, for example, Bryan Palmer, *Descent into Discourse: The Reification of Language and the Writing of Social History* (Philadelphia: Temple University Press, 1990).

for the emergence of what Foucault calls "discourse," we turn to Benedict Anderson's *Imagined Communities*. As far afield from French poststructuralism as it seems in method and subject matter, not to mention in presuppositions about language, Anderson's is perhaps the one
study of the modern period to describe the formation of national cultures as the direct result of a specific type of literacy. Sharply at odds
with notions of causality that would place his account within the
parameters of European social or cultural history, Anderson readily
identifies a cause for modern nationalism, because he is interested in
the nations that emerged from European colonies rather than in European nationality per se. To explain how the colonies' relation to the
European metropoles made writing in the print vernacular far more
important than speech when it came to determining the national identity of colonial Europeans, Anderson inadvertently provides a model
that obtains for modern England, too, and eventually for the rest of
Europe. His logic can be brought to bear on the overargued and still-
unsubstantiated questions of the origins of the English middle class
and the reason for its so-called rise.[5]

According to Anderson, an entirely new kind of nation came into
being as the functionaries and bureaucrats who did the business of
Europe throughout the New World produced and distributed information in vernacular English, French, Spanish, Dutch, and Portuguese
within their territories and between those territories and their respective countries of origin. In the seventeenth century, Anderson reminds
us, "the diversity of spoken languages, those languages that for their
speakers were (and are) the warp and woof of their lives, was immense;
so immense, indeed, that had print-capitalism sought to exploit each
potential oral vernacular market, it would have remained a capitalism
of petty proportions" (46–47). However, he also reminds us that the
many idiolects quickly dwindled to a handful once phonemes were
represented graphically. As print vernaculars circulated among readers who no longer lived in their countries of origin, print called into

---

5 Anderson, *Imagined Communities: Reflections on the Origin and Spread of Nationalism*
(London: Verso, 1983). Anderson's logic is discussed in Nancy Armstrong, "Reclassi-
fying Clarissa: Fiction and the Making of the Modern Middle Class," in *The Clarissa
Project: The Critical Controversy—New Commentaries*, ed. Edward Copeland and Carol
Houlihan Flynn (New York: AMS Press, 1998).

being a new individual who understood himself or herself as part of a community of individuals who shared a body of knowledge acquired from newspapers and novels. The information that crossed the Atlantic connected the New World European to Europe. It distinguished individuals who could read and write in what would soon become standard English, French, Spanish, Dutch, or Portuguese from both the non-Europeans among whom they lived and worked and the Europeans of other nationalities who carried on the business of the nation in their own vernaculars.

But their peculiar kind of literacy also made those who were of English, French, Spanish, Dutch, or Portuguese birth understand what they shared with the people with whom they lived and worked in America. They were bound together by their exclusion from the homeland. Though a decided minority in relation to those with whom they did business in Europe as well as to the indigenous populations among whom they lived in America, according to Anderson, the New World Europeans "constituted simultaneously a colonial community and an upper class" (59). "Neither economic interest, Liberalism, nor Enlightenment could, or did, create *in themselves* the *kind*, or shape, of imagined community to be defended from these regimes' depredation; to put it another way, none provided the framework of a new consciousness—the scarcely-seen periphery of its vision—as opposed to the centre-field objects of its admiration or disgust. In accomplishing *this* specific task, pilgrim creole functionaries and provincial creole printmen played the decisive historic role" (65). New World nationalism as a community created and sustained by a half dozen print vernaculars is potentially compatible with Foucault's story of the formation of modern institutions.

However differently they may identify a cause or place the emphasis in their accounts of the rise of writing, both Anderson and Foucault argue that the emergence of print cultures cannot be distinguished from the emergence of a class of people whose purpose in life was to reform themselves and others in compliance with abstract norms of thought, speech, and behavior conveyed in writing. By staging this transitional chapter of English history in North America, however, Anderson shows us certain things about modern English culture that Foucault does not. For example, as writing provided an umbilical cord between the monarch's agents in the New World and bureaucracies in Europe, it began to take on a life in the New World apart from England and apart from speech.[6] The extension of writing to New England made it the primary means of holding together a nation that existed on both sides of the ocean. As print vernaculars acquired such importance, furthermore, they empowered the people who controlled the means of producing information over and above those, presumably, who could whisper in the ear of the nobility. This change in what writing did effectively changed what it was. By consolidating into a readership those who possessed a specific cultural and linguistic competence, Anderson argues, writing produced an "imagined community" that became the basis of British-American nationalism.

Like most historical scholars, Anderson allows modern national boundaries to organize his view of early modern culture, and so he has no difficulty abandoning his account of European nationality precisely when the European nations were about to change significantly. He shifts his focus to America. He never finds it necessary to consider how England or any of the seventeenth-century monarchies became the great imperial bureaucracies of the nineteenth and twentieth centuries, more similar to than different from the United States. Anderson notes that print vernaculars had been available in England well before print began to proliferate in British America; still, he acknowledges,

6 New England had a higher rate of literacy and more presses in the seventeenth century than England. For discussions of the print culture of colonial New England see, for example, David Cressy, *Coming Over: Migration and Communication between England and New England in the Seventeenth Century* (Cambridge: Cambridge University Press, 1987); Ian K. Steele, *The English Atlantic, 1675–1740: An Exploration of Communication and Community* (New York: Oxford University Press, 1986); David D. Hall, *World of Wonder, Days of Judgment: Popular Religious Belief in Early New England* (Cambridge, Mass.: Harvard University Press, 1990); Michael Warner, *The Letters of the Republic: Publication and the Public Sphere in Eighteenth-Century America* (Cambridge, Mass.: Harvard University Press, 1990); Richard D. Brown, *Knowledge Is Power: The Diffusion of Information in Early America, 1700–1865* (New York: Oxford University Press, 1989); George Parker Winship, *The Cambridge Press, 1638–1693* (Philadelphia: University of Pennsylvania Press, 1945); Douglas C. Murtrig, *A History of Printing in the United States*, vol. 1 (New York: Bowker, 1936); and George Emery Littlefield, *The Early Massachusetts Press, 1638–1711*, 2 vols. (Boston: Club of Old Volumes, 1907). Hall and Warner are particularly useful for explaining the importance of print in New England, while Brown offers the most detailed discussion of the means by which information was distributed in the colonies.

"nothing suggests that any deep-seated ideological, let alone proto-national, impulses underlay this vernacularization where it occurred" (44). Print vernaculars simply provided "well positioned would-be absolutist monarchs" with an instrument of centralization; "there was no idea of systematically imposing the language on . . . various subject populations" (44). But when the instruments of centralization were extended overseas, they were indeed systematically imposed. By thinking forward across the Atlantic, we can identify the conditions under which print not only became more important than speech in defining a community but also transformed the very notion of community from the group with whom one lived and worked to a disembodied and generalized readership.

Becoming a Modern Individual in Europe

To consider how writing changed those who used it once it had acquired the power to constitute a nation, however, it is necessary to think backward, from British North America to England. Anderson is not concerned with the kind of individual that the new national literacy produced. He simply assumes that such an individual preexisted the fact of writing. Foucault, in contrast, refuses to locate agency in authors or in the class from which they come. He inverts the functions of cause and effect that organize traditional accounts of modernity and tries to imagine how writing and the institutional practices that gave it the power of discourse in turn wrote both the subjects (*The History of Sexuality: An Introduction*) and human objects (*Discipline and Punish*) of knowledge. If Foucault is among the handful who locate agency in print itself on the grounds that it permanently changes the very nature of those who use it, then he is practically alone in identifying the most personal recesses of the human subject as precisely the territory that writing opened to social exploration and conquest. By resisting the impulse to posit an economic cause for a textual effect, he forces his readers to reconsider the relationship among personal feelings, the government external to one's self, and the textualizing practices generally assumed to mediate them.

Foucault begins his multivolume *History of Sexuality* by invoking the conventional wisdom that the advent of modernity was marked by a puritanical censorship leveled against individual sexuality: "The seventeenth century . . . was the beginning of an age of repression emblematic of what we call the bourgeois societies, an age which perhaps we still have not completely left behind. Calling sex by its name thereafter became more difficult and more costly."[7] England, arguably, provides the clearest example for this phase in Foucault's larger story of modernity, as it does for the unfolding of capitalism. Although the monarch's official censor was thrown out during the interregnum, rigid censorship was nevertheless exercised under Cromwell. (The double meaning of the term *puritan* testifies to the pervasive and long-lasting cultural impact that moderns attribute to his regime.) With the Restoration, the Licensing Act was renewed, and control of the press again passed to the licenser, who was appointed by the secretary of state. If the office of licenser was now answerable to Parliament, however, continued restrictions on the number of printers, on where presses could function, and on what could be licensed for print indicate that an equally harsh system of censorship was nevertheless in effect. After 1695, when Parliament refused to renew the Licensing Act, the government could no longer arbitrarily prevent publication, and print culture does indeed appear to have undergone a revolution in the kinds as well as the volume of information in print.[8] Government censorship had been superseded by one that differed in effect as well as in object and means. As Foucault contends, whole new areas of social life had become subject to "tact and discretion: between parents and children, for instance, or teachers and pupils, or masters and domestic servants. This almost certainly constituted a whole restrictive economy, one that was incorporated into [the] politics of language and speech" (1:18).

Thus he launches an argument that stands the conventional notion of censorship on its head. Silences may have been "imposed" where

---

7 Foucault, *The History of Sexuality*, trans. Robert Hurley (New York: Pantheon, 1978), 1:17.

8 John Feather, *A History of British Publishing* (London: Routledge, 1988), 50–63; "From Censorship to Copyright: Aspects of the English Book Trade, 1695–1775," in *Books and Society in History*, ed. Kenneth E. Carpenter (New York: Bowker, 1983), 173–81; John Walker, "The Censorship of the Press during the Reign of Charles II," *History* 25 (1950): 219–38; Raymond Astbury, "The Renewal of the Licensing Act in 1693 and Its Lapse in 1695," *The Library*, 5th ser., 33 (1978): 291–322.

previously statements had been made and desires enacted, but in practice the opposite phenomenon occurred at the level of what he calls discourse. By shifting our attention away from social history, or *what* people are supposed to have said and done, toward *how* they were saying and doing it, Foucault explains why the repressive hypothesis that informs conventional wisdom no longer holds up. Sexuality was not repressed but produced: "There was a steady proliferation of discourses concerned with sex—specific discourses, different from one another both by their form and by their object: a discursive ferment that gathered momentum from the eighteenth century onward" (1:18). In England, the explosion of information in print during the century following the interregnum is particularly apparent. Raymond Williams has named it "the long revolution," as if to acknowledge that it was the logical realization of the revolutionary moment that began in the 1640s and 1650s.[9] He claims the suspension of licensing during this period set in motion an irreversible process of cultural change delayed by the reestablishment of licensing in 1662 and then accelerated by Parliament's failure to renew it in 1695. According to the logic Foucault unfolds in *The History of Sexuality*, however, any form of censorship that occurred during or after the revolution in writing should be considered an acknowledgment of the revolution underway and would only have increased its activity.

Even when the Stuarts were returned to the English throne in 1660, then, the power of the monarchy was not the same; the power of words had too profoundly changed, and no renewal of censorship could reverse the course of history, as the proliferation of written forms immediately after the Restoration indicates. The urgency with which the licenser, Roger L'Estrange, sought to restore the government's monopoly on printed information suggests the difficulty of carrying on the old style of monarchy in the new semiotic environment.[10] In effect, the iconicity of Renaissance iconography had disintegrated with the severing of the monarch's head, and the most cherished signs and symbols of English culture had promptly taken on a life independent

9 Williams, *The Long Revolution* (New York: Columbia University Press, 1965).

10 For a discussion of L'Estrange's tactics see, for example, Christopher Hill, "Censorship and English Literature," in *The Collected Essays*, 3 vols. (Amherst: University of Massachusetts Press, 1985), 1:41.

of his body. No longer under the control of church and state, meaning could be decided elsewhere and serve other interests. Williams argues that it quickly came to be determined by what made sense to a community of educated people. As the locus of meaning changed, according to Foucault's theory of discourse, the power of determining how and what kind of meaning was achieved in print increased dramatically. Followed to its conclusion, his line of reasoning reveals how the practices that began to cluster around writing sometime near the end of the seventeenth century might have produced new class affiliations and a new form of nation-state as well.

To imagine English history in terms of the change that Anderson uses to explain the difference between the Old World and the New, we do not have to add a new class to the familiar three. Nor do we have to turn up new evidence of social change. But we do have to modify the Eurocentric assumption that the traditional middle class consisted chiefly of money owners. Anderson contends that ownership of money was not the primary basis for class affiliation in the North American colonies, for the very reason that it is not what amalgamated certain groups of people into a nation. Where the old aristocracy could be illiterate, according to the modern definition of the term, and still be powerful, the new bourgeoisie could come into being as a class only "in so many self-replications" (74). Indeed, if there is any lesson to be learned from Anderson's account of New World nationalism, it is that print capitalism had to be in place before certain artisans, businessmen, merchants, and professional people could imagine, much less achieve, economic independence from England. To suggest how literacy might have remodeled the mother country in the image of her former colony, however, we must attend to an omission common to Foucault's and Anderson's very different accounts of the rise of writing.

According to Foucault, the new prohibitions on sexuality produced what the exponents of an emergent middle class sought to regulate and what twentieth-century intellectuals thought their predecessors had repressed: a desire present in the individual's body at birth, an identity prior to the one given by the state, an energy hostile to social order and requiring new managerial procedures. Male sexuality during the eighteenth and female sexuality during the nineteenth century became the objects and sources of meaning for a range of genres.

Anderson, Williams, Roger Chartier, and others identify the period with an unprecedented increase in printed information about the private feelings and intimate relationships of ordinary individuals.[11] Sexuality had to be taken into account not only in medicine but also in the law and in political theory. During the nineteenth century, the literatures of sociology, anthropology, and psychology, respectively, sprang up in response to the problems of working-class sexuality, the sexuality of colonial populations, and the sexuality of middle-class women. "Sex was not something one simply judged; it was a thing one administered. It was in the nature of a public potential; it called for management procedures; it had to be taken charge of by analytical discourses" (1:24).

It is difficult to imagine how writing could have acquired so much authority in such a short time had its decentralization in Europe not coincided with the growth of the idea that consciousness harbored sexual secrets that called for detection and analysis. At present, no other historical or theoretical explanation for the information revolution exists. Moreover, it can be argued that the discourse of sexuality made its most lasting impact through literature that could be reproduced and distributed on a mass basis. Throughout the eighteenth and nineteenth centuries, British theater moved steadily toward melodramas that turned on the repression or absence of sexual gratification and family affection. Poetry began to favor dramatic monologues that articulated the same sense of longing. The fiction that had come into fashion by the end of the eighteenth century rearticulated social relationships in terms of a single urge—however misunderstood, thwarted, displaced, or deformed—to formulate a modern family unit. Similar changes occurred within French, German, and Spanish cultures. On the discovery, containment, and redeployment of what was understood as a universal reproductive drive thus came to depend not only the wholeness of the individual qua individual but also the survival of the collective as a free and all-embracing nation.

11 Chartier, "The Practical Impact of Writing," in *A History of Private Life: Passions of the Renaissance*, ed. Roger Chartier, trans. Arthur Goldhammer, 5 vols. (Cambridge, Mass.: Harvard University Press, 1989), 3:111–59; and Nancy Armstrong and Leonard Tennenhouse, "The Interior Difference: A Brief Genealogy of Dreams," *Eighteenth-Century Studies* 23 (1990): 458–78.

Being Subject to Fiction

Filtered through Anderson, Foucault's account of modern European culture asks us to think of discourse as the precondition or cause rather than the reflection or consequence of money's compulsively imperialistic behavior. Filtered back through Foucault, Anderson's account invites us to think of modern European culture as an emergent culture governed by a class of people who controlled the production and distribution of information, including credit notes and paper currency. Contrary to the impression we receive from most accounts of the rise of the modern middle class in England, remarkably few people actually qualified for membership in it—if the definition of the middle class is based on economic status. When to the professions of clergymen, lawyers, and doctors we add the more amorphous group of bankers, merchants, brokers, agents, clerks, shopkeepers, and intellectuals involved in literature, science, and the fine arts, the 1841 census yields a total British population of 214,000.[12] Even when we include civil servants and parochial, town, church, and police officers (some of whom fell short of the criteria for educated persons), fewer than 250,000 people fit the loosest economic definition of the middle class in England. Of a total population of 4.5 million, then, the middle class comprised a mere 5.55 percent. Anderson and Foucault focus on the rise of "print capitalism" and "discourse," respectively, to explain how writing began to produce the readership it addressed and the human source from which it came. But neither can help us face the discrepancy between the rapidly swelling body of texts that addressed a middle-class readership during the century preceding the 1841 census and the economically based demographic information recorded in the census. Even as the readership underwent a tremendous expansion, the middle class, economically defined, remained a small minority of the English population.[13]

12 We draw on the statistics provided in Norman Gash, *Aristocracy and People: Britain, 1815–1865* (Cambridge, Mass.: Harvard University Press, 1979), 20–21.

13 See Margaret Hunt, "Time-Management, Writing, and Accounting in the Eighteenth-Century English Trading Family: A Bourgeois Enlightenment," *Business and Economic History*, 2d ser., 18 (1989): 150–59; "Wife-Beating, Domesticity, and Women's Independence in Early Eighteenth-Century London," *Gender and History* 4 (1992): 10–33; *The Middling Sort: Commerce, Gender, and the Family in England, 1680–1780* (Berkeley: University of California Press, 1996); and Leonore Davidoff and Catherine Hall, *Family Fortunes: Men and Women of the English Middle Class, 1780–1850* (Chicago: University of Chicago Press, 1987).

To what can the discrepancy be attributed? We believe that texts addressing a community of readers had to precede the self-definition of the literate sectors of the population as readers first and foremost. The production of texts also exceeded the number of people capable of living according to the norms they conveyed; otherwise, the community Anderson describes could not have existed in and as writing before it entered everyday life and reorganized the way people imagined their relationship to one another and understood their place within the nation. Upon such cultural priorities, according to Althusser, rests the modernity of our culture and the exercise of state control through a national education system rather than a national religion.[14] Still, Althusser would insist that culture (or the ideological interpellation of individual subjects through cultural rituals that reproduce class relations) ensures the material conditions necessary for capitalism. Given this proposition, one does not kneel down to pray because one believes; one believes because one kneels down to pray (167–69). By analogy, then, one does not read because one is middle class; one is middle class because one reads.

Foucault claims that modern sexual desire began in prose and passed into speech, where it was used to interpret behavior. In this capacity, writing eventually gave rise to thoughts, feelings, wishes, and dreams. Matthew Arnold, for one, existed at the moment when it became impossible to ignore the degree to which words and images had displaced feelings and things and determined how one carried on relations both with other people and with the world of objects. He shared his phobia of mass culture not only with Morris, Ruskin, and others resolved to salvage traditional culture but with Marx and Freud as well.[15] Even if we reject Arnold's conviction that the world would be a better place if popular culture lost some of its energy and appeal, we must concede his point that a modern nation governs far more effectively through education and consent than through censorship and

---

14 Louis Althusser, "Ideology and Ideological State Apparatuses (Notes towards an Investigation)," in *Lenin and Philosophy*, trans. Ben Brewster (London: Monthly Review Press, 1971), 155.

15 Arnold, *Culture and Anarchy: An Essay in Political and Social Criticism*, ed. J. Dover Wilson (Cambridge: Cambridge University Press, 1960); Andreas Huyssen, "Mass Culture as Woman," in *After the Great Divide: Modernism, Mass Culture, Postmodernism* (Bloomington: Indiana University Press, 1986), 44–62.

coercion. As Marx once observed, people may be perfectly aware of the precise nature of their exploitation and still go to work with perfect regularity. Who they think they are when they think they are out from under the thumb of government has much more influence over what they consider true, normal, natural, desirable, or right. The power to determine what they think freedom is and how they want to practice it is arguably what keeps the populations of modern nations in line.

To give the nineteenth-century idea of government through culture a Foucauldian turn of the screw, we simply have to entertain the possibility that the capacity to give pleasure has a wider-reaching political effect (as defined not only by literature, especially fiction, but also by paintings, sketches, newspapers, photo albums, and, more recently, radio, sound, and video recordings, television, and film) than political or economic oppression. The formation of leisure as a space to be progressively occupied, managed, and commodified is perhaps responsible for the proliferation of unruly behavior that Arnold called on an elite tradition to control. On the other hand, in trying to dampen contemporary enthusiasm for cultural studies, traditional humanism fails, much as Arnold failed, to understand that the expanding domain of popular culture produces the very subject who is most likely to feel subordinated by traditional literary authority. Far from acknowledging the information revolution that accompanied the development of the modern industrial nations, a traditional literary education in the United States suppresses the story of how reading produced a cultural space in which people did not feel that they were at work or under the supervision of the state. And when it allowed its readers to bask in that form of freedom we call leisure, literature began to infiltrate their fantasies and dreams and whisper in their heart of hearts just who they could be and still be English or American.

Anderson and Foucault recognize the relationship between nationality and mass culture, only to discount and ultimately deny it. Both describe a major event that occurred during the late seventeenth and early eighteenth centuries and involved the rise of writing. Yet European modernity and colonial nationalism remain dissociated in each account. While Foucault explains how literate individuals not only were written into being as such but also became capable of writing others, Anderson surveys the conditions under which they began to understand themselves as a new collective entity, or nation. It is only reasonable to assume that when, combined with Anderson, Foucault should provide a way of rethinking modern England as an emergent culture. But in fact Foucault and Anderson do not yield a total explanation; they merely supplement each other, together revealing a question that neither asks. It is the question of fiction, or why narratives that claim to represent imaginary communities are the most reliable markers of a nation's emergence.

As a given culture develops the kind of imagined community associated with New World nationalism, Anderson reminds us, it invariably produces great novels: works of fiction in the creole language that simultaneously declare what is specific to the emerging nation and place it among the other novel-producing nations. Indeed, of all writing in print, only the novel offers a simulacrum of the community that Anderson has in mind; only the novel is composed of various acts that may all be "performed at the same clocked, calendrical time, but by actors who may be largely unaware of one another" (31). Fiction welds otherwise disconnected bits of information into a unity that can be contained "in the mind of omniscient readers. Only they see the links" (31). But Anderson grants, only to deny, fiction primacy in creating the sense of community that distinguished the New World from the Old. For what controlled the selection and arrangement of information in print, he declares, was "not fiction but the very structure of the colonial administration and the market system itself" (62). The moment he accepts the principle that economic production necessarily precedes social reproduction, his theory of imagined communities reverts to a traditional narrative of national development in which causes occur in Europe and have their effects in North America.

Foucault's theory of discourse also depends on fiction. Whenever words begin to produce an object that is not already there, they behave like little fictions, especially when they presume to describe nothing but the object itself. Foucault concentrates on the fictional dimension of nonfictional genres that multiplied during the late seventeenth and eighteenth centuries—memoirs, medical treatises, social-scientific writing, educational pamphlets, and personal confessions—to support his hypothesis that such intellectual activity actually called into being the recesses of self and the regions of private experience that authors presumed to be discovering. He identifies the properties and powers we associate with modern fiction in a wide array of cultural materials, but he does not consider, in turn, the historical impact of fiction. Here, as in his Eurocentricity, Foucault remains true to philosophical and historical tradition.

To factor the sudden proliferation of printed information into the story of modernity, Foucault finds it necessary to replace the repressive hypothesis—that writing suppresses a more genuine voice and authentic feeling—with what might be called the productive hypothesis. He argues that discourse produces the voice that writing claims to imitate and thus the consciousness from which it seems to come. The inversion of speech and writing, by which writing grants speech a priori external existence, thus provided the means of producing an individual whose voice, thoughts, body, and behavior constitute the source of writing as well as the ultimate object of knowledge. To account for the discursive takeoff that made the inversion possible, however, we must replace the productive hypothesis with what might be called the reproductive hypothesis; we must ask how the kinds of writing that individuated the source of language became curiously and compulsively reproducible. On this question hinges the relationship between New World nationalism and the rise of a new class of literate people in England. To forge a nation of such individuals, there had to be a mechanism that compelled their individuation. It was not enough for members of the emergent class, decidedly in the minority, to testify to their own unique humanity. To become dominant, they had to universalize their self-definition; they had to define other people as more or less lacking their humanity. Anderson identifies print, especially newspapers and novels, as the means by which the modern middle class consolidated and expanded its power into that of a nation.

More than any other medium, however, fiction proved able to represent the inner world of the solitary individual. In this respect, it was very much like modern love: a relationship among people who did not work with one another but shared a private world. Newspapers may well have prompted the reader to imagine all the other readers of the morning news and momentarily to feel part of a community of readers. Fiction interpellated a readership in much the same way. Yet it also resembled a diary, because it gave special access to information that by definition was not publicly shared. It was so personal that, short of living it oneself or violating someone else's privacy, one did not have access to such information. And without access to it, privacy itself could not provide the common ground that individuals, regardless of their other differences, might occupy. Fiction was the public form of the very information that it designated as private. If fiction is the unmistakable mark of a nation's emergence, it is because only fiction can pull off this peculiar sleight of hand.

Let us conclude by pointing to an instance where fiction ensured the social reproduction of the kinds of individuals necessary for a modern industrial nation. Nationality entered into this mutually transforming relationship with fiction in the English diaspora. In *The Imaginary Puritan* we describe how the process took root and spread in areas of New England where presses were abundant and literacy was especially high, and we suggest how the same model of diaspora can explain the onset of European modernity as well. The fiction whose development cannot be distinguished from that of the modern middle classes can be described in New World terms. It invariably looks backward with longing toward a Europe that supposedly existed before the reign of writing, and its nostalgia implies that neither it nor the writing that preceded and accompanied it into cultural prominence was out to formulate a new, more democratic society. There is a great deal of evidence that the fiction emerging with the new class of authors and readers was simply trying to reproduce a nation of sovereign landowners that, depending on one's station in early modern British society, was either about to vanish forever because of the upheavals of the 1640s or about to appear on the horizon of real possibility because of the opening of a new land to colonies and the enclosure of common land within England. The novels of Defoe, Richardson, Fielding, Radcliffe, Austen, and the Brontës all focus on the utter vulnerability of a lone individual (dis)located on a terrain that threatens his or (more often) her identity and the extinction of something uniquely English. Such fiction transforms the nation into one of self-enclosed subjects who through writing make contact with a community of similarly solitary readers and who feel that their survival depends on maintaining not only this contact but also their self-enclosure.

What we have just said about exemplary English novels can also be said about the narratives written by Englishmen and women taken captive by Indians in North America.[16] Separation from some kind of speech community seems in each case to be what compels them to translate that community into writing that subsequently becomes the basis for community existence. In looking forward to the new society—first in North America and later in England—they cast their narratives backward. Their desire to return to a more authentic, pure society, where relationships do not have to be mediated by print, inspires them to reproduce it in the print vernacular. But the same desire also reproduces a profound sense of lack—lack of the very community that written words, especially print, can never fill. Language loses whatever innocence it may have had as speech; it begins to behave as signs, writing, or the supplement. In replacing an originary community, however fantastic it was to begin with, writing inevitably replaces speech and relocates the originary community still farther in the past with each successful replication. Although the nations that emerged through the discourse of diaspora can be classified as fictions, the changes that English culture underwent in venturing to New England suggest that the power of those nations increased as they took on new life in the print vernacular. Nations that appeared to emerge repeatedly between the covers of a novel grew with their readerships as nation and readership became virtually if not explicitly the same. What is more, the nations that existed as the imaginary sources of print vernaculars—as, say, England was for English—rapidly constituted communities that exceeded the boundaries of the nation. Together these communities eventually defined themselves as a first world over and against "oral," "native," "subaltern," "immigrant," or "ethnic" forms of literacy.

16 Nancy Armstrong and Leonard Tennenhouse, "The American Origins of the English Novel," *American Literary History* 4 (1992): 386–410.

Catherine Gallagher

Nobody's Story: Gender, Property, and the Rise of the Novel

We literary critics often exaggerate the ease with which boundaries can be crossed; we only half acknowledge the borders between disciplines, between national cultures, between historical periods. We don't deny the usefulness of such divisions; after all, they allow us to describe ourselves as interdisciplinary as well as to organize our texts and define cultural and historical differences. But deep down we don't really believe they constrain *us*. Rather, we tend to imagine ourselves to be cosmopolitan citizens of the whole intellectual world.

It was with this typical literary critic's naïve self-assurance that I set out six years ago to write a book about eighteenth-century English women writers. Trained primarily in nineteenth- and twentieth-century British literature, I'd nevertheless read the canonical eighteenth-century works, and like most Victorianists I knew that the truly important trends in the eighteenth century were those that anticipated the nineteenth anyway. With its early and imperfect novelistic realism, its minor women writers and their undeveloped domestic ideology, its primitive industrialism and nascent market economy (to name just a few features that were relevant to my particular project), I knew at the

Originally presented as a lecture before the American Society for Eighteenth-Century Studies, Seattle, March 1992.

outset that I was going to encounter an immature version of a very familiar culture.

Well, you can easily see what's coming: plunked down abruptly into eighteenth-century studies, I was extremely disoriented. At the outset, I was looking for early-eighteenth-century novels, and I couldn't find any. Indeed, I couldn't find any fiction, properly speaking, at all. Women writers of the period seemed especially powerful to me, but not in ways that anticipated Jane Austen or George Eliot. Both formally and thematically, they were simply unfamiliar. Finally, I could not perceive in the mainstream culture recognizable foreshadowings of nineteenth-century capitalist ideology; the assumptions of my writers eluded the categories of economic thought I had been taught.

After feeling panic, dejection, elation—all the things one experiences when arriving in a place that is not just foreign but unexpectedly so—I decided to foster my sense of alienation, hoping that it might produce some insights that, if not authoritative, could at least be provocative. So I come to you today as a determined outsider with a few eccentric findings about eighteenth-century British culture. Put in their baldest and most outlandish language, they are that the category of pure fiction, properly speaking, was an invention of the mid–eighteenth century; that realism was not a way of trying to hide or disguise fictionality but was, rather, the formal sign of fiction; that eighteenth-century readers identified with novel characters *because* the latter were fictional and not in spite of that fact; and that these readers had to be taught how to read fiction (it didn't come naturally), and as they learned this skill, new emotional dispositions were created.

I wouldn't be surprised if you were now quite suspicious of the phrase "pure fiction, properly speaking." What exactly do I mean by it? I can't, after all, be claiming that romances, fables, allegories, fairy stories, dramas, narrative poems—in short, all forms of literature that were not taken to be the literal truth and that we usually therefore categorize as fictional—were virtually nonexistent before the mid–eighteenth century. Surely, you're thinking, I have some special definition of "pure fiction, properly speaking" that's going to create the illusion of a questionable identity between fiction and the realist novel. This suspicion is, indeed, half right. I do have a quirky definition of fiction, but I think it's a justifiable one and will lead to an argument that isn't merely tautological.

A pure fiction is, first of all, distinguishable from a lie. Here the word *pure* is meant to carry a moral charge: a pure fiction is innocent of any design to deceive. As one mid–eighteenth-century writer put it, a fiction, properly speaking, has no "intention to be credited."[1] Nevertheless, literary scholars have understandably ignored this part of the definition. For example, in his introduction to *A Check List of English Prose Fiction, 1700–1739*, William Harlin McBurney admits he included works claiming to be true as long as he judged them to be "full of improbable lies."[2] In this statement, McBurney, I believe, gives a historically accurate account of the usually stated narrative options of the early eighteenth century: truth telling and lying. But fiction writing, I would argue, cannot be said to exist as a marked and recognized category in a culture until it can be effortlessly told apart from deception. Only at that point does it become pure. The fact that so many of the books on McBurney's list are full of gross and obvious lies is not what links them to the actual fiction of the mid–eighteenth century, but what distinguishes them from it.

McBurney's phrase, "improbable lies," implies, however, that some lies are so absurd that they can't really be said to claim credit and should therefore meet my first criterion for fiction. Flagrant lies, on this account, show such a wanton disregard for their own credibility that they could not be said to practice deceit seriously and hence can be told apart from normal lies. Literary historians have, therefore, reasonably pointed to numerous pre-eighteenth-century writings that can now be called "fictional" because they made no serious truth claims. Before the mid–eighteenth century, though, there was no consensus that such genres shared any common trait; instead, they were classified according to their implied purposes (e.g., moral fables), their forms (e.g., epic), or their provenance (e.g., oriental tales). The dis-

1 Charlotte Lennox, *The Female Quixote; or, The Adventures of Arabella*, ed. Margaret Dalziel, intro. Margaret Anne Doody, World's Classics (Oxford: Oxford University Press, 1989), p. 376.

2 *A Check List of English Prose Fiction, 1700–1739* (Cambridge, Mass.: Harvard University Press, 1960), p. ix.

cursive practice we now call "fiction" was, at the most, a "wild space," unmapped and unarticulated.

The fact that there were plenty of narratives that might have fit into the category of fiction before fiction had been fully differentiated from falsehood in the culture at large seems to me significant.[3] It indicates that although there were many reasons for telling improbable lies— political, pedagogical, erotic, magical, religious, and heroic, among others—there was not yet a reason for fiction per se. Moreover, the category problem indicates that as long as stories could only announce what we would now call their fictionality by their flagrant improbability, the idea of fiction was not really available. Fiction should allow one to distinguish between probable stories and lies.

You may wonder why I'm spending so much time on this point: what difference does it make whether the category of fiction preceded the rise of the realist novel or was coterminous with it? It matters because different versions of the novel-fiction relationship will lead to very dissimilar accounts of the novel's appearance. Because histories of the novel had long assumed that its genealogy lay in explicitly fictional forms, they tended to focus on the issue of realism. Where, they asked, did the taste for *realistic,* novelistic fiction come from?—assuming that the textual universe was already divided, like the best-seller list today, between fiction and nonfiction. They imagined that a taste for fiction and an understanding of its nature already existed. But once we see that explicit fiction and realism came into view at the same historical moment, we must address a prior question. Instead of asking why the novel became the preferred form of fiction, we should ask why fiction became the preferred form of narrative and what role realism played in defining its nature.

Both Lennard Davis and Michael McKeon have recently helped redefine the issues along these lines. By denying that the novel developed out of the romance and by asserting that its origins lay instead in

3 My argument does not deny that there were occasional, quite sophisticated discussions of fiction (under different names) prior to the mid–eighteenth century. Sir Philip Sidney's *Defense of Poesy* is an obvious case in point. Most of these followed Aristotle, however, in linking the fictional to the heroic, and none of them succeeded in creating a widespread cultural consensus. It is a generalized understanding of the status of fiction that concerns me here.

what he calls the "news-novel matrix," Davis points to the legal and political pressures that eventually created an explicit discourse of fiction.[4] He shows that fiction became a topic of discourse in ways that made it seem innocent in contradistinction to the seditious libels popular in the early eighteenth century. Hence, he helps us understand the appeal of what I am today going to call "nobody's story." The fact that the novel is nobody's story, I'll argue, is what makes it the prototypical form of fiction and simultaneously necessitates its realism. And so we have arrived at the second component of my definition of "pure fiction, properly speaking": it is not only a story that claims *not* to be credited but also a story about nobody. Indeed, it is a narrative that differentiates itself from lies and scandalous libels *by* being about nobody. Historically, the category of fiction consolidates itself around this simple but generally overlooked formal feature: the denial, through a variety of conventions, of any particular extratextual referent for the characters' proper names.

If Lennard Davis helps us see where Nobody came from, Michael McKeon offers clues about why realism should be Nobody's mode of representation.[5] McKeon adheres to the romance-novel connection and identifies a dialectical development inside of romance that created an imperative for verisimilitude. The movement from romance to novel, according to McKeon, rests on an underlying epistemological shift from truth as historical accuracy to truth as mimetic simulation. He claims that it was the widespread acceptance of verisimilitude as a form of truth, rather than as a form of illusion, that made fiction a category and simultaneously founded the novel as a genre. Before the late seventeenth century, verisimilitude had been simply considered a form of illusion. The likely story was the false one.[6] McKeon seems to provide ample evidence for my contention that there is no prior category of fiction to which mimetic realism is added in order to produce the

4 *Factual Fictions: The Origins of the English Novel* (New York: Columbia University Press, 1983), pp. 25–70.

5 *The Origins of the English Novel, 1600–1740* (Baltimore, Md.: Johns Hopkins University Press, 1987), pp. 25–64.

6 For an excellent discussion of the intertwined notions of probability and fiction as well as the special properties of fictional belief, see Robert Newsom, *A Likely Story: Probability and Play in Fiction* (New Brunswick, N.J.: Rutgers University Press, 1988).

novel. According to his argument, the legitimation of the verisimilar as opposed to the historical, of the realistic as opposed to the real, allowed the separation of the fictional from historical components of the romance and the development of the former as The Novel. Hence McKeon could conclude (although he doesn't quite) that pure (in the sense of unmixed) fiction *is* realism. Moreover, the corollary of this conclusion, it seems to me, is that realism is the sign of fiction. Instead of being an extraneous ingredient added to make fiction palatable, to excuse or disguise it, realism is the mark, the code of the explicitly fictional.

I depart from McKeon's account by questioning the role he gives to changes in the idea of verisimilitude as the motor for this history. By stressing the identity between fiction and realism, McKeon, like numerous scholars before him, avoids the question "Why fiction?" My account reverses McKeon's causality; a desire to read Nobody's story, I believe, was the primary impulse behind the rise of the novel, and realism came to be valued partly because it signaled that the story was Nobody's, that is, that it was fictional.

Before turning to the question of why people started wanting to read fiction, let me briefly fill in a few salient facts about Nobody and his or her connection to realism. When I speak of the prehistory of fictional Nobodies, I have a particular set of popular jokes and puzzles in mind, all of which turned on the possibility of speaking of someone, namely Nobody, of whom you simultaneously deny the existence.[7] Frances Burney, for example, tapped into this tradition when she began writing her first diary. In this quotation, listen to the easy transition she makes from joking about Nobody to creating a fictional character:

> To Nobody, then will I write my Journal! since To Nobody can I be wholly unreserved—to Nobody can I reveal every thought, every wish of my Heart, with the most unlimited confidence, the most unremitting sincerity to the end of my Life! For what chance, what

7 Greta Calmann traces the history of Nobody in "The Picture of Nobody: An Iconographical Study," *Journal of the Warburg and Courtauld Institutes*, 23 (1960): 60–104, beginning with the trick Odysseus played when he told the Cyclops his name was Noman, thus causing the monster's fellows to ignore him when he called out that Noman was tormenting him.

accident can end my connections with Nobody? No secret can I conceal from No-body, & to No-body can I be ever unreserved. . . . I will suppose you, then, to be my best friend; tho' God forbid you ever should! my dearest companion—& a romantick Girl, for mere oddity may perhaps be more sincere—more *tender*—than if you were a friend [in] propria personae [*sic*]—in as much as imagination often exceeds reality. (Calmann, p. 2)

Although I have no intention of deriving fictional characters in general from the widespread use during the early modern period and the eighteenth century of the figure of Nobody, I would like to point out that comic novelists used this tradition frequently as a popular precedent for the overt fictionality of their own discourse. Indeed, the fact that this tradition lived on longer in England than anywhere else in northern Europe (Calmann, pp. 93ff.) might be attributed to the lively interest that early novels created in the ontological puzzles of fictionality.

Perhaps Nobody also lived longer in England than elsewhere because the English word *Nobody*, in contradistinction to *Nemo* or *Niemand*, invites jokes about the idea of bodilessness specifically. Nobody was a name without a material referent in the world, without, emphatically, a physical existence. He or she was, if you will, the site of a material lack and an open invitation, as Burney indicated, to imagine in detail. The very specificity and particularity of realist representation, I contend, should be viewed as signs of a similar lack of material referent. Realist fiction's wealth of circumstantial and physical detail, class, gender, and regional characteristics are all overtly illusionistic confessions that the particulars of the novel character have no extratextual existence. The character came into *fictional* existence most fully only when he or she was developed as nobody *in particular*; that is, the particularities had to be fully specified in order to ensure the felt fictionality of the character. A generalized character would too easily take on allegorical or symbolic reference, just as one rendered in mere hints would have been read at the time as a scandalous libel. Thinness of detail at the time almost always indicated specific extratextual referent. But the more characters were loaded with circumstantial and even insignificant properties, the more the readers were assured that the text was at once assuming and making up for the fact that it referred to nobody at all. Roland Barthes has pointed out that the contingent, unmotivated detail was the code of the real in realist fiction, but he didn't draw what seems to me an obvious conclusion that realism was the code of the fictional.

Let me mention just one more of Nobody's general features before moving on to the question of why people wanted to read his or her story. The name had come to signify a common person, a person of no social consequence. Henry Fielding, for example, defined Nobody as "all the people in Great Britain, except about 1200."[8] Somebody was used throughout the seventeenth and eighteenth centuries as Nobody's foil; the figures were common enough, for example, to form a pair in a deck of playing cards. Often a fop, Somebody "was a person of consequence, whose name was perhaps intentionally suppressed" (Calmann, p. 93). Hence, just as Nobody might be seen as related to fictional characters, Somebody might be seen as the abstract type of scandalous reflections.

The contrasting pair of Somebody and Nobody reminds us that the eighteenth-century preoccupation with reference in representation was always tied very closely to issues of social status. True stories and lies were generally about Somebody; that was their raison d'être. But stories about nonentities with common names like Pamela Andrews or Tom Jones, or even Clarissa Harlowe, unless they were adventurers or criminals, could generally be counted on to be fictional because there was no market in true stories—scandal or gossip—about such people. The ordinariness of realism, therefore, like its detailed particularity, would have been taken at the time as an indication of fictionality.

The burden of this first half of my remarks has been to suggest that realism was valued as a sign of fiction. But this leaves us with a large question still looming: why did people start wanting to read Nobody's story? In the middle of the eighteenth century, such a desire couldn't be taken for granted. The heroine of Charlotte Lennox's *The Female Quixote* expresses a common eighteenth-century objection to the new form when she complains:

8 *Covent Garden Journal*, 14 January 1752.

He that writes without intention to be credited, must write to little purpose; for what pleasure or advantage can arise from facts that never happened? What examples can be afforded by the patience of those who never suffered, or the chastity of those who were never solicited? . . . When we hear a story in common life that raises our wonder or compassion, the first confutation stills our emotions and however we were touched before, we then chase it from the memory with contempt as a trifle, or with indignation as an imposture. (p. 376)

Arabella's two main challenges here—that self-proclaimed fictions can neither instruct nor *move* the hearer—are met by her interlocutor inside the novel with classic midcentury assertions of the peculiar truth and pleasure of the verisimilar. But there is a mismatch between the objections and their refutation, for Arabella has asked why one should *care* about people who never existed, not why one should take aesthetic pleasure in a well-accomplished mimesis. To respond that the accuracy of the mimesis is the foundation of the emotional response, and is therefore a register of artistry, is to miss the force of Arabella's question. Why introduce disbelief simply in order to suspend it, however artfully? How would disbelief, however suspended, contribute to what Arabella calls "compassion"?

For "compassion," "identification," and "sympathy" were generally acknowledged to be the ends of fiction. As we've often been told, fiction was thought to be an important tool in the eighteenth century for the education of the moral sentiments. It was said to exercise sympathy, that process by which one feels the joys and sufferings of another and may thereby be motivated to perform benevolent actions. Benevolence and imaginative identification, we know, were linked in some ethical systems, and certain historians of the novel argue that the new cultural prestige of fiction depended on this link. Fiction, the argument assumes, makes it easy to appropriate another's point of view, to sympathize.

This formulation has all the self-evidence of long acquaintance, but the process by which fiction and sympathetic identification were linked has been more often assumed than traced. To trace it, we have to begin by denaturalizing it. Arabella does just that by pointing out that we might expect our emotions to be "stilled" if we understand that their objects do not have, and never had, any actual existence remotely like our own. And Arabella was by no means unique in her opinion; it is common to find early- and mid-eighteenth-century commentators assuming that a real hero would more easily arouse compassion than a fictional one: "To pity a feign'd Hero," as one "novelist" tells us, "is commendable, because it is a sure Argument that Compassion would not be wanting to a real one."[9] If, then, there is a "natural" link between fiction and sympathy, it was certainly not taken for granted in the period, and it has yet to be fully articulated. As Arabella and a good many other eighteenth-century skeptics were fond of remarking, there is something odd, even absurd, about making up people to sympathize with. Why not just sympathize with the people who were already there?

Normally at this point in my argument I would turn to certain moral-sense philosophers to demonstrate that sympathy for actual people was thought to be a very difficult thing to achieve in the eighteenth century; that it was not a feeling about someone else but rather the process through which someone else's feelings became your own; and that the process was almost never completed unless that someone else was already related to you as a family member or business partner or, in the optimal case, as both. In short, the tendency of other people to be really other—to have other bodies, other relatives, and other property—was perceived as a constant impediment to sympathetic identification.

Today I don't have time to document these claims about the problematic nature of sympathy in eighteenth-century moral discourse; I must ask you to take them on faith.[10] But even in this truncated form they provide the beginnings of an answer to that common question,

9 *The Unfortunate Duchess; or, The Lucy Gamester: A Novel, Founded on a True Story* (London, 1739, quoted in Michael Crump, "Stranger than Fiction: The Eighteenth-Century True Story," in *Searching the Eighteenth Century: Papers Presented at the Symposium on the Eighteenth Century Short Title Catalogue in July 1982*, ed. Michael Crump and Michael Harris (London: British Library in association with the University of London, Department of Extra-Mural Studies, 1983), p. 67.

10 Most of these contentions are supported by passages from David Hume's *A Treatise of Human Nature*.

"Why not just sympathize with the people who were already there?" Because they were *other* people. What the element of disbelief contributes to sympathy is the removal of any suspicion that the character might in fact be somebody else. Since nobodies and their stories didn't belong to anyone in the real world, they didn't create the same barriers to identification that almost everybody else did. They could become a species of utopian common property, potential objects of universal identification. Another way to put this might be to say that since the stories were nobody's, everybody could have an equal interest in them. The questions that clustered around putatively true stories in the eighteenth century—is the story libelous? who should be allowed to tell it? whose interest does it serve to tell it this way?—vanish, and a new kind of interest takes their place, a gratuitous or sentimental interest. Fiction allowed readers to be, in Burke's words, "acquisitive without impertinence."

Despite Arabella's objection, therefore, it did make sense for eighteenth-century readers to identify with characters *because* they were fictional and not in spite of that fact. However, the identification was not automatic; readers had to be taught to do it. Indeed, even nonsentimental, satirical writers of the midcentury took pains to stress that their characters were nobody in particular; otherwise, the general satirical import would be lost. In *Joseph Andrews*, for example, Fielding underscored fiction's peculiar ability to avoid the scandal inherent in the satire of individuals while maintaining, indeed increasing, the effectiveness of satire aimed at general types:

> I question not but several of my Readers will know the Lawyer in the Stage-Coach [a character who'd just been introduced], the Moment they hear his Voice. . . . To prevent therefore any such malicious Applications, I declare here once for all, I describe not Men, but Manners; not an Individual, but a Species. . . . [The lawyer's depiction] is calculated for much more general and noble Purposes; not to expose one pitiful Wretch, to the small and contemptible Circle of his Acquaintance; but to hold the Glass to thousands in their Closets, that they may contemplate their Deformity, and endeavour to reduce it, and thus by suffering private Mortification may avoid public Shame. This places the Boundary

between, and distinguishes the Satirist from the libeller; for the former privately corrects the Fault for the Benefit of the Person, like a Parent; the latter publickly exposes the Person himself, as an Example to others, like an Executioner.[11]

Because a fictional characterization refers to nobody in particular, it *indirectly*, Fielding's narrator claims, refers to everybody of a certain "species." Only when readers are prevented from seeing somebody *else* in the textual reflection (that is, when they understand that they're reading fiction) will they become capable of seeing themselves. Self-knowledge, in this case a knowledge of selfishness, is achieved by a reader's identification with a character taken to be typical *because* of his fictionality. The resulting chastisement is, therefore, benignly private, for readers refer the representation to themselves as a solitary exercise. Libelous satire, on the other hand, had publicly exposed living examples, thereby merely discouraging certain forms of behavior. Fielding's satirist has what he calls a "nobler" aim: to give readers the habits of quiet self-reflection and rational self-improvement. These aims could only be met by a referential generality that had superseded nonfictional, individual reference.

Fielding's distinction between public execution (libel) and private, parental correction (fiction) certainly gives weight to the claims of recent critics, such as D. A. Miller, John Bender, and Nancy Armstrong, that the realist novel is associated with specifically modern modes of discipline that contrast themselves with crude or "inhumane" public punishments. I would only want to add to their analyses a rider stressing that the disciplinary impact of the novel relies on readers who understand that they are reading fiction; it is because the story refers to Nobody that it can so easily refer to them. Fictionality was thus the specific trait upon which the novel supported its claim to be a benign instrument of self-discipline, at once regulating, normalizing, and individuating its readers.

In the 1740s and 1750s, fiction writers like Fielding and Charlotte Lennox often explicitly told their readers what *not* to do (don't waste time trying to figure out who the characters really are) and what *to* do

---

11 *Joseph Andrews*, ed. Martin C. Battestin (Middletown, Conn.: Wesleyan University Press, 1967), p. 189.

(read this story as if it were indirectly about you; that is, identify with Nobody). Fielding's narrator scolded the naïve reader who was vainly looking for a particular referent, and Lennox satirized such literal-minded naïveté in the person of Arabella, whose objections to fiction I read earlier. As in the case of her prototype, Don Quixote, Arabella's inability to separate the historical from the verisimilar in romances leads her to "mistake" reality, to misinterpret real people and contemporary situations. She needs to learn to read fiction as fiction by reading novels like *The Female Quixote*, which are too realistic to be mistaken for mere notations of historical truth.

The naïve reader never quite disappeared from the metadiscourse of the novel but was increasingly replaced by the sentimental reader in the later years of the eighteenth century. We can easily understand this development if we reflect for a moment on the relationship I've been outlining between the epistemological or cognitive and the affective dimensions of fiction. If it is true that the suspended awareness of their fictionality makes characters easier to sympathize with, then the reader who has an accurate knowledge of the characters' status would be all the more emotionally involved in the story. Once Arabella is cured of her naïve reading, in other words, we might expect her to become a sentimental reader, one who has inappropriately strong emotional reactions to books she knows are fictions. After all, a correct reading of a novel can hardly fail to be sentimental, since the emotion felt for a person the reader knows never existed is ipso facto excessive, and yet the reader feels it *because* the character never existed.

After 1760, this paradox became a scandal in its own right. Both inside and outside of novels, complaints mounted about what one doctor called a "disproportionate activity of the representative faculties."[12] According to this influential medical writer, "the faculty of fiction too frequently exercised" aroused "strong passions" and led to unsteadiness of character and other nervous disorders. The medical literature on this point, moreover, echoed the attacks of moralists who were particularly concerned about fiction's effect on women. The following

12 Alexander Crichton, *Inquiry into the Nature and Origins of Mental Derangement*, vol. 2 (London, 1799), pp. 10–11. I am grateful to Thomas Laqueur for bringing this passage to my attention.

quotation from a 1795 periodical is typical: "I have actually seen mothers, in miserable garrets, crying for the imaginary distress of an heroine, while their children were crying for bread: and the mistress of a family losing hours over a novel in the parlour, while her maids, in emulation of the example, were similarly employed in the kitchen. I have seen a scullion-wench with a dishclout in one hand, and a novel in the other, sobbing over the sorrows of a *Julia* or a *Jemima*."[13] Another writer blamed what he called the "identifying propensity" encouraged by the novel for a host of women's ills.[14]

Fiction writers, oddly enough, rather cheerfully joined in to this apparently antifictional barrage, and their manner of doing so gives us one final insight into the functions of fiction in the late eighteenth century. Regulation, individuation, the encouragement of an identifying propensity that could facilitate emotional response and speculative exchange—all these have been mentioned. But when novelists scolded and satirized sentimental readers, they stressed the need not only to experience but also to disown emotional responses. The novelistic character whose concern for nonexistent people diverted her care and attention away from her own family was a stock figure designed to show the reader how absurd it would be to accede completely to Nobody's (always excessive) emotional demands. Satirizing the sentimental reader thereby helped establish a new form of emotional practice: that of sympathizing with characters because they are fictional and then ceasing to feel the transferred emotions upon closing the book, because, after all, the characters are only fictional. This deliberate creation of emotional discontinuity allowed for a separate dimension of affective life, one in which emotions are only "practiced," in which the feelings themselves take on the same suppositional, conjectural status as the nobody in whom they supposedly originated.

Such emotional practice was especially important for women in an age when the new affective demands of family life came into conflict with the still-prevalent patriarchal habit of encouraging marriages for

---

13 *Sylph*, 6 October 1795, p. 35. For this and numerous similar quotations, see John Tinnon Taylor, *Early Opposition to the English Novel: The Popular Reaction from 1760 to 1830* (New York: King's Crown, 1943), p. 53 and passim.

14 *Eclectic Review*, June 1812, p. 606.

economic advantage and status. Hence the early domestic novel, especially, is full of comic or otherwise parodic representations of sentimental reading that doesn't know how to stop sympathizing. The lesson to be learned from such books was not only that sentimental identification is ultimately egotistical but also that it gives no practice in the various modes of having emotions, of trying them out, of "holding" them in a speculative, tentative way, without fully incorporating them. Some fictions, and I have in mind particularly Maria Edgeworth's domestic tales, went so far as to manipulate the processes of identification and disidentification, to teach readers to break off the sympathetic response especially in moments of romantic indulgence.

Let me give just one brief example of Edgeworth's method before concluding. In her lengthy tale *Patronage*, almost every time a crisis occurs, we are explicitly told that our novelistic expectations will not be met; the pleasures of succumbing to a series of familiar emotions will not be allowed us, nor will any other preference for mere feeling. When, for instance, a young man has been discovered to be a cad, the heroine's mother warns her daughter against behaving like typical novel heroines:

> You may recollect more than one heroine of a novel, who discards a lover upon such a discovery as was made by you last night. It is a common novel incident, and, of course, from novels, every young lady, even [those] who might not have felt without a precedent, knows how she ought to express herself in such circumstances. But you will observe, my dear, that both in novels and in real life, young ladies generally like and encourage men of feeling, in contradistinction to men of principle.[15]

This lecture on novels gets right to the heart of the problem. Although they may be seen as a school for the moral sentiments, they will ultimately fail if they work sentimentally, that is, by merely encouraging identification. Thus the sentimental reader, who has no feelings of her own and learns to feel rightly only by adopting those of the novel heroine, can never learn the important lesson from fiction: how to stop sympathizing and will inappropriate feelings away. The wise

15 Maria Edgeworth, *Patronage*, intro. Eva Figes (London: Pandora, 1986), p. 141.

matron goes on to advise her daughter not to engage in the melodramatic reproaches of common heroines, and the matter is quietly, anticlimactically, dropped.

Patronage is a conscious attempt to school women, primarily, in the necessary discontinuities of feeling that must be suffered so that larger continuities (of property and family) might be built. The interruption of our narrative expectations by such didactic interpolations is thus itself didactic, for it does not simply draw a moral out of an incident; rather, it puts the sentimental process into reverse, converting feeling into principle, impression into idea, and thus giving practice in that all-important skill, emotional extrication.

Such didactic tales, for all of their harsh words about novels, are quite logical extensions of the discourse of fiction I've been outlining. For learning to recognize Nobody's numerous particular guises and then to identify with them one after another created a new kind of overburdened and therefore tentative emotional being. It was almost inevitable that sophisticated techniques for managing this emotional plurality would evolve in the very genre that had created the perceived problem in the first place. I am suggesting, finally, that the telos of emotional overload was its management, and that Nobody's story, simply by virtue of its fictionality, has played a very real role in the creation of the modern self.

Reading Shakespeare's

Novels: Literary

History and Cultural

Politics in the

Jonathan Brody Kramnick | Lennox-Johnson Debate

Few cultural products are as important for the discipline of English as the novel and Shakespeare, yet their simultaneous emergence in the eighteenth century is seldom analyzed.[1] Mid-eighteenth-century

I would like to thank Jonathan Goldberg, John Guillory, Ronald Paulson, and Mary Poovey for their attentive responses to this essay.

1 Contemporary criticism, as far back as the eighteenth century, is dominated by the novel. See among others Nancy Armstrong, *Desire and Domestic Fiction: A Political History of the Novel* (New York: Oxford University Press, 1987); John B. Bender, *Imagining the Penitentiary: Fiction and the Architecture of Mind in Eighteenth-Century England* (Chicago: University of Chicago Press, 1987); Lennard J. Davis, *Factual Fictions: The Origins of the English Novel* (New York: Columbia University Press, 1983); J. Paul Hunter, *Before Novels: The Cultural Contexts for Eighteenth-Century English Fiction* (New York: Norton, 1990); Michael McKeon, *The Origins of the English Novel, 1600–1740* (Baltimore, Md.: Johns Hopkins University Press, 1987); and Patricia Meyer Spacks, *Desire and Truth: Functions of Plot in Eighteenth-Century English Novels* (Chicago: University of Chicago Press, 1990). A recent and suggestive discussion of the profession of writing the "elevation of the novel" is given by William B. Warner in "The Elevation of the Novel in England: Hegemony and Literary History," *ELH* 59 (1992): 577–96. For more on eighteenth-century Shakespeare criticism see Margreta de Grazia, *Shakespeare Verbatim: The Reproduction of Authenticity and the 1790 Apparatus* (New York: Oxford University Press, 1991); Colin Franklin, *Shakespeare Domesticated: The Eighteenth-Century Editions* (New York: Scholar, 1990); R. B. McKerrow, "The Treatment of Shakespeare's Text by His Early Editors, 1709–68" (London, 1933), rpt. in *Studies in Shakespeare: British Academy Lectures*, ed. Peter Alexander (New York: Oxford University Press, 1964); and Gary Taylor, *Reinventing Shakespeare: A Cultural History, from the Restoration to the Present* (New York: Weidenfeld and Nicolson, 1989).

critics, however, understood the rise of the novel to generic stability and that of Shakespeare to the pinnacle of the vernacular canon within an overall sense of cultural transformation. Whereas the novel represented the problem of a larger reading public and a commodified exchange of texts, Shakespeare (along with Milton, and to a lesser degree Spenser) signified the high-vernacular tradition, separate in time and value from mass-cultural and "feminine" forms.[2] In *The Progress of Romance* (1785), Clara Reeve characterized the 1740s and 1750s as a time when "the press groaned under the weight of novels, which sprung up like mushrooms."[3] Perhaps feeling that weight, the Shakespearean critic John Upton complained in 1748 that "the manly and nervous Shakespeare and Milton . . . so little please our effeminate taste" and situated them specifically against novels and contemporary drama. Joseph Warton echoed Upton's complaint in the *Adventurer* (1753–54), charging his culture with being an "academy of effeminacy" in which "the tinsel of the burletta is now preferred to the gold of Shakespeare."[4] The opposition between Shakespeare and the novel culminated in the controversy surrounding Charlotte Lennox's critical text, *Shakespeare Illustrated* (1753). Lennox registered the impact of the novel on the ordering of literary culture, as did other critics, but by arguing that the novel is *the* canonical genre.

2 The classic formulation of the English reading public in the eighteenth century is offered in Richard Altick, *The English Common Reader* (Chicago: University of Chicago Press, 1957) and Ian Watt, *The Rise of the Novel: Studies in Defoe, Richardson, and Fielding* (London: Chatto and Windus, 1957). Altick and Watt propose that along with the expansion and hegemony of the "middle-class" grew a larger and more inclusive reading public, aided by the circulating library and the novel. See also Jeremy Black, *The English Press in the Eighteenth Century* (Philadelphia: University of Pennsylvania Press, 1987); Robert DeMaria, "Samuel Johnson and the Reading Revolution," *Eighteenth-Century Life* (November 1992): 86–102; Alvin Kernan, *Samuel Johnson and the Impact of Print* (Princeton, N.J.: Princeton University Press, 1989); and Lawrence Lipking, "Inventing the Canon: Samuel Johnson and the Common Reader," in *Interpretation and Cultural History*, ed. Joan H. Pittock and Andrew Wear (London: Macmillan, 1991), 153–75.

3 Reeve, *The Progress of Romance through Times, Countries, and Manners* (London, 1785), 2:7.

4 Upton, *Critical Observations on Shakespeare* (London, 1748), 28; Warton, *Adventurer*, nos. 139, 113, in *The British Essayists*, ed. A. Chalmers (London, 1823), 21:291, 124.

Though best known for her novels, particularly *The Female Quixote* (1752), Lennox was also a literary critic, a colleague of Samuel Johnson, and part of the circle he dominated.[5] Her knowledge of continental and classical languages prompted Johnson to engage her in translating Shakespeare's source material and thus in the larger historical project of categorizing and ranking English texts. The result, *Shakespeare Illustrated*, offered in three volumes, for the first time in English criticism, a translation and summary of Shakespeare's major sources.[6] Johnson not only solicited these volumes from Lennox but dedicated them in her name to the aristocratic patron Lord Orrery. Despite collaborating on *Shakespeare Illustrated*, however, Johnson and Lennox strongly disagreed on the value and location of certain genres. Hence, even though much of Lennox's antiquarian research appeared in the footnotes of Johnson's edition of Shakespeare's plays twelve years later, his dedication to Orrery was highly ambivalent about the claims of *Shakespeare Illustrated* and ultimately argued against its literary history. Johnson's response became the norm, and subsequently Lennox's preference for source material has often been considered, or dismissed, as simply an attack on Shakespeare.[7] Yet Lennox's noto-

5 Lennox criticism has tended to focus on *The Female Quixote*. Recent work on that novel that has been important for my understanding of *Shakespeare Illustrated* includes Catherine A. Craft, "Reworking Male Models: Aphra Behn's *Fair vow-Breaker*, Eliza Haywood's *Fantomina*, and Charlotte Lennox's *Female Quixote*," *Modern Language Review* 84 (1991): 821–38; Laurie Langbauer, "Romance Revised: Charlotte Lennox's *The Female Quixote*," *Novel: A Forum on Fiction* 18 (fall 1984): 29–44; James J. Lynch, "Romance and Realism in Charlotte Lennox's *The Female Quixote*," *Essays in Literature* 14 (spring 1987): 51–74; Ronald Paulson, *Satire and the Novel in Eighteenth-Century England* (New Haven, Conn.: Yale University Press, 1967); Deborah Ross, "Mirror, Mirror: The Didactic Dilemma of *The Female Quixote*," *Studies in English Literature* 27 (1987): 455–73; Patricia Meyer Spacks, "The Subtle Sophistry of Desire: Dr. Johnson and *The Female Quixote*," *Modern Philology*, no. 85 (May 1988): 532–42; and Helen Thompson, "Charlotte Lennox's *The Female Quixote*: A Novel Interrogation," in *Living by the Pen: Early British Women Writers*, ed. Dale Spender (New York: Teachers College Press, 1992).

6 Lennox's only precursor in this practice is Gerard Langbaine's *Account of English Dramatick Poets* (1691). Langbaine accounts for the source of a dozen plays but does not reprint or translate them as does Lennox's larger survey, nor does he focus exclusively on Shakespeare.

7 Though Franklin dismisses the work in these terms, Taylor and de Grazia simply overlook her text. Analyses that have devoted more time to *Shakespeare Illustrated*

rious difficulty with Shakespeare actually amounts to an argument on behalf of the novel; she responds to what she sees as the antinovelistic "improbability" of his plots and the "immodest" "indecency" of his female and upper-class characters. The Lennox-Johnson debate thus concerns the shape of literary history and the relative canonical value of the novel and Shakespeare.

"The Foregoing Novel"

Lennox repeatedly terms Shakespeare's sources "novels and histories" and follows each translation with "observations on the use Shakespeare has made of the foregoing novel" (or "history").[8] Whereas the term "novel" is by no means settled during the period, Lennox is one of the first critics to use it in the modern sense as an imaginative and "probable" prose narrative. Her career indicates in fact an abiding concern with defining the form. In *The Female Quixote* she is primarily interested in the question of that text's own genre; no common set of conventions or terms covers both the implacable romanticism of Arabella and the quotidian realism of her suitors.[9] *Shake-*

---

nonetheless recapitulate this reading, beginning this century with Thomas R. Loundsbury, *Shakespeare as a Dramatic Artist with an Account of His Reputation at Various Periods* (New York: Scribner, 1901), through Lennox's biography, Miriam Rossiter Small, *Charlotte Ramsay Lennox: An Eighteenth Century Woman of Letters* (New Haven, Conn.: Yale University Press, 1935), 184–228, to the only post–World War 2 study of *Shakespeare Illustrated*, Margaret Doody, "Shakespeare's Novels: Charlotte Lennox Illustrated," *Studies in the Novel* 19 (fall 1987): 296–310.

8   For this sense of the term Lennox is well in advance of Johnson, whose definition in the *Dictionary* is "a small tale, generally of love" (Johnson, *A Dictionary of the English Language in which the words are deduced from their originals and illustrated in their different significations by examples from the best writers to which are prefixed a history of the language, and an English grammar* [London: Robinson, 1828], 800).

9   Whereas criticism once assumed that Lennox was burlesquing the "romance" (understood in the restricted sense as the tradition of "extravagant" French narratives by Scudéry and so forth), recent feminist studies have pointed to Lennox's complex and ambivalent relation to this critique. The romance's attention to the etiquettes of courtship and the powerful, female realm of enchantment, according to Craft and Thompson, represented to women readers something of a utopian alternative to the misogynist realities of the eighteenth century. Lennox's understanding of Arabella's library hence records the loss of this domain of female literariness to the harsh necessities of real life. Langbauer makes the Derridean point that even as an

speare Illustrated complicates this Manichaean dynamic by continually invoking "the novel" as a third term distinct from romance and realism alike.

Lennox's theorization of the novel in *Shakespeare Illustrated* begins by comparing the comedies to their largely Italian sources. Like Fielding in *Tom Jones*, Lennox centers the elaboration and defense of the novel on "probability."[10] In the probable unfolding of the narrative (or "fable," "story," "action," and the like) and the probable delineation of character, Lennox finds the generic standards to evaluate Shakespeare's plays and their sources. Bandello's "novel" is preferable to *Twelfth Night*, for instance, because "the *novelist* is much more careful to preserve probability in his narration than the *poet* in his action: The wonder is that Shakespeare could task his invention to make those inci-

---

"anti-romance" it is predicated on, and contaminated by, that which it subordinates and refuses, namely the "romance" but also "the feminine," which are in her argument tantamount to the same thing. Patricia Meyer Spacks suggestively discusses the twin generic modes of romance and antiromance as matters of reader response or "desire." I shall argue below that *Shakespeare Illustrated* might be understood on a different set of terms having to do with the novel's relation to women readers and "effeminate" culture and with Lennox's coordinate understanding of the regulative value of female character.

10 We might consider Lennox's work, therefore, as part of the process in which, according to Douglas Patey, eighteenth-century critics elevate "probabilistic inference" from its earlier association with rhetoric and lesser truth to a type of knowledge continuous with scientific, or "demonstrative," certainty. Lennox's particular sense of "probability," further, seems to square with Patey's claim that the discourse of "probability" had, in addition to a central, mediating status in "Augustan literary theory," a particular grounding in the emergent novel, which was understood by the midcentury to combine and condense probabilistic theories of narrative with those of character (Patey, *Probability and Literary Form: Philosophic Theory and Literary Practice in the Augustan Age* [Cambridge: Cambridge University Press, 1984], 89, and passim). Patey's thesis wants to square the rise of the novel with neo-Baconian accounts of "probabilistic inference"; Lennox's understanding of the term is far more flexible and, in fact, demonstrates the resiliency or recrudescence of the Aristotelian model. For more general accounts of the "probabilistic" discourse in the eighteenth century see Ian Hacking, *The Emergence of Probability: A Philosophical Study of Early Ideas about Probability, Induction, and Statistical Inference* (London: Cambridge University Press, 1975) and Barbara J. Shapiro, *Probability and Certainty in Seventeenth-Century England: A Study of the Relationships between Natural Science, Religion, History, Law, and Literature* (Princeton, N.J.: Princeton University Press, 1983). See also Fielding, *The History of Tom Jones, a Foundling* (New York: Norton, 1973), esp. bk. 8, chap. 1.

dents unnatural and absurd."[11] Lennox's Shakespeare, a "poet" and a writer of "romance," fails to deliver the novelistic "probability" of a believable and meticulously constructed narrative. Comparing Cinthio's "novel" to *Measure for Measure*, Lennox writes that "the incidents in the novel are fewer, and less complex than in the play," but the advantage goes to the former: "wherever Shakespeare has invented, he is greatly below the novelist; since the incidents he has added are neither necessary nor probable" (1:21, 24). The "natural" events of the novel are preferable to Shakespeare's overweening and improbable "contrivance." Lennox repeats these terms virtually every time she juxtaposes the novel and Shakespeare. Boccaccio's "novel" outstrips *Cymbeline* because "the catastrophe of the story, though the same in the play as the novel . . . is very differently conducted in each: there is more *probability* in the incidents which lead to it in the *novel*, and more *contrivance* in the play" (1:146). The critique of Shakespeare by the source—of "romance" by "the novel"—is most evocatively discussed in connection with *The Winter's Tale*, where Lennox finds "poetic" and "romantic" machinery throughout the narrative.

> In the novel the *accidents* that happen to the exposed infant are governed by *chance*; the boat into which it was put being left in the midst of the ocean, is driven by the winds to the coast of Bohemia, and being spied by a sheaperd is drawn to Land.
>
> In the Play, Antigonous, who is bound by oath to leave the child in some desart place quite out of his father's dominiouns, is warned in a dream to call the infant Perdita, and carry it to Bohemia, and there leave it.
>
> Antigonous obeys, and this done, it is absolutely necessary he should not return to Sicily, otherwise it may be discovered where the Princess is left, and all the future adventures would fall to the ground; therefore a bear rushes out of the woods and devours him; the good natured bear, as it should seem, resolved not to spoil the story, passes by the little princess, who is to make so great

11 Lennox, *Shakespeare Illustrated; or, The Novels and Histories on which the Plays of Shakespeare are Founded, Collected and Translated from the Original Authors, with Critical Remarks in Three Volumes, by the Author of the Female Quixote* (London, 1753–54), 1:245; all italics, unless otherwise noted, are mine.

a figure hereafter, and a violent storm arising, splits the ship in which she was brought thither, so that all the sailors perishing, though they were near enough the shore to have saved themselves, no one is left to carry back any account of the affair to Sicily, and thereby prevent the adventures which are to follow.

All this is very *wonderful*: Shakespeare multiplies *miracle upon miracle* to bring about the same events in the Play, which *chance*, with so much *propriety*, performs in the *novel*. (2:80)

Lennox's account of Shakespeare's "improbable" narrative proposes a historical scheme for the development of novelistic narration. By reversing the sequence of cultural causality Lennox locates modern narration *prior* to Shakespeare in Robert Greene's "novel." Thus Shakespeare is conflated with the worldview of the cultural past when "wonder" and "miracle" guided narratives. The source or novel, in turn, is retroactively assigned the modern, desacralized strictures of "accident," "chance," and "propriety." Before Shakespeare, both in chronology and value, Lennox finds "probable" novels, the very novels she claims to write.[12] Lennox's metaleptic literary history argues that before Shakespeare's plays are contemporary novels, the very mass-cultural form that other critics find not only to come after Shakespeare but in fact to bespeak his canonicity.

"Only Interesting As They Are True"

With the history plays Lennox further develops the heterodox distinction between the novel and Shakespeare, prose and poetry, or probability and romance. She locates the former (in all its contemporaneity) prior to Shakespeare. Discussing *Hamlet* in the second volume, Lennox notes that "the Danish history of Saxo-Grammaticus [is] a story so full of incredible fancies, wild and improbable circumstances [that it] has

---

12 Loundsbury, Small, and Doody at various points this century have all claimed that Lennox's criticism is somehow anachronistic, that it looks back to the heyday of early-eighteenth-century neoclassicism. Both Small and Doody cite and accept Loundsbury's verdict, even if the latter would like to see the resurgence of such "Restoration" theory as "advancing upon" Shakespeare, understood as a monument of patriarchal culture (Small, 184–228; and Doody, 296–310). My reading, by contrast, attempts to place Lennox in the context of midcentury criticism.

more the appearance of *romance* than *historical fact*" (2:267). Yet "the historian, romantic as his relation seems, has the advantage of the poet in probability" (2:269). Lennox's equivocation over the source's "factual" status is nonetheless resolute in the categorical boundary it establishes around different species of prose texts. Whereas the novel offers probabilistic stories, history sets forth demonstrative fact; as the epistemological negation of both these narratives, in its turn, lies *poetry*, again bearing the name "romance."[13]

The category Lennox places before Shakespeare in the "observations" on the history plays is "history," a textual tradition found in such works as Holinshed's *Chronicles* and Hall's *Union of the Noble and Illustre Families of Lancaster and York*. She argues that histories must be evaluated on entirely different terms than novels; *Richard II*, for example, contains "several . . . instances in which Shakespeare's inattention to the history is plainly proved; and is therefore the less pardonable, as the subject of it is not one entire action, wrought up with a variety of beautiful incidents, which at once delight and instruct the mind; but *a dramatic narration of historical facts*, and a successive series of actions and events which are only interesting as they are true, and only pleasing as they are gracefully told" (3:109). Here Lennox invokes two narrative paradigms, first the novelistic "one entire action," and next the historical "narration of facts"; held to the latter's strictures, Shakespeare fails (moderately in the Henriad, extensively in *King Lear*) in comparison to the source. The failure, a departure from "fact," bears the name "fiction." The manner of the Duke of Suffolk's death in *Henry VI*, for instance, "is not to be found, either in Hall or Holinshed; and . . . *it has greatly the air of fiction*" (3:154). Whereas the novel's fiction is probabilistic (the opposite of the history's facts), Shakespeare's misplaced fiction in the history plays is insufficiently novelistic: "That little *fiction* which Shakespeare has introduced into [*Richard II*], is *imagined* with his usual carelessness and inattention to *probability*" (3:119). Thus

13 In *The Origins of the English Novel*, McKeon finds the stigmatized meaning of "romance" to be a touchstone in the dialectic of "naive-empiricism" and "extreme skepticism"; according to his account, "romance" emerges as such in this "open ended reversal" of literary and social polarities, thus enclosing otherwise random and disparate texts and discourses in a single, complex unit, or "simple abstraction" (25–65).

Shakespeare doubles the error; he slips from historical fact to fiction but once there foregoes novelistic probability for poetic romance. Holinshed and prose texts marked "history" are by contrast repositories of facts, "only interesting as they are true."

"Romance" thus names the position of negativity where Shakespeare is neither a novelist nor a historian although somehow defining of them both. His mistaken representation of the Queen in *Henry VI*, for example, is explained by his having "been misled by romance, or oral tradition, to give such improper manners to a Queen, and in an historical play, contradict the known facts on which it was founded" (3:144). In distorting both manners and facts, Shakespeare represents the dimness and barbarity of the cultural past, before novels, print, and even writing itself. According to the quasi-Aristotelian system in which the discourse of probability originates, the novel now supplants poetry as the oppositional term to history and so bears a version of imaginative truth different in kind from empirical facts. Lennox thus recasts novels in the grandest and oldest scheme for the ranking of literary forms as nothing less than the displacement of poetry.[14] *Shakespeare Illustrated* in this sense generically underscores *The Female Quixote*'s maxim that "truth is not always injured by fiction" by placing "the pleasing dress of the novel" against Shakespeare's fictional extravagance.[15] Unlike Fielding, or her closer associates Richardson and Johnson, Lennox proleptically identifies the novel with fiction and fiction with imagination.[16]

14 Even those who write directly on *Shakespeare Illustrated*, like Doody, have assumed that Lennox's interest in the history plays is not "careful," merely a contractual necessity bearing the marks of boredom and haste (299). Doody assumes that Lennox is only interested in "romances" and "comedies," because these are somehow more essentially "female," an assertion that would have difficulty explaining how the history plays are clearly Lennox's favorite; she reserves some of the highest praise in the whole work, for example, for *Henry VI*, where "the poet has given us the finest picture of true heroism, paternal tenderness, and filial love," and for *Henry VIII*, which is full of "pathetic eloquence," "propriety," and "inexpressible grace and beauty" (3:144, 177).

15 Lennox, *The Female Quixote; or, The Adventures of Arabella* (New York: Oxford University Press, 1982), 377.

16 The one time Johnson uses the term "fiction" in the dedication to *Shakespeare Illustrated* it is as a pejorative: "Shakespeare's excellence is not the fiction of the tale, but the representation of life" (x). Lennox's discussion of the history plays distin-

"Pious, Innocent, and Tender Maids"

Lennox's supplanting of poetic and romance narratives by the novel obtains also in the analogous domain of gendered character. As Margaret Doody has pointed out, Lennox focuses on Shakespeare's inattention to the etiquette of female characterization.[17] For Lennox,

guishes her account of the novel from Fielding's too. Since *Tom Jones* is called a "history" and defended on these grounds, Fielding cannot make Lennox's Aristotelian defense of the novel as the genre that has supplanted poetry in countervailing form to history; thus he writes, "It is by falling into fiction, therefore, that we generally offend against this rule, of deserting probability, which the historian seldom if ever quits, till he forsakes his character, and commences a writer of romance" (*Tom Jones*, 305). Raymond Williams argues that "fiction" became "almost synonymous with novels" only at the end of the century (*Keywords: A Vocabulary of Culture and Society* [London: Fontana, 1983], 134–45). See also Williams, *Marxism and Literature* (Oxford: Oxford University Press, 1977), 51–52.

17 In her reading of *Shakespeare Illustrated*, Doody argues that *The Female Quixote* and *Shakespeare Illustrated* share a common project of rescuing the "romantic" female world from the predations of masculine culture; just as Arabella's "romances" are misunderstood and defeated by male Augustans, so too the "romantic" source is misunderstood and defeated by Shakespeare. In both works Lennox looks back to "romance" for a "common and large-scale world of literary reference where women could be at home," and where the "private experience" of every woman writer would be inscribed. *Shakespeare Illustrated*, Doody concludes, exemplifies how "the romance was of great importance because it *allegorized every woman's life* for her" (Doody, 299–300). Lennox's work would suggest, however, that constructions of literary history and genre in the midcentury are not so reducible to the gender identity of critics, or collapsible into a simple binarism in which women are commensurate with "romance" and men with "Shakespeare." For how could we explain by this logic the enthusiasm in which some women critics read Shakespeare's plays? (most notable in this regard is Elizabeth Montagu, whose *Essay on the Genius and Writings of Shakespeare* [1769] outperforms Johnson in its nationalist bardolatry). Moreover, the antiromantic terms of Lennox's *Shakespeare* had been provided in part by such other critics as Mary de la Rivière Manley, whose *Secret History of Queen Zarah and the Zarazians* (London, 1705) begins by observing that "the prodigious length of the ancient romances, the mixture of so many extraordinary adventures, and the great number of actors that appear on the stage, and the likeness which is so little managed . . . has given a distaste to persons of good sense, and has made romances so much cry'd down"(A2). Although Lennox would find Manley's text itself to be a "romance," her critique of Shakespeare repeats Manley's generic terminology (its juxtaposition of the simple and the complex, the extraordinary and the probable, and so forth). The novelistic critique of romance, which revolves around the depiction of female characters, thus has a long sedimented prehistory in attempts to define late-seventeenth- and eighteenth-century narratives, dating back at least to the preface of Congreve's *Incognita*

Shakespeare and the novel represent two historically specific regimes of gender. Her elaboration of female character derives its terms, I would suggest, from what Nancy Armstrong argues is the emergent novel's singular concern with presenting and policing female behavior according to "domestic ideology" (Armstrong, esp. 96–160). Lennox locates in the sources what Armstrong calls "domestic women," finding there the "propriety" she had initially constructed around narrative. In *Measure for Measure*, for instance, Isabella is superior to Cinthio's Epitia when she refuses to sleep with the Duke as Claudio requests in order to save his life, but unpalatably coarse and violent in her refusal, rather than (like Epitia) decorous and feminine: "The character of Isabella in the play seems to be an improvement upon that of Epitia in the novel; for Isabella absolutely refuses, and persists in her refusal, to give up her honour to save her brother's life; whereas Epitia, overcome by her own *tendernous* of nature, and affecting prayers of the unhappy youth, yields to what her soul abhors, to redeem him from a shameful death" (*Shakespeare Illustrated*, 1:33). Even though Isabella is properly virtuous, she "is a mere vixon in her virtue" when compared to the "modest, tender" speech of Epitia (1:33). Lennox then imagines how she might rewrite them both into an idealized paragon of female propriety:

> From her *character*... one might have expected *mild expostulations, wise reasonings, and gentle rebukes*: his desire of life, though purchased by methods she could not approve, was a natural frailty, which a sister might have pitied and excused, and have made use of her superior understanding to reason down his fears, recall nobler ideas to his mind, teach him what was due to *her honour* and his own, and reconcile him to his own approaching death, by arguments drawn from that religion and virtue of which she made so high a profession; but that torrent of abusive language, those *coarse and unwomanly* reflexions ... her exulting cruelty to dying

(1692). Lennox is distinctive in placing the novel before romance (identified with Shakespeare); the notion that the novel supplants romance (by virtue of its empirical adequacy) becomes axiomatic for English criticism later in the century, as in for example Reeve, *The Progress of Romance through Times, Countries, and Manners* (London, 1785): "no writings are more different than the ancient *Romance* and the modern *Novel*" (7).

youth, are the manners of an affecting prude, outrageous in her seeming virtue, not a *pious, innocent, and tender maid.* (1:33–4)

Lennox's chastening combination of Epitia and Isabella (where the former's femininity is retained along with the latter's virginity) invokes a notion of female character as at once a formal and social ideal. Probabilistic "expectation," in Lennox's reading, hinges on the propriety of female characters, who should act in predictably domestic ways. For this reason Lennox is equally puzzled by Isabella's inability to recant her lie about having given in to the Duke: "Is this *natural?* Is it *probable* that Isabella would thus publicly bring a false imputation of her honour, and, though innocent and unstained, suffer the world to believe her violated?" (1:34). As the countervailing romance, Shakespeare's immodest narrative is redoubled by his unchaste and unwomanly characters. Lennox's construal of probable "women" thus repeats her metalepsis, this time by viewing the past through the lens of a contemporary ideal of restraint, propriety, and domestic moralism.[18]

In constructing probable female character, Lennox strongly opposes Shakespearean cross-dressing, which demonstrates a disregard not only for female propriety but above all for the very gender boundaries that ground her novelistic practice. In *Twelfth Night,* for instance, Shakespeare "very much lessens the probability of the story" by focusing on Viola's transvestism: "a very natural scheme this," Lennox ironically notes, "for a beautiful and virtuous young lady to throw off all at once the *modesty and reservedness of her sex,* mix at once among men, herself disguised like one: and, prest by no necessity, influenced by no

---

18 On this ideology of female propriety and its connection both to the novel and to social structures in the eighteenth century see Mary Poovey, *The Proper Lady and the Woman Writer: Ideology as Style in the Works of Mary Wollstonecraft, Mary Shelley, and Jane Austen* (Chicago: University of Chicago Press, 1984). Poovey argues that ideologies of female conduct emerge out of the "complex social role that actual women played" during the eighteenth century, on the one hand as ballast in familial property structures (the "settlement" and transfer of estates and moneys) and on the other as a totem for the "political and economic triumph of the middle classes" (15, 10, and passism). Although thematically linked, Poovey's account of the emergence of the "proper lady" over the long course of the eighteenth century is at implicit odds with Armstrong's, insofar as the former understands ideologies of conduct as effects of larger historical structures and transformations, whereas the latter sees them as causes.

passion, expose herself to all the dangerous consequences of so unworthy and shameful a situation" (1:233–44). Lennox here rests what Doody calls her "running argument in favor of women" on a restricted set of behavior and codes that are affronted by Viola's slippage into male attire and actions and by the absence, in Olivia's desire for the cross-dressed Viola, of "any of those emotions which bashfulness, delicacy, and . . . the decorum of her sex and birth oblige" (Doody, 300; and Lennox, 1:246). Novels are better suited to the project of fixing gender in the appropriate body. Since they tell restrained stories (with no excess of events) through chaste characters (with no excess of desire), it is characteristic when "we find this incident managed with much more decency in the novel" (1:244).

The problematic of female character may now be understood under the historical rubric of genre. Lennox does take issue with Shakespeare's tendency to "humiliate his women," as Doody argues, but in order to imagine novelistic or *proper* female characters (Doody, 305–6). Comparing *The Winter's Tale* to its source, Robert Greene's novel, Lennox notes that Hermione ought to be "a virtuous and affectionate wife" and asks why she "conceal[s] herself during sixteen years in a solitary house, though she was sensible that her repentant husband was all that time consuming away with grief and remorse for her death?" (2:85). Shakespeare's cruelty is "a mean and absurd *contrivance*" that is to be faulted for confounding the formal probability of the novel (2:85). "How ridiculous also in a great queen, to submit to such buffoonery as standing on a pedestal, motionless, her eyes fixed, and at last to be conjured down by the *magical* command of Paulina. . . . The novel has nothing in it *half so low and improbable as this contrivance* of the statue," a judgment based at once on the behavior of the novel's characters and the secular rationality of its narrative (2:87). *Shakespeare Illustrated* targets the "humiliating" treatment of Hermione on behalf of constructing more probable narratives, more probable female characters, and more modest and tender maids; that is, on behalf of an ideology inseparable from the form of the novel itself.

This process is not simply generic, however, but responds to the situation of the novel within the hierarchically structured domain of culture. Lennox's understanding of the novel stakes a modern (or "bourgeois") gender system against the older "Shakespearean" system because she is constructing the novel as a response to a reading public imagined to include women. The attention to female characterization, in this sense, momentarily reinvents Shakespeare as unable to represent gender difference in order to advertise how the novel regulates female reading. Considered from this perspective, Lennox is part of the larger attempt by midcentury criticism to understand female literacy and mass-culture. For many eighteenth-century critics the novel signified women readers, and its predominance augured the "effeminizing" of cultural life. Responses to this situation varied from Upton's "masculine and nervous Shakespeare," to Fielding's hostility to the domestic novel, to what we shall see as Johnson's anxious dedication to *Shakespeare Illustrated*. Lennox by contrast emphasized the redemptive value of "pious and innocent" characters and the "imaginative" truth of narrative.

"Sex and Birth"

Lennox's attempt to elevate the novel works through class problems as well as those of gender and thus underscores the generic and social dimension to her criticism. Novelistically proper and decorous behavior, she claims, is not only the province of "tender maids" but also and inseparably that of "quality." The cross-dressing incident in *Twelfth Night* "is handled with much more decency in the novel," where it is given to a lower-class woman: "Catella acts the same part in the novel that Olivia does in the play; but Catella is a young gay libertine girl, whose birth was but mean, and education neglected; it was not therefore surprising that she should so easily fall in love with a page, indecently court him, and resolve to marry him, such an inconsiderate conduct was agreeable to her *character*; but in the *noble and virtuous* Olivia, 'tis unnatural and absurd" (1:247). Lennox regularly demands that Shakespeare's characters act in ways "proper" to their social rank. If any part of *Shakespeare Illustrated* is anachronistic, as Lennox's biographer Miriam Rossiter Small and Margaret Doody both claim, it may be the insistence on the one-to-one correspondence between birth and worth, between what Lennox calls here "nobility" and "virtue."[19] Yet

19 For the reading of Lennox as anachronistic, or as a belated neoclassicist, see n. 12.

even this apparent anachronism is launched from new social and aesthetic coordinates. In a telling philological exchange with Thomas Rymer, Lennox reprimands the critic for mistaking Cinthio's Desdemona for a "middle rank" woman rather than one "of high birth": "Cinthio calls her Cittadina, which Mr Rymer translates a simple citizen; but the Italians by the phrase mean a woman of Quality. If they were, for example, to speak of a woman of the middle rank, in Rome, they would say, Una Romana; if a noble lady, Una Cittadina Romana: So in Venice they call a simple citizen Una Venitiana; but a woman of Quality, Una Cittadina Venitiana" (1:132). The novel's formal consistency depends on Desdemona's high birth, since "there is less improbability in supposing a noble lady, educated in sentiments superior to the vulgar, should fall in love with a man merely for the qualities of his mind than that a mean citizen should be possessed of such exalted ideas, as to overlook the disparity of years and complexion, and be enamored of virtue in the person of a Moor" (1:132). Lennox understands Quality as opposed not simply to a generalized "vulgar" but more directly to that new and equivocal class, the middle rank. The "simplicity in manners, . . . virtue and innocence" that define novelistic women by this measure also define the aristocracy (1:131).

The social problem of a culturally ambiguous middle rank also underlies Lennox's difficulty with *Cymbeline*, which is faulted for shifting from Boccaccio's novelistic setting in a tavern filled with middle-class players to a court stocked with nobility. As with the discussion of *Othello*, social struggle is distilled into the middle rank and quality: "Shakespeare makes the Lady in question, not the wife of the merchant, but the heiress of a great kingdom. . . . The husband, who lays so indiscreet a wager, not a simple trader intoxicated with liquor, but a young noble" (1:156). Since Boccaccio's novel does not represent Quality but rather stigmatizes the middle rank, we may understand Lennox's point to be that the novel best represents the social order according to the probabilities of character and narrative. According to Lennox's reading, Shakespeare confounds social class by letting heiresses and nobles enact the indecorous behavior suitable for traders and merchants. Lennox argues in other words that the novel is the best genre to depict status or rank and that Shakespeare's social problems are intrinsically formal, bringing about "strange adventures . . . at the expense of probability" (1:162). Reiterating that Shakespeare "has given the manners of a tradesman's wife, and two merchants intoxicated with liquor, to a great Princess, an English hero, and a noble Roman," Lennox adds, "to this injudicious change of the characters is owing all the absurdities of this part of Shakespeare's plot" (1:156). The novel, in this way, is advanced specifically against the middle rank, figured as the reborn and highly problematic vulgar class.

The novel's relation to social class is less a result of identity (whether the author's, the critic's, or the characters') than a response to the genre's position in literary culture.[20] Lennox adverts to the class of characters so as to elevate the "class" of the novel on the hierarchy of forms, to strip it of any conflation with the unruly reading practices of emergent mass-culture. Her commitment to status is not simply conservative nostalgia, then, but an attempt to render the novel in such a way as to combat its social ambiguities. The continual recourse to the landowning aristocracy restrains the declassing connection of the novel to the mass-cultural public by placing the novel in the past, before Shakespeare's romantic confusion of social rank. Lennox is thus concerned with sex and birth to the degree that they correspond to the historical development of genre and forms. Her positing of the novel in a superseded aristocratic world in which female virtue held sway is aimed at a certain configuration in the present: the novel is the fully modern and paradigmatic genre, able to represent gender and social rank with probability at the level of both narrative and character. Lennox's formulation equips the novel with the formal means to solve problems besetting literary culture; its elevated position in her thought, in this sense, has the imaginary authority of history itself.

"Entertaining Novels"

The reception of Lennox's work immediately problematized the placement of the novel against romance, the mass-culture of the middle

20 In Lennox's case, any personal identification with the aristocracy can only be at the level of class longing. Her own position was precarious throughout her entire life. For Lennox's biography see Small (n. 7) and Kathryn Shevelow, "Charlotte Lennox," in *A Dictionary of British and American Women Writers, 1660–1800*, ed. Janet Todd (Totowa, N.J.: Rowman and Allenheld, 1985), 196–8.

rank. Soon after its printing, *Shakespeare Illustrated* received its first public notice from *The Gentleman's Magazine* (1753), in a monthly catalog of new publications and an excerpt and review a month later. The magazine divided new publications into eleven discursive categories—divinity, morality, physic, policy, history, antiquities, biography, poetry, entertainment, misc., and sermons. *Shakespeare Illustrated* fell under "entertainment," along with travel narratives, true histories, novels, ballads, and so on.[21] "These volumes contain entertaining novels, and a play of Plautus, elegantly translated from the Italian, French, Latin, and Danish; the author submits them as the original stories, on which the following plays of Shakespeare are founded. . . . A parallel is then drawn between the play and the novel and the difference critically marked" (*Gentleman's Magazine*, 250 n. xxiii). The classification of *Shakespeare Illustrated* thus rests on the "entertaining novels" Lennox translates and condenses for the reader, the assumption being that one would go to Lennox's text not out of a scholarly or aesthetic interest in Shakespeare but for the pleasure of reading novels. As befits one of the first truly mass-produced periodicals, the "first *magazine*," in Carl Carlson's words, *The Gentleman's Magazine* classifies novels according to their cultural status as light reading, as that new and unstable category "entertainment" staked in opposition to the heavy weight of "poetry" or "antiquities."

The Gentleman's Magazine responds to Lennox's conception of the novel, in other words, by assimilating it into the larger class of works purchasable for imaginative "entertainment" (a term that Johnson tellingly associates in the *Dictionary* with "lower-comedy" [404]). The following month, the magazine printed Lennox's discussion of *Romeo and Juliet* to demonstrate the attractiveness of the play's source for their readers: "We have selected *Romeo and Juliet* for a specimen of what has been done by this writer to illustrate Shakespeare, because it is one of

21 *The Gentleman's Magazine* awaits critical analysis, although it is for my mind a crucial instrument not only in the long-term structural transformation of the public sphere in the direction of mass-produced commodity journalism but also in the related history of the division and dissection of discourses and knowledge, which their categorization of new publications at once records and instances. The only extensive study of the magazine is Carl Carlson, *The First Magazine: A History of the Gentleman's Magazine* (Providence, R.I.: Brown University Press, 1938).

his most regular pieces, and at present more generally known than any other. But whoever would make a just estimate of his merit should see the whole work in which his resources are displayed, his faults detected, and many beauties of which he was supposed to be the inventor, restored to those whom they were borrowed" (*Gentleman's Magazine*, 256 n. xxiv). Like Lennox, *The Gentleman's Magazine* prefers the novel to Shakespeare, applauding the critic's evaluative restoration of beauty to the source and noting that Shakespeare's most popular play will prove an even more entertaining novel. The "novel" of *Romeo and Juliet*, they go on to promise, is one of many entertaining narratives offered by Lennox's text. Unlike Lennox, the magazine is interested in the popularity of the novel, a position that might be understood according to the magazine's presumptive audience and their relative proximity to the exchange of printed goods. The magazine's founder, Edmund Cave, was himself a middle-class printer-publisher, and the subtitle for his periodical was "Trader's Monthly," positioning his readers within the very middle rank Lennox finds culturally debasing. From its position within the circuits of print culture, *The Gentleman's Magazine* claims to grasp the desire of the reading public for "entertainment," for monthly periodicals and novels. The magazine's misreading of Lennox's high-cultural resistance to the market and the middle rank is not so much an error, therefore, as an institutional misrecognition.

"Absolutely Necessary to a Perfect Knowledge of the Abilities of Shakespeare"

Though *The Gentleman's Magazine* slots *Shakespeare Illustrated* as "entertainment," Johnson's singularly fraught and ambivalent dedication of the volumes to Lord Orrery, written in Lennox's name, places Shakespeare in the high-cultural position mapped by Lennox for the novel.[22] Johnson begins by announcing Lennox's claims to antiquarian

22 At some point during the writing of *Shakespeare Illustrated,* Johnson wrote to an apparently ill Lennox that "I hope you take care to observe the Doctor's prescriptions, and take your physick regularly, for I shall soon come to enquire. I should be sorry to lose criticism in her bloom. Your remarks are I think all very judicious, clearly expressed, and incontrovertibly certain. When Shakespeare is demolished your wings

cultural capital: "I have no other pretence to the honour of a patron-age, so illustrious as that of your Lordship, than the merit of attempt-ing what has by some considerable neglect been hitherto omitted, though absolutely necessary to a perfect knowledge of the abilities of Shakespeare" (*Shakespeare Illustrated*, iii–iv); he continues, "I have *dili-gently* read the works of Shakespeare, and now presume to lay the results of my searches before your Lordship, before that judge whom Pliny himself would wished for his assesor to hear a literary cause" (vi–vii). Though Johnson reduces the work to a compilation of sources, this reduction confirms "the perfect knowledge" of Lennox and "the abilities of Shakespeare." Johnson attempts to fix Lennox's work within the larger designs of his criticism and thus elevate the critic (as "diligent" reader of high-cultural texts) and Shakespeare (as the cultural capital of the aristocracy). Johnson's nomination of *Shake-speare Illustrated* as "a literary cause" is not at all a misnomer, then, except that what "literary" signifies in the dedication is at some odds with its meaning in the rest of the work (vii).

Johnson is well aware that Lennox does not share the same under-standing of the "literary." The bulk of the dedication discounts the crit-ical work to follow. Johnson dismisses in advance the central terms of Lennox's criticism, finding probability and plot to be equally insignifi-cant to a true understanding of Shakespeare's genius. "The truth is, a very small part of the reputation of this mighty genius depends upon the naked plot or story of his plays"; hence "it is not perhaps very nec-essary to inquire whether the vehicle of so much delight and instruc-tion be a story probable, or unlikely, native or foreign" (viii, xi). John-son prefers the categories of endurance and universality, whereby Shakespeare's value derives from his lasting depiction of "human

will be full summed and I will fly you at Milton; for you are a bird of prey, but the bird of Jupiter" (Johnson, *Letters* [Princeton, N.J.: Princeton University Press, 1992], 1:71). The editor's dating of the letter as May 1753 because of the *Shakespeare Illus-trated* reference (which was published that month) seems to me to be erroneous, since Johnson is clearly referring to work in progress. It is, I would argue, undecidable whether Johnson privately enjoyed Lennox's work but found it necessary to discount it in pub-lic, or if his initial response changed as he continued to read, or if he is simply con-soling a sick friend. For whatever reason, however, Johnson never sent Lennox after Milton.

actions, passions, and habits" (viii). Johnson's attempt to generalize against the overweening particularities of the novel is managed by placing Shakespeare in what he understands, against Lennox, to be the author's cultural context, the "disposition of the age" (ix): "He lived in an age when the books of Chivalry were yet popular, and when therefore the minds of his auditors were not accustomed to balance *probabilities*, or to examine nicely the proportion between *causes and effects*" (viii–ix). To straighten Lennox's metalepsis, Johnson claims that Shakespeare's sources in fact lead the author to write in ways contrary to the reading habits of the eighteenth century. *Romances*, not novels, are what lay behind and determine the formal structures of Shakespeare's plays, he argues; such "books of chivalry" explain Shakespeare's difference from the present, whose signal cultural form, the novel, "balance[s] probabilities" (ix). Shakespeare is to be credited, however, for transcending the romantic source material to appeal to all humans at all times. Johnson's and Lennox's literary histories are thus strikingly different. According to Johnson romances or books of chivalry are either rewritten into the canon by Shakespeare or persist in literary history until they are revived by novelists in the eighteenth century. Whereas Shakespeare transfigures romance into the literary, contemporary authors remake romance into the novel, a genre whose literary status is entirely unclear. The romance reemerges in commodity culture as the novel, whose particularities signal the ephemerality of demand. Like Lennox, Johnson emphasizes the relationship between the source material and the novel but insists that it is one of continuity rather than identity; from his perspective, "probability" is an eighteenth-century invention, newly invented to manage the domain of literary culture.

Johnson responds to Lennox in this fashion as part of his larger engagement with the novel as an emergent genre. His complex and ambivalent response to the works of Fielding, Richardson, and Smollett is well known. Three years before the dedication to *Shakespeare Illustrated* he warned in the *Rambler* no. 4 (arguably the most cited of his critical essays) that the curious "works of fiction with which the present generation seems . . . delighted, . . . are written chiefly to the young, the ignorant and the idle, to whom they serve as lectures of conduct, and introductions into life. They are the entertainment of minds unfurnished with ideas, and therefore easily susceptible of impressions; not fixed by principles, and therefore easily following the current of fancy; not informed by experience, and consequently open to every false suggestion and partial account."[23] Elsewhere Johnson will celebrate the taste of the "common reader" and position himself against cultural elitism, but the popularity of the novel only makes him uneasy.[24] Patricia Meyer Spacks has argued that Johnson's relation to Lennox demonstrates how his "anxiety about women was massive and manifest"(*Desire and Truth*, 241). In *Shakespeare Illustrated*, this anxiety impinges greatly on the position Johnson accords the novel in literary history. He has Lennox apologize, in the dedication, for the problems that "my sex" may have broached in the valuation of texts, namely, the preference for novels (vi). Whereas in the *Rambler* Johnson tries to solve the problem of the novel by stressing its exclusively didactic vocation to "increase prudence without impairing virtue" (177), in the dedication to Lennox's work he pitches Shakespeare against the novel as a masculinized high-cultural form. This "literary cause," he contends, is quite a serious matter: "Some danger there is, lest [Shakespeare's] admirers should think him injured . . . and clamour as at the diminution of the honour of that nation, which boasts herself the parent of so great a poet" (vii).

Lennox's revisionary and heterodox derogation of Shakespeare might threaten national honor. Saving Shakespeare and the national canon requires demoting the novel on the very terms of Lennox's criticism. Justifying Shakespeare's negligence with "the naked plot or story," Johnson writes: "Of all the *novels and romances* that wit or idleness, vanity or indigence have pushed into the world, there are very few, of which the end cannot be conjectured from the beginning; or where the authors have done more, than to transpose the incidents of

23 Johnson, *Rambler* no. 4, in *The Yale Edition of the Works of Samuel Johnson*, ed. W. J. Bate and Albrecht B. Strauss (New Haven, Conn.: Yale University Press, 1969), 21.

24 Johnson's edition of Shakespeare, for instance, leaves the final adjudication of textual problems to the "reader." His notion of the "common reader" is famously trumpeted years later in the life of Gray, where he "rejoices to concur with the common reader" in enjoying the Elegy; this occurs however as a response to Bell's mass-marketed editions of "English Poets." Johnson's concurrence in this sense is an attempt to secure the boundaries of elite culture from the commodification of high-cultural texts.

other tales, or strip the circumstances for one event for the decoration of the other" (vi). Whereas Lennox labors to distinguish the novel from romance, Johnson collapses the two in order to oppose them at once to Shakespeare. According to Johnson, novelists founder in the ruck of narrative while Shakespeare writes of timeless human feeling. Not a simple matter of style, the difference implies a distinction at the level of value and cultural status. Shakespeare's transcendent position in the vernacular canon is predicated on his inattention to the very etiquettes of plotting upon which novelists are ineradicably bound. Lennox's focus on the probability of narrative, by this measure, simply indicates the novel's mass-cultural status as romance.

Johnson's account in the dedication is mediated, however, by the novel form it intends to bracket. The danger in *Shakespeare Illustrated* has to do with its reversal of novel and Shakespeare only in the domain of narrative. Lennox's focus on the probability of character is not addressed because, rather than discount character as inconsequential to literary works, Johnson takes the different approach of describing it as constituting Shakespearean "genius." For Lennox, Shakespeare's characters act "improbably" and "unbelievably"; Johnson asserts that Shakespeare deserves credit for having "exhibited many characters, in many changes of situation" (x). "These characters are so copiously diversified, and some of them so justly pursued, that his works may be considered a map of life, a faithful miniature of human transactions, and he that has read Shakespeare with attention, will perhaps find little new in the crouded world" (x). For as much as he dismisses the novel (on the plane of narrative) as an "idle" venture sprung from commodity culture, Johnson celebrates Shakespeare's delineation of character in the novelistic manner of the conduct book, complete with attentive advice on the human transactions that enable one to better get along in the world.[25] The imaginary situation of reading Shakespeare, at this point in Johnson's account, converges with that of reading novels as Johnson understands the practice in the *Rambler*, where "common readers" are to "fix their eyes upon [a character] with closer attention, and hope by observing his behaviour and success to *regulate their own practices*, when they

---

25 The eighteenth-century conduct book is essential to both Armstrong's and Poovey's account of the rise of the novel (see Armstrong, 28–96; and Poovey, 3–48).

shall be engaged in the like part" (21; emphasis added). A novel's characters must be undiluted, although probable, moral paragons for the "common mind": "I cannot discover why there should not be exhibited the most perfect idea of virtue; of virtue not angelical, nor above *probability*, for what we cannot credit we shall never imitate, but the highest and purest that humanity can reach" (24). The dedication's repetition of the *Rambler*'s understanding of how one ought to read a novel, in which Shakespeare's characters are as regulative and imitable as a conduct book, allows Johnson briefly to approximate Lennox's aesthetic. For nowhere is the *Rambler*'s ideal of character more programmatically installed, perhaps, than in the main body of *Shakespeare Illustrated*, which finds the "perfect idea of virtue" in Shakespeare's sources.

Lennox does not disagree with Johnson over how to read novels, then—her citation of the *Rambler* at the close of *The Female Quixote* discusses just this question; rather, she diverges from Johnson over where to place the novel in the canon and over the relative value of transcendence and probability. Lennox applies Johnson's understanding of novelistic character onto Shakespeare and finds him wanting, a move that makes Johnson reconsider what in Shakespeare (or in high-canonical literature in general) outstrips the novel. Johnson's rendering of Shakespeare in the regulative, although culturally declassing, manner of the conduct book is thus countered by a "literary" distinction he draws between Shakespeare and the novel soon after he appears to identify them around character. Here Johnson shifts discussion away from the quasi-novelistic ideal of Shakespearean conduct. "It has hitherto been unnoticed that his heroes are men, that the love and hatred, the hopes and fears of his chief personages are such as are common to other human beings, and not like those which later times have exhibited, peculiar to phantoms that strut upon the stage" (x). The characters in the "world" that Shakespeare paints so accurately as to be a "faithful miniature" are ultimately different from those "humanity can reach" because of their "generality," or transcendence of the "peculiar phantoms" more suitable for instruction in conduct. Shakespeare's personages are ultimately what distinguishes his works from the novels that "later times have exhibited" because, now returning to the narrative argument, unlike novels "Shakespeare's Excellence is not the fiction of a tale, but the representation of life and his reputation is therefore safe, till human nature shall be changed" (xi). To distinguish Shakespeare from the novel, Johnson describes the former's characters in the language that he had reserved for narrative, abandoning the didacticism of character for the aesthetics of transcendence. Johnson's depiction of the universal and timeless humanity of poetry places Shakespeare outside characterological particularity by situating him against the later times of Lennox's novel, that is, against the present moment of probability and commodity culture, women readers and fiction.

At its most extreme, Johnson's literary history aims to sunder the novel from Shakespeare and so from "the literary" on all generic and social counts. Yet his argument depends on Lennox's novel. Lennox prompts Johnson to describe Shakespeare in terms that remain central to his doctrine in the preface to the plays twelve years later, where Shakespeare is cast as an "adamant" withstanding the buffeting tides of history.[26] The persistence of the novel in Johnson's thought represents not only Lennox's influence but also the common historical situation of the two critics. Seen as a cultural problem, the particular conjuncture of "novels and romances" brings about and informs the language of Johnson's formation of the vernacular canon. Johnson's devaluation of the source material is directed at the same conditions as Lennox's elevation. Whereas Lennox reverses Shakespeare and the novel, Johnson reinscribes their constitutive distance on the hierarchy of literary

26 Johnson's preface reaches its rhetorical crescendo in a recapitulation of his response to Lennox: "As his personages act upon principles arising from genuine passion, very little modified by particular forms, their pleasures and vexations are communicable to all times and to all places; they are natural and therefore durable; the adventitious peculiarities of personal habits, are only superficial dies, bright and pleasing for a little while, yet soon fading to a dim tinct without any remains of former lustre; but the discriminations of true passion are the colours of nature; they pervade the whole mass, and can only perish with the body that exhibits them. The accidental compositions of heterogeneous modes are dissolved by the chance which combined them; but the uniform simplicity of primitive qualities neither admits increase, nor suffers decay. The sand heaped by one flood is scattered by another, but the rock always continues in its place. The stream of time, which is continually washing the dissoluble fabricks of other poets, passes without injury by the adamant of Shakespeare" (Arthur Sherbo, ed., *The Yale Edition of the Works of Samuel Johnson*, vol. 7 [New Haven, Conn.: Yale University Press, 1968], 69–70).

forms. Considered from this perspective, their critical positions share certain underlying assumptions: if Lennox placed Shakespeare in the distance of a brutish past that did not yet know how to construe probable narratives and characters, then Johnson rewrites this literary history as the sign of Shakespeare's value. Likewise, both critics posit value at the greatest distance from the pressure of the market. (Only *The Gentleman's Magazine*, in this instance, can imagine the market as culturally elevating.) The similarity of Johnson and Lennox's otherwise very different constructions of the vernacular tradition demonstrates how Shakespeare and the novel emerge together, in this moment, as compensatory responses to the conditions of cultural production and consumption—the encroaching identity of print culture with the market as such, the "groaning of the press under the weight of novels," and the transformation of the reading public so as to include more women and a greater number of the middle rank. Recent work on the emergence of the novel has importantly contextualized the genre in terms of large-scale social transformation culminating at this historical moment.[27] The Lennox-Johnson debate suggests that the novel was one element in a larger formation, which among other things positioned "Shakespeare" as the high-canonical solution to the problem of the reading public. By this measure, the debate is a particularly evocative moment in the social origins of literary history.

27 See the texts listed in n. 1.

Godwin and the Republican Romance

Jon Klancher

A crisis of literature and of the left: William Godwin's great half-decade, from 1793 to 1798, spans a moment in literary history that was to prove ruinous to the British republic of letters and to its central category, the larger Enlightenment classification of "literature." It was a time when literature itself—still the spacious universe of eighteenth-century written genres that included natural philosophy, moral philosophy, historiography, and political economy, as well as poetry, drama, and criticism—had become associated in Britain with the Dissenters, who edited the four leading literary reviews, and with intellectuals such as Godwin or Paine, who modeled the progressive's ideal political republic upon the republic of letters.[1] Fractious and fragile by the mid-1790s, the republic of letters formed the modernized, much-expanded version of the old *Respublica literaria*, of which the most decisive renunciation in the years to come would be Coleridge's *Biographia Literaria*, and toward which Godwin would direct his own

---

1 My reading of this situation in the British 1790s will exploit the ambiguity of Jürgen Habermas's remark: "The two forms of public sphere"—literary and political—"blended with each other in a peculiar fashion" (*Structural Transformation of the Public Sphere: An Inquiry into a Category of Bourgeois Society*, trans. Thomas Burger [Cambridge: MIT Press, 1989], 56). For the political context of later eighteenth-century reviewing I rely in part on Derek Roper's detailed account, *Reviewing before the "Edinburgh": 1788–1802* (Newark: University of Delaware Press, 1978).

searching, troubled inquiries following the original publication of *An Enquiry Concerning Political Justice* in 1793. It was above all in *The Enquirer: Reflections on Education, Manners, and Literature* (1797) that Godwin's writing complicated our historical sense of those divisions that figured into his fin-de-siècle moment in one way and in our own in another: between Enlightenment and romanticism, history and fiction, genre and politics, necessity and contingency, modernity and its critics.

In January 1797 the author of *Caleb Williams* drafted an essay on narrative genre theory, "Of History and Romance," for a projected second volume of the *Enquirer*, which he planned to follow from the first. Instead of being revised and published, however, Godwin's essay was dropped into a drawer of manuscript; it appeared for the first time in print as an appendix to Maurice Hindle's 1988 Penguin edition of *Caleb Williams*. Like the Enquirer as a whole, "Of History and Romance" was written when the progressive sector of England's public sphere was about to collapse, and the machinery of the publications industry that had been central to it was being taken over by a new generation of sophisticated conservative intellectuals.[2] Today, "Of History and Romance" may well appear to be the first of those romantic critical programs that promoted literary genre-reform as the means to induce greater social and ideological reform in history. I refer to genre-reforming agendas of Wordsworth, Coleridge, Joanna Baillie, or Shelley, all sharing in one political sense or another the ambition of transforming a received poetic, dramatic, or narrative genre to produce, as Shelley phrased it, "the seeds at once of its own and of social renovation."[3] Along such lines, Godwin forged a critique of Enlightenment universal history—as the mystified collective autobiography of modern Britain—and promoted in its place the reflexive historical romance as a superior mode of historiography capable of changing the ideologies of modern history. Recent commentators on this work have been especially impressed by what appears to be Godwin's final and most provocative claim, that "the writer of

2 On Godwin's intellectual and social context in the 1790s see Mark Philp, *Godwin's Political Justice* (Ithaca, N.Y.: Cornell University Press, 1986), esp. 214–30.

3 Shelley, "Defense of Poetry," in *Shelley's Poetry and Prose: Authoritative Texts, Criticism*, ed. Donald H. Reiman (New York: Norton, 1977), 493.

romance is to be considered as the writer of real history; while he who was formerly called the historian, must be contented to step down into the place of his rival, with this disadvantage, that *he* is a romance writer, without the arduous, the enthusiastic, and the sublime licence of imagination."[4]

Yet, while "Of History and Romance" makes the genre-reforming moves that would shortly become a characteristic gesture of British romantic criticism, Godwin also provocatively complicated the reflexive effort to transform genre in order to change history. I will take Godwin's 1797 text as an unusual guide to the late eighteenth century's political crisis of the Enlightenment category of literature as generally educated discourse. Whether prose fiction was or should be one of the genres encompassed by the Enlightenment category of literature was a question Godwin took up in "Of History and Romance"; by so doing, he tested the boundaries and internal principles of this category at a time of extraordinary political pressure. Godwin confronted in this essay the two most striking narrative developments of the later eighteenth century: what recent cultural historians have called the quantitative rise or culture-industrial "takeoff" of the British novel between 1770 and 1800, on the one hand; and the power of that new and imposing account of the evolution of modernity, Scottish "philosophical history," on the

---

4 Godwin, "Of History and Romance," app. 4 of *Things as They Are; or, The Adventures of Caleb Williams*, ed. Maurice Hindle (New York: Penguin, 1988), 372. All page references will refer to the Hindle text. The essay has subsequently appeared as "Essay on History and Romance," in *Political and Philosophical Writings of William Godwin*, ed. Mark Philp (London: William Pickering, 1993), 5:290–301. For brief commentaries on this essay see Paul Hamilton, "Coleridge and Godwin in the 1790s," in *The Coleridge Connection*, ed. Molly Lefebure and Richard Gravil (London: Macmillan, 1990), 41–59; Pamela Clemit, *The Godwinian Novel: The Rational Fictions of Godwin, Brockden Brown, Mary Shelley* (Oxford: Clarendon, 1993), 79–81; Mark Philp and Marilyn Butler, introduction to *Collected Novels and Memoirs of William Godwin*, ed. Mark Philp (London: William Pickering, 1992), 23–4; Clifford Siskin, "Eighteenth-Century Periodicals and the Romantic Rise of the Novel," *Studies in the Novel* (1994): 38–9. The first and still the most complete discussion to date is David McCracken, "Godwin's Literary Theory: The Alliance between Fiction and Political Philosophy," *Philological Quarterly* 49 (1970): 113–33. On Godwin's reflexivity more widely see Tilottama Rajan, "Wollstonecraft and Godwin: Reading the Secrets of the Political Novel," in *The Supplement of Reading: Figures of Understanding in Romantic Theory and Practice* (Ithaca, N.Y.: Cornell University Press, 1990), 167–96.

other.[5] But unlike Walter Scott, who was to fuse such narratives into the nationalist historical vision of the Waverley novels, Godwin probed and exploited their potential for antagonism, thereby invoking a generic model I will call the "republican romance." How that romance played against the neo-aristocratic romance visions of Burke and other cultural ideologues in the romantic period is one question; why it would be ultimately unpublishable—along with the essay that speculatively invented it—is another. I begin, however, at an earlier point in Godwin's odd and still little-discussed writing career. In one of his earliest and least-read texts, *The Herald of Literature*, Godwin tried to comprehend the fast-shifting relation between historiographic and fictional narrative genres through the context encountered most often by eighteenth-century readers and least often by modern students of cultural history—the so-called literary review, chief mediator of the republic of letters.

In 1784 Godwin introduced himself to the British publications industry by writing *The Herald of Literature*, a parody of the eighteenth-century literary reviews and thus of nearly all the current literary genres of the time, from historiography and political discourse to poetry, drama, and reviewing as such. Here Godwin presented reviews of books he claimed were forthcoming from well-known authors, inventing lengthy "quoted" passages from such nonexistent works as volumes 3 and 4 of William Robertson's *History of America*, volumes 4 through 7 of Edward Gibbon's *Decline and Fall of the Roman Empire*, a novel *Louisa* by Frances Burney, a Pope-like poem on fiction and criticism by William Hayley called "An Essay on Novel," and two imagined political tracts by Thomas Paine and Edmund Burke. The *Herald* mimed the Enlightenment literary review so persuasively as to mislead several modern Godwin scholars into accepting these texts as authentic reviews of actual works.[6] Insiders of the eighteenth-century reviewing business, know-

5 On the "takeoff" of the novel see James Raven, *Judging New Wealth: Popular Publishing and Responses to Commerce in England, 1750–1800* (Oxford: Clarendon, 1992); Siskin, 21–40.

6 I have used the facsimile edition in Burton Pollin, ed., *Four Early Pamphlets by William Godwin* (Gainesville, Fla.: Scholar's Facsimiles, 1966), 205–319. The text also appears, in a modernized form without the typographical features I refer to below, in

ing better, greeted the *Herald* as a canny piece of culture-industry one-upmanship performed at their own expense.

But its greater significance was that the eighteenth-century reviews themselves—the *Monthly* (1749), the *Critical* (1758), the *English* (1783), and the *Analytical* (1788)—were not throwaway periodicals but rather were "conceived as installments of a continuous encyclopedia, recording the advance of knowledge in every field of human enterprise" (Roper, 36).[7] By imagining himself as a reviewer, Godwin invented a simulacrum of the broad Enlightened category of literature as learned discourse. He made visible its internal relations between truth and fiction, history and novel, style and author by fictionalizing long "quoted" passages of putative historiography he had written himself, then setting them alongside such passages as those "quoted" likewise from the imagined Frances Burney novel. Meanwhile, to William Hayley's celebrated actual poem published four years earlier, "Essay on History," Godwin matched the virtual poem "An Essay on Novel," a generic shift in which he transformed verse on the history of historiography into a prospectus for what in 1784 was as yet unwritten anywhere—a history of the novel, from Homer's epics to the "modern French writers of fictitious history" and the English novelists as well (288).

What literary history has taken to be the chief limitation and defect of eighteenth-century reviewing—the reviewer's seeming deference to lengthy quotes from the book under review—Godwin could thereby refashion as a revealing trope: quotation as a power of invention, the book reviewer as text-producer in the guise of mere text-commentator. Godwin never needed actually to write the faked works he attributed to Hayley, Robertson, Burney, or Gibbon—he needed only to "quote" from and to comment upon them to produce the reflexive effects of the *Herald.* The Edward Gibbon review is the most instructive of these, since it intervenes in a historiographical work that in 1784, three years

---

Philp, *Political and Philosophical Writings* 5:23–71. On the reception of the *Herald* by contemporary reviewers and some modern scholars see William St. Clair, *The Godwins and the Shelleys* (Baltimore, Md.: Johns Hopkins University Press, 1989), 22; Pollin, xiv.

7 On reviews from the eighteenth century through the 1820s see also Marilyn Butler, "Culture's Medium: The Role of the Review," in *The Cambridge Companion to British Romanticism,* ed. Stuart Curran (Cambridge: Cambridge University Press, 1993), 120–47.

after the publication of its first three volumes, was only half completed. To draw Gibbon's unfinished historical narrative through the looking glass of a carefully authenticated historiographic fiction was, in one sense, to replicate the older narrative conceit according to which novels entered the world appearing as "true histories." But by the second half of the eighteenth century, the generic confusion of histories and fictions was no longer possible in the self-presentation of the novel as such; it was rather possible—and interestingly productive—in the printed form and medium of the literary review as the eighteenth-century publishers and writers had constructed it. By momentarily quoting himself as "Gibbon," "Robertson," "Burney," or "Burke," Godwin made the *Herald* a peculiarly performative literary review. In its pages the thickly accumulated quotation marks on the left margin of the eighteenth-century reviewing page appear to reverse their usual implication in the eighteenth-century review—which was to attest to the separate existence of the book being reviewed (223–43). In the *Herald* those typographic marks instead signal inversion, mimesis, or, to borrow a term from Bakhtin perfectly apt for this event, *novelization*. It was as though the material form of the literary review, as reproduced by the *Herald* with exhausting exactness, would now permit the greater Enlightenment category of literature itself to become unexpectedly readable as a fictive world—as though it had abruptly become through Godwin's text what in fact the category of literature would become in the nineteenth century, a realm of fictive or imaginative genres. Hence the virtual reviewer of *The Herald of Literature* became momentarily the master artificer of that array of genres upon which the Enlightenment category of literature had heretofore depended.

Thus, without seeming to have intended it, Godwin exposed how the eighteenth-century review had worked to materially, visibly register what is never fully representable—that is, the *form* of the prevailing category or canon of literature rather than any particular writers or texts that may belong to it.[8] Following the victory of vernacular literacy in the armed struggle of the Battle of the Books, the *Monthly* and

<hr />

8 John Guillory's work on the history of literary canon-formation locates for us the sense in which "the canon is an *imaginary* totality of works," not reducible to a syllabus or a reading list; it is a totality or form to which "no one has access" directly and which is predicated upon a certain architecture of genres (see *Cultural Capital: The*

Critical reviews of the mid–eighteenth century introduced the modernized forms of learning called "literature" to the nascent British culture industry, becoming the chief exchange medium of both scholarly and commercial writing. Godwin's 1784 experiment revealed, in retrospect, that the new commercial media of modern learning could also have destabilizing, genre-shifting effects upon the authority of the very category they were so successful in promoting to reading audiences, "literature" as the modern discourses of truth. As novel production in Britain more than quadrupled between 1750 and 1800, the literary reviews increasingly crowded their pages with both the promotion and the critique of commercial popular and novelistic culture (Raven, 19–60). As a metacommentary on that process, the contingent effects of *The Herald of Literature* belong to a preoccupation in Godwin's career that was to be deepened and complicated by his more searching texts of the 1790s. In Godwin's career the parodist was the earliest form of the cultural inquirer.

Godwin's reflexivity was to be obscured by William Hazlitt's later portrait of him as a "metaphysician engrafted onto the Dissenting Minister."[9] It was also obscured by *An Enquiry Concerning Political Justice* in 1793, a work in which the Dissenting Minister grasped the shape of philosophical criticism and the virtue of rational principle, effectively defending the political public sphere as the realm of the private judgment and consensual public communication of truth. If the Godwin of 1793 thereby also corresponded to Habermas's ideal speaker in the bourgeois public sphere—where "the power of the better argument was the claim to that morally pretentious rationality that strove to discover what was at once just and right" (Habermas, 54)—the post-1793 Godwin engaged in the precarious self-critique of that sphere, with unpredictable results.[10]

   In the 1793 edition of *Political Justice*, Godwin proceeded as if Britain

---

Problem of Literary Canon-Formation [Chicago: University of Chicago Press, 1993], 29–38).

   9 Hazlitt, "Mr. Godwin," rpt. in *The Spirit of the Age; or, Contemporary Portraits* (London: Oxford University Press, 1954), 37.

   10 For a different but complementary sense of *Political Justice* as "Godwin's most perfect fiction"—a description that in my view holds only for the 1793 edition—see

had no culture industry, as if there were only a world of public conversation and private judgment undistorted and unselected by contexts of publication and publicity. And this was the only edition of the work in which Godwin held fast to the most sensitive category of the British public sphere.

> Few engines can be more powerful than literature. . . . Literature has reconciled the whole thinking world respecting the great principles of the system of the universe, and extirpated upon this subject the dreams of romance and the dogmas of superstition. Literature has unfolded the nature of the human mind, and Locke and others have established certain maxims respecting man, as Newton has done respecting matter. . . . the race of speculative reasoners in favor of despotism, are almost extinct.[11]

In fact, far from being extirpated, the "dreams of romance" were fast being restored in the great British romance revival of the later eighteenth century, a generic event that would shortly give rise to spectacular ideological and literary confrontations with the narratives of enlightened modernity; meanwhile, the "almost extinct" speculative defenders of despotism were to have their species reanimated by such political claims for the Enlightenment category of literature as Godwin was mounting in *Political Justice* itself.

Godwin's seemingly confident passage of 1793 disappeared from the next two editions of *Political Justice* in 1796 and 1798. What British audiences of 1796 could read instead was the polemical gloss upon this passage published by T. J. Mathias in the third installment of his work of Malthusian poetics, *The Pursuits of Literature.* "Literature, well or ill-conducted, is the great engine by which all *civilized* States must ultimately be supported or overthrown."[12] Mathias belonged among the anti-Jacobins who struggled to replace Godwin's culture-historical narrative, in which the enlightened literary genres battled the super-

Gary Handwerk, "Of Caleb's Guilt and Godwin's Truth: Ideology and Ethics in *Caleb Williams*," *ELH* 60 (1993): 939–60.

11 Godwin, *An Enquiry Concerning Political Justice, 1793*, ed. Jonathan Wordsworth, facs. ed. (New York: Woodstock, 1992), 20.

12 [Thomas James Mathias], *The Pursuits of Literature*, 14th ed. (London, 1808), 244.

stition, myth, and romance fictions of the past, with a conception of literature as an "engine" or technology of civil war *within* enlightened British culture itself. Anti-Jacobin conservatives, not radical intellectuals, were producing this politically correct and starkly instrumentalized conception of literature by the mid-1790s, with great effect: Mathias's *Pursuits of Literature* would become a widely read manual of British literary population-politics at the turn of the century, published in sixteen editions by 1812. Its popularity coincided with the insurgent rise of the journal that bears an antithetical relation to Godwin's *Herald of Literature*, the more crudely and effectively parodic *Anti-Jacobin Review*.[13] What was now underway—the neoconservative takeover of large parts of the British publications industry and the opening of the culture wars of the next two decades—would play out their contradictory consequences in the genre-reform arguments of romantic criticism and the emergence, in 1814, of the Scottish historical novel.

Chief among Mathias's targets was Godwin's new book, the *Enquirer*, which Mathias mistakenly read as if it were the mere extension of *Political Justice* into the realms of cultural criticism and theory. In fact, the *Enquirer* was far more revisionist: it was a methodologically self-conscious attempt to reconstruct a progressive English intelligentsia by literary, educational, and canon-reorganizing means. It required Godwin to relinquish the overarching ambition of the original *Political Justice*—the task of philosophical totalization that by 1797 he was reluctantly calling "incommensurate to our powers"—so that instead of high theory, Godwin now pursued local "investigations," open-ended inquiries into "education, manners, and literature," which demanded questioning the method, the motive, and the reflexive position of the

13 Thomas De Quincey and Samuel Rogers reported it was widely read from 1797 through 1810; by 1818 Coleridge was still using it to refer to the "sting of *personal* malignity in the tail" of contemporary criticism and literary politics (Coleridge, *The Friend* [London, 1818], 2:12–3). See also Joseph Sheldon Mabbett, *Thomas James Mathias and "The Pursuits of Literature"* (Switzerland: University of Fribourg, 1973). For a wider exploration of the crises of the British literary and political public sphere from 1798 to 1830, and their implications for Habermas's classic model of the bourgeois public realm, see "Romanticism and Its Publics: A Forum," *Studies in Romanticism* 33 (1994): 523–88.

cultural inquirer himself.[14] Many of the essays entailed reeducating the educators; or, in the hermeneutic context recently explored by Tilottama Rajan, of comprehending the complexity of authorial intentions and textual "tendencies" entailed by the construction and reception of meaning in history (168–9).

Yet none of the *Enquirer*'s published essays spoke to the Enlightenment category of literature with quite the polemical and methodological self-consciousness of the essay "Of History and Romance." Romance, as Ian Duncan has suggested, is Britain's version of a written constitution, a national text revered and reinterpreted countless times in its novelistic production. As articulated by Edmund Burke in the 1790s and later transfused into the historical novel fashioned by Scott in 1814, Britain's conservative ideology of history and romance entailed the staying power of romance as a historically obsolete genre that had nonetheless persevered into a modernity continuing to require its highly mediated and fictionalized presence.[15] Between Burke and Scott, however, fell the shadow of Godwin, who in 1797 struggled to convert the conservative uses of romance against Enlightenment historicity into a new, reflexive, and progressive—if ultimately and paradoxically impossible—mode of historical knowledge.

In "Of History and Romance" Godwin mounted an aggressive critique of the Edinburgh Enlightenment's universal history, charging its conjectural historians—among them Hume, Robertson, and Gibbon —with refashioning the European past through abstraction, what in Adorno's sense could be called the abstracting process endemic to the enlightening project itself.[16] The older testimony of antiquities had largely disappeared into the philosophical historians' effort to steer readers away from annals and sources, permitting whole continents of

14 Godwin, preface to *The Enquirer: Reflections on Education, Manners, and Literature* (1797), in Philp, *Political and Philosophical Writings* 5:77–9; cf. Rajan, 168–70.

15 Duncan, *Modern Romance and Transformations of the Novel: The Gothic, Scott, Dickens* (Cambridge: Cambridge University Press, 1992), 59. For complementary arguments, used to different ends, see also Michael McKeon, *The Origins of the English Novel, 1600–1740* (Baltimore, Md.: Johns Hopkins University Press, 1987); and Jerome Christensen, *Lord Byron's Strength: Romantic Writing and Commercial Society* (Baltimore, Md.: Johns Hopkins University Press, 1993).

16 Theodor Adorno and Max Horkheimer, *The Dialectic of Enlightenment*, trans. John Cumming (New York: Continuum, 1972), chap. 1.

context, by the magic of abridgment, to vanish into the abstract national geographies of the universal historians' narrative machine. Their method was the "collation and comparison of successive ages"; their product was the autobiography of British nationhood—a collective or "mass" subject called England (in Hume's case) in which "individualities" on the one hand, and the particularities of such conjunctures as the English Civil War on the other, were equally abstracted away.[17] Hence, according to Godwin, the philosophical historians have produced the ineluctable logic of "probability," the "dull repetition" of a "general history" in which Hume, Robertson, and implicitly Burke connive to "furnish us precedents in abundance, . . . show us how that which happened in one country has been repeated in another . . . that what has occurred in the annals of mankind, may under similar circumstances be produced again" (362). Hume's intolerable credo—that "history teaches us nothing new or strange"—had made it scarcely conceivable how history could ever tell the moderns what they did not already know.[18] Universal history's cancellation of possible, unrealized futures prohibits us from conceiving "what it is of which social man is *capable*" (363; my italics), sentencing us, as Godwin puts it with a somewhat Foucauldian flourish, to the institutional order of modernity, where we "dance in fetters," "blight[ed] . . . in every grander and more ample development of the soul" (365).

To probe behind the unacknowledged fictions of universal history, Godwin briefly promotes a localist, agent-centered historicism that would overcome enlightened abstraction by grasping the "materials" and "motives" through which history is made, and thereby could replace the ideological trope of probability with the constructionist figure of possibility:

> Laying aside the generalities of historical abstraction, we must mark the operation of human passions; must observe the empire of motives whether grovelling or elevated; and must note the influence that one

17 For an interesting discussion of such abstraction in both eighteenth- and twentieth-century public spheres see also Michael Warner, "The Mass Public and the Mass Subject," in *Habermas and the Public Sphere*, ed. Craig Calhoun (Cambridge, Mass.: MIT Press, 1992), 377–401.

18 David Hume, *Enquiry concerning Human Understanding*, ed. Eric Steinberg (Indianapolis, Ind.: Hackett, 1977), 54–5.

human being exercises over another, and the ascendancy of the daring and wise over the vulgar multitude. It is thus, and thus only, that we shall be enabled to add, to the knowledge of the past, a sagacity that can penetrate into the depths of futurity. We shall not only understand those events as they arise which are no better than old incidents under new names, but shall judge truly of such conjunctures and combinations, their sources and effects, as, though they have never yet occurred, are within the capacities of our nature. (363)

This was less a substitute for philosophical history than a drastic revision. The historical "subject" is to be shifted from the collective subject of the emergent nation to the individual agents whose public and private acts connive to produce "things as they are."

To this end, Godwin's skeptical historicism would carry out an investigative agenda designed to follow the agents of history off the public stage and into their closets, to reexamine the public man as a private "friend and father of a family," to perform close readings of his works and letters, friendly or suspicious hermeneutics of his public orations and private behaviors (364). Indeed, it would even be to investigate, if ultimately to reinforce, the very distinction between "public" and "private" upon which the British public sphere itself had been built and which the 1793 edition of *Political Justice* had itself, perhaps too vehemently and unselfconsciously, defended. It was the same privacy that other liberal writers of the late 1790s—notably Joanna Baillie in her "Introductory Discourse" to *A Series of Plays* (1798)—also set out to investigate in literary projects ultimately poised to reform the public, political world.[19]

More reflexively than Baillie's, however, Godwin's project looped back into the history of disciplines and to the outcome of the great quarrel over the authority of modern literary canon-formation in the Battle of the Books. The historiographic model he summons to testify against the abstractionist universal historian is not the early modern

19 Baillie defined her own program of theatrical genre-reform as the project of moving it from the realm of the state ("classical tragedy") to the domestic interiors of civil society ("plays on the passions")—and then back to the public world again (see "Introductory Discourse," in *A Series of Plays, 1798*, ed. Jonathan Wordsworth, facs. ed. (New York: Woodstock, 1989), 1–72.

historian who vanquished the ancients by compiling tomes of antiquary based on the "evidence of the senses." It is rather the ancient historian himself—Sallust, Livy, Plutarch—who furnishes a prototype of intellectual agency otherwise unavailable to the Humean or Burkean moderns who groan under the institutional weight of "prejudices and precedents." Downclassed by moderns as "a species of fable," the ancient histories have no cachet among the current rivals for historical authority. Yet, Godwin imagines, they may still serve pragmatically as "a genuine praxis upon the nature of man" (367), a *licentia historica* for imagining possible pasts and futures as something other than probabilistic versions of the world ratified by the Revolution of 1689 and the imposing narratives of philosophical history. Moreover, the moderns' accusation that the ancients fabulated their histories can easily be turned against the moderns themselves: "All history bears too near a resemblance to fable" (367). By this logic, the novel or the romance itself, "strictly considered, may be pronounced to be one of the species of history" (370). Hence it is little wonder why "the man of taste," despairing of foundational historiography, might exclaim, "Dismiss me from the falsehood and impossibility of history, and deliver me over to the reality of romance" (371).

The precursors for such skepticism toward modern claims to historicity were the conservative critics of early modern empirical historiography, the Shaftesburys and the Swifts whose "extreme skepticism" forms an essential basis for Michael McKeon's account of the institutionalizing of the British novel in the 1740s. By exposing the stealthy persistence of aristocratic idealism in modern progressive knowledge, and thereby "the inescapability of romance in true history," McKeon argues, such "extreme skepticism appear[ed] also to pursue a far more radical conclusion, the unavailability of narrative truth as such" (119). In rescue of "narrative truth," the symbolic resolution of the conflict between conservative skepticism and progressive empiricism in the early eighteenth century was the sophisticated novelistic "realism" of Richardson and Fielding, whose new genre would mime the unfolding of action in history through the logic of a "probability" that located the genre equidistantly between invention and actuality. A similar resolution, but well beyond the scope of the English novel itself, could also produce the probabilistic narratives of Scottish philosophical history

—and the affinity between the assumptions of the English novel and the historical logics of the Scottish Enlightenment were finally what Walter Scott himself would come to "discover" in fabricating the historical vistas of the Waverley novels.

In a sense, "Of History and Romance" replays this scenario in 1797 but with striking differences. Godwin's far regions of "romance" were not those of Burke's immemorial English antiquity or aristocratic idealism but the Roman republic and the age of Cromwell. What Godwin calls "historical romance" has the political charge of a *republican* romance, which seeks imaginatively to reopen that possibility in English history—the moment of 1642—which the Scottish philosophical historians, and most notoriously Hume in the first volume of *The History of England* (1763), had been especially anxious to close.[20] The great ideological fiction of Scottish historiography was the necessity of the post-1689 modernity, which Godwin calls the most "insipid" period in British history. One of Godwin's later, pessimistic historical novels would return to the Revolution scenarios of the mid–seventeenth century to diagnose in detail the failures of a historical transformation that produced 1689 rather than the possible worlds of republican imagining.[21] Likewise, his single extended work of political history, *History of the Commonwealth of England*, would open in 1824 with the epigraph, "To attend to the neglected, to remember the forgotten."[22] But in 1797 the deeper subtext of the essay "Of History and Romance" is the unavailability to modern Britain of its own revolutionary moment—except as what can be *fictionally* reconstructed and investigated by the historiographer capable of grasping the multitudinous

20 Though the republican romance is specific to Godwin as I have defined it here, a wide range of modern romance genres and subgenres were at work in later eighteenth- and early-nineteenth-century fiction, discriminated superbly by Miranda Burgess in "The Work of Romance: The British Novel and Political Discourse, 1740–1830" (Ph.D. diss., Boston University, 1995).

21 I refer to *Mandeville: A Tale of the Seventeenth Century in England* (1817), a novel Clemit links to Godwin's lengthy meditations on the English Revolution as well as to Baillie's play *De Montfort*. Doubtless one stimulus to Godwin's imagining was the historical romance of Abbé Prévost, especially the fiction Godwin read in translation while writing *Caleb Williams*—Prévost's *Life and Adventures of Mr. Cleveland, Natural Son of Oliver Cromwell* (1733–34). Cf. Clemit, introduction to *Mandeville*, in Philp, *Collected Novels and Memoirs* 4:v–vii; and Clemit, *Godwinian Novel*, 70–104.

22 Godwin, *History of the Commonwealth of England* (London, 1824–28).

"conjunctures and combinations" of historical possibility, what the English revolutionary moment might now look like if it were narrated by the historical romancer, whose "express stamp of invention" investigates past revolutionary failures and those potential conjunctures of thought and action yet to be made. The republican romance would thereby refute the necessity of British history as the universal historians had narrated it, the better to locate the unrealized possible futures that proliferated from the mid–seventeenth century.

This line of implication, I believe, is the basis for claiming that the romance writer should be considered the author of "real history." It also entails the crucial claim, more modernist than antimodern, that the superiority of the self-conscious "writer of romance" over the "writer of history," who unconsciously creates his own fictions, lies in the argument for reflexivity that grants the romancer full powers of knowledge about the speculative world being constructed. The historian who haplessly conjectures about the *motives* of distant historical actors fills modern histories with error, an unbridgeable gap in his knowledge. But the romance writer "must be permitted, we should naturally suppose, to understand the character which is the creature of his own fancy" (372). Such knowledge of one's own constructions also makes the romancer the narrator of true or "real history": the republican romancer is not right because he is virtuously republican, but because he is reflexively self-conscious, thus comprehending the manifold circumstances and the consequences that motivate and contextualize his own characters or creations. The notion that such reflexivity makes a *political* difference has no counterpart, to my knowledge, in the discourse about novels and romances that filled British prefaces, reviews, histories, and polemics from 1750 through 1800;[23] it has since, of course, become a familiar claim in post-1900 modernist arguments, from Brecht to *Tel Quel* and beyond, which equate the self-reflexivity of the fiction maker with a progressive exposure of ideology and mystification in history.

Unlike all later romantic genre-reforming critical arguments, "Of History and Romance" posits no break between political theory and

---

23 Much of this discourse is collected in Ioan Williams, *Novel and Romance, 1700–1800; A Documentary Record* (New York: Barnes and Noble, 1970), though Godwin's is not.

imagination's practice.[24] Unlike the Jacobin novel, it also imagines no mere fusion of republican politics and novelistic narrative. The trope of "possibility" weighs in against the Jacobin novel's figure of "necessity" as much as against the philosophical historian's claim for "probability," especially if, as I will now argue, Godwin's rhetoric of possibility is only the more polite and wishful form of that harder thing, *contingency* properly so called.

Unexpectedly, in the remarkable and self-undoing final paragraphs of the 1797 essay, Godwin ceases to promote the genre-reform I have just outlined and abruptly forestalls it. Hence it will now appear that his own, apparently romantic argument for narrative genre-transformation must itself be read as a fiction—a thought experiment in both the possibility and the difficulty of changing genres to change history. What he had written about the project of philosophical totalization at the beginning of the *Enquirer*—that it is a project "incommensurate to our powers"—must now be said of the reflexive romancer as well: "To write romance is a task too great for the powers of man . . . [for it] requires a sagacity scarcely less than divine" (372). Nearly two decades before *Waverley*, Godwin glimpses and declines—at least in theory—the spectral return of a divine placeholder or surreptitious theologian in the powerful act of authorship that makes things happen in the parallel universe of the British historical romance. In the nineteenth century such acts would constitute the aesthetic frisson of the modern novel, its magical working out within the novel's boundaries of all those contingencies of action, motive, and poetic justice that can hardly be foreseen or managed in the referential world beyond the novelistic sphere.[25] Certainly Godwin himself can be read as contributing to this authorial revolution by way of engineering the first modern "psychologi-

24 Even the genre-reforming argument closest in tendency to Godwin's own, Shelley's "Defense of Poetry" (1821), was to be formally, textually disengaged from the work in which several of its parts first crucially appeared, *A View of Philosophical Reform* (1819). For an important discussion of the connection between Shelley's "Defense" and his *View* see James K. Chandler, "Representative Men, Spirits of the Age, and Other Romantic Types," in *Romantic Revolutions: Criticism and Theory*, ed. Kenneth R. Johnston et al. (Bloomington: Indiana University Press, 1990), 117–27.

25 Duncan writes excellently of Scott's and Dickens's harnessing such powers in chap. 4 of *Modern Romance and Transformations of the Novel.*

cal" novel (*Caleb Williams*), the minor tradition of "the Godwinian novel," or even, in such novels, the "decisive shift . . . from theatrical and rhetorical to novelistic modes of social control."[26] Yet all readings of Godwin that would assimilate him to the ideology of the modern authorial *subject* will have to contend with the end of the essay "Of History and Romance," which draws back, as if by reflex, from the subject-position projected by the imagined author of the historical romance ("scarcely less than divine").

Against the powerful act of knowing authorship he has attributed to the historical (or republican) romancer, Godwin now invokes the counterprinciple of contingency, which he borrows from yet another eighteenth-century narrative mode: natural history. "Naturalists tell us that a single grain of sand more or less on the surface of the earth, would have altered its motion, and in process of ages, have diversified its events. We have no reason to suppose in this respect that what is true in matter, is false in morals" (372). A similar passage about "matter" appears in the 1796 edition of *Political Justice*, which revises the original 1793 edition away from the discourse of "necessity" toward that of unforeseen and consequential circumstances. There the "single grain of sand" produces "an infinite variation" in the earth's history, and the principle counts "much more so" in human history.[27] This theme would again appear in an important chapter of the *Enquirer*, "Of Choice in Reading," where Godwin argues that the contingent "tendencies" or effects of a text, unlike its intended "moral," can be neither foreseen nor captured and finalized at any given moment of historical reception.[28] As for historians and romancers, the principle of contingency turns both kinds of narrator into well-nigh Darwinian competitors in the universe of narrative genres. "The historian seems to recover his advantage upon the writer of romance" since, despite the former's failures of knowledge about "character" or subjectivity, "the events [of the past] are taken out of his hands and determined by

26 Christensen's rationale for Godwin as pioneering "novelistic modes of social control" appears in *Lord Byron's Strength*, 286–7; on authorship see also Siskin, 39.

27 Godwin, *Enquiry Concerning Political Justice*, (1798), ed. Isaac Kramnick (Harmondsworth: Penguin, 1976), 192.

28 Godwin, "Of Choice in Reading," in *The Enquirer*, in Philp, *Political and Philosophical Writings* 5:140–1.

the system of the universe, and therefore, as far as his information extends, must be true" (372). The romancer, meanwhile, "knows" the character he constructs but cannot possibly set that character into the motion of "events" without plotting them toward the false inevitability of a narrative ending. It is as though the modern narrative universe is divided into halves, "character" and "action," which cannot add up, or as if the division of intellectual labor has now sundered the ancient historian's unification of enlightened agency into the rival and mutually negating narrative modes of historiography and fiction writing in the epoch of modernity.

In the unsettling conclusion of 1797 Godwin has neither returned to the generic hierarchy of the Enlightenment category of literature, in which historiography outflanks the novel/romance, nor provided the first romantic rationale for fictional narrative's higher symbolic truth of history. Natural history's conceit of contingency has instead the effect of producing the epistemological and political conflict of genres that Franco Moretti—alluding to the contingent evolutionism of Stephen J. Gould—refers to by calling for "a Darwinian history of literature, where forms fight one another, are selected by their context, evolve and disappear like natural species."[29] In the period 1780–1820 of British cultural history, those fights, those selections by economic and political context, and those disappearances would entail not only a population of written genres and genre-experiments as diverse, and today sometimes as hard to recognize, as the fossils of the Burgess Shale interpreted by Gould. They would also involve, on the larger scale, the meaning, generic composition, politics, and historical transformation of the category "literature" itself.

Having read the *Political Justice* of 1793, Wordsworth urged his peers to consult "Godwin on Necessity"; in a major self-revision, Godwin renounced the theoretical discourse on necessity and introduced in much of the *Enquirer* project a more polite and reflexive Godwin on Possibility. Forgotten republics and lost opportunities in history could be recovered in that discourse, under the sign of fiction and its possible or virtual worlds. But the moment of Contingency, as Slavoj Žižek

---

29 Moretti, "The Moment of Truth," and "On Literary Evolution," in *Signs Taken for Wonders* (New York: Verso, 1989), 254, 262–78.

proposes, is neither especially polite nor wholly reflexive: "There is always something of an 'encounter with the Real' in contingency, something of the violent emergence of an unheard-of-entity that defies the limits of the established field of what one holds for 'possible,' whereas 'possible' is, so to speak, a 'gentrified,' pacified contingency with its sting plucked out."[30] Recent invocations of "contingency" in American cultural criticism have more often been pragmatist, comfortable variants of the "possible," in Žižek's sense, than bewildering, dislocating encounters with the "unheard-of."[31] Such an encounter takes place as an unplanned reversal, a reflex. In "Of History and Romance" Godwin's reflex was a moment of writing that undid the earlier moments of a reflexive argument by responding to the kind of contingency that is always material, unimaginable, unheard-of—that is, one's own place and act in the moment of comprehending "history."

30 Slavoj Žižek, *For They Know Not What They Do: Enjoyment as a Political Factor* (New York: Verso, 1991), 195–6.

31 For example, Richard Rorty's in *Contingency, Irony, and Solidarity* (Cambridge: Cambridge University Press, 1989). Žižek's lengthy meditation on contingency appears also in *Tarrying with the Negative: Kant, Hegel, and the Critique of Ideology* (Durham, N.C.: Duke University Press, 1993), 150–9.

Feminine Identity Formation in *Wilhelm Meisters Lehrjahre*

Jill Anne Kowalik

Natalie, the "beautiful soul," and Therese have been treated almost without exception in commentaries on *Wilhelm Meisters Lehrjahre* as examples of idealized types, representing static categories or principles of feminine existence. Scholars explicitly or implicitly adopt Schiller's view, expressed in a letter to Goethe dated 3 July 1796: "Es ist zu bewundern, wie schön und wahr die drei Charaktere der *Stiftsdame, Nataliens* und *Theresiens* nuanciert sind. Die zwei ersten sind heilige, die zwei andern sind wahre und menschliche Naturen; aber eben darum, weil Natalie heilig und menschlich zugleich ist, so erscheint sie wie ein Engel, da die Stiftsdame nur eine Heilige, Therese nur eine vollkommene Irdische ist" (It is admirable how subtly the three figures of the canoness [the beautiful soul, J. K.], Natalie, and Therese are so beautifully and truly portrayed. The first two are saintly; the other two have a true and human character; but because Natalie is both saintly and human, she appears as an angel, whereas the canoness is only a saint and Therese only a perfect earthly type).[1]

---

1 *Der Briefwechsel zwischen Schiller und Goethe*, ed. Emil Staiger (Frankfurt am Main: Insel, 1966), p. 225. All translations of the German are my own. Schiller's praise of these women was not universally repeated in the case of the beautiful soul, although critics continued to view her as a type, albeit a negative one. The most notable contemporary disagreement came from Wilhelm von Humboldt and Friedrich Schlegel.

Schiller arrived at his judgment by ignoring those sections of the novel in which the histories of these characters are recounted. His oversight exemplifies the androcentric ideology of German Classicism, which constructed feminine identity as a timeless, ahistorical existence for which the concept of development or *Bildung* was irrelevant. Kept off the historical stage to play institutionalized "natural" gender roles in the private sphere, women were represented also in theoretical documents on gender as passive, "emotional" creatures whose lives did not and could not contain a dynamic dimension.[2]

In *Wilhelm Meisters Lehrjahre*, however, Goethe radically departed from the masculine notion of feminine stasis to offer a detailed and insightful account of the early childhoods—the histories—of the three women whom Schiller idealized. By analyzing Goethe's representation of the interaction between these women as children and their primary caregivers, we can draw some important conclusions about the process of feminine identity formation in late eighteenth-century Germany. This process, as I shall attempt to show, displays certain pathological features of which Goethe, the *Augenmensch* and master observer of human behavior, was keenly aware. I use the term *pathological* here and throughout my essay as a descriptive rather than a normative designation; I am not interested in whether the three women in question are "good," an issue that has obsessed critics for decades. I want instead to examine how their particular adult identities evolved and what their evolution tells us about the social-historical and psychohistorical context in which the novel was produced. Our task is

See *Wilhelm Meisters Lehrjahre* ("Hamburger Ausgabe"), ed. Erich Trunz (Munich: Beck, 1981), p. 658 (hereafter cited as *WML*), for Humboldt's letter of 4 December 1794 to Schiller and p. 674 for Schlegel's comments on this figure in his *Athenäum* review. Klaus F. Gille (*"Wilhelm Meister" im Urteil der Zeitgenossen* [Assen: Van Gorcum, 1971], esp. 13–16, 47–50) discusses the early reception of these women. Susanne Zantop ("Eignes Selbst und fremde Formen: Goethes 'Bekenntnisse einer schönen Seele,'" *Goethe Yearbook*, 3 [1986]: 73–92) gives a historical overview of misogynist versus feminist interpretations of the beautiful soul.

2 The most lucid account of women's ahistorical image in late-eighteenth-century Germany is Silvia Bovenschen's now-standard work *Die imaginierte Weiblichkeit: Exemplarische Untersuchungen zu kulturgeschichtlichen und literarischen Präsentationsformen des Weiblichen* (Frankfurt am Main: Suhrkamp, 1979), pp. 9–11, passim. For a discussion of Schiller's androcentric attitudes (but without reference to his discussions of the *Lehrjahre*), see pp. 74–76, 220–56.

not to assign moralistic labels to its figures but to look into complexities of characterization in order to understand better what the book is actually about.[3]

In my analysis I employ one of several possible psychoanalytic constructs of the personality, namely, the model of psychosexual development proposed by Freud.[4] Although some readers may find it ahistorical

3 A dominant trend in *Wilhelm Meister* scholarship has been to reduce one or more members of the feminine triad to "aspects" or "symbols" of Wilhelm's development. This approach was most explicitly defended by Jürgen Rausch ("Lebensstufen in Goethes 'Wilhelm Meister,'" *Deutsche Vierteljahrsschrift*, 20 [1942]: 65–114) and has been continued, for example, by Emil Staiger, *Goethe* (Zurich: Atlantis, 1962), 2:128–74; Hans Eichner, "Zur Deutung von 'Wilhelm Meisters Lehrjahren,'" *Jahrbuch des Freien Deutschen Hochstifts* (1966): 165–96; Peter Pfaff, "Plädoyer für eine typologische Interpretation von 'Wilhelm Meisters Lehrjahren,'" *Text und Kontext*, 5 (1977); 37–55; Ilse Graham, *Goethe: Portrait of the Artist* (Berlin: de Gruyter, 1977), pp. 182–226; Hellmut Ammerlahn, "Goethe und Wilhelm Meister, Shakespeare und Natalie: Die klassische Heilung des kranken Königssohns," *Jahrbuch des Freien Deutschen Hochstifts* (1978): 47–84; Ivar Sagmo, *Bildungsroman und Geschichtsphilosophie: Eine Studie zu Goethes Roman "Wilhelm Meisters Lehrjahre"* (Bonn: Bouvier, 1982); Clark S. Muenzer, *Figures of Identity: Goethe's Novels and the Enigmatic Self* (University Park: Pennsylvania State University Press, 1984); and Monika Fick, *Das Scheitern des Genius: Mignon und die Symbolik der Liebesgeschichten in "Wilhelm Meisters Lehrjahren"* (Würzburg: Königshausen und Neumann, 1987).

4 While there are a few studies that rely wholly or in part on a Freudian model (e.g., Friedrich A. Kittler and Gerhard Kaiser, *Dichtung als Sozialisationsspiel: Studien zu Goethe und Gottfried Keller* [Göttingen: Vandenhoeck und Ruprecht, 1978]; David Roberts, *The Indirections of Desire: Hamlet in Goethe's "Wilhelm Meister"* [Heidelberg: Winter, 1980]; Jochen Hörisch, *Gott, Geld und Glück: Zur Logik der Liebe in den Bildungsromanen Goethes, Kellers, und Thomas Manns* [Frankfurt am Main: Suhrkamp, 1983]; Dorrit Cohn, "Wilhelm Meister's Dream: Reading Goethe with Freud," *German Quarterly*, 62 [1989]: 459–72), I have not been able to locate a single psychoanalytic study of any of the three idealized women. Frederick J. Beharriell's essay "The Hidden Meaning of Goethe's 'Bekenntnisse einer schönen Seele'" (in *Lebendige Form: Festschrift für Heinrich E. K. Henel*, ed. Jeffrey L. Sammons and Ernst Schürer [Munich: Fink, 1970] is unfortunately always cited as a Freudian reading of the "Confessions." Beharriell uses terms such as *sexual neurosis* in a trivial popular sense, however, and displays no understanding of childhood psychosexual development as set forth by Freud. In fact, he does not even discuss the early childhood of the beautiful soul. Some critics have used this essay, quite unfairly, I think, to attack all Freudian approaches to the "Confessions" as reductive (cf. Zantop; Christine Oertel Sjögren, "Pietism, Pathology, or Pragmatism in Goethe's *Bekenntnisse einer schönen Seele*," *Studies on Voltaire and the Eighteenth Century*, 193 [Oxford: Cheney, 1980], pp. 2009–15; and Lothar Müller, *Die kranke Seele und das Licht der Erkenntnis: Karl Philipp Moritz' Anton Reiser* [Frankfurt am Main: Athenäum, 1987], p. 306).

to apply an interpretive model developed in the twentieth century to an eighteenth-century text, it is apt for *Wilhelm Meisters Lehrjahre* because the work constantly thematizes, as does psychoanalysis itself, the function of the past in the present. Every character in this novel about development has at some point either to come to terms with the past, as Wilhelm has been seen to do, or to be destroyed by it, as the harpist is—indeed, as is his entire family, whose youngest member is celebrated in the *Saal der Vergangenheit* (chamber of the past). While none of the figures I discuss can be said to have been destroyed by her childhood, I shall argue that the contours of their early experience lend their existence a tragic dimension that has not been sufficiently appreciated.

Readers may also harbor the reservation that interpreting the text according to a Freudian model is invariably reductive and simplifies or distorts its dense symbolic structure.[5] Such complaints are rarely heard today with regard to sociocultural readings; few contemporary critics would dispute, for example, that the *Lehrjahre* addresses, in any number of controversial ways, the relationship between the aristocracy and the middle class in eighteenth-century Germany. Yet it has not been generally recognized that Goethe likewise deals with the problem of gender identity in this period and that it might well be approached from a psychoanalytic perspective. Thus a Freudian model does not close off but rather allows us access to crucial sections of the novel that have resisted interpretation for almost two centuries.[6]

5 Wilhelm Emrich ("Symbolinterpretation und Mythenforschung: Möglichkeiten und Grenzen eines neuen Goetheverständnisses," *Euphorion*, 47 [1953]: 38–67) rightly attacks the ahistorical quality of Jungian approaches to literary interpretation (which he mistakenly conflates with all psychoanalytic readings) and observes: "Literary studies confront specific historical manifestations and transformations of the human psyche. These differentiated phenomena are what have to be investigated if we are to produce exact, meaningful, and concrete conclusions rather than empty generalizations" (p. 57). But Emrich effectively takes back his insight by reducing all of the symbols in Goethe's texts to expressions of "Goethe's own spiritual conflicts" (p. 55).

6 "'Gender'—as distinct from categories such as 'class,' 'social class,' or 'social standing'—does not as a category have a conceptual [*begriffsgeschichtliche*] tradition" (Bovenschen, p. 14). The best illustration of Bovenschen's point is that the androgynous aspects of the women figures in the *Lehrjahre* have, astoundingly, never been interpreted with respect to historical problems of gender identity. Instead, the entire matter has been reduced to a merely symbolic or mythological theme. The only exception to this rule, to my knowledge, is Ursula R. Mahlendorf's essay "The Mystery

In the pages that follow I shall be concerned especially with the details of Goethe's presentation. For in the passages that might be dismissed as less significant embellishments of the main plot (if they are mentioned at all), Goethe reveals his ability as a narrator to locate major issues of the *Lehrjahre* within the apparently incidental fact or event, the seemingly offhand remark. His narrative strategy enables him not only to integrate important information about the childhood of the three women figures into his text but also, and perhaps most importantly, to represent the attitude of the novel's characters toward this information. While the author is obviously concerned with the etiology of feminine identity, his protagonist is not. Wilhelm is the only character who clearly knew the childhood stories of Natalie, the beautiful soul, and Therese, but his response is silence. He has no comment on the early experience of the woman who was later to become his wife, or on that of her aunt, or on that of Therese, whom he almost married.[7] This curious lacuna exemplifies (and I believe Goethe meant it to exemplify) the male, and specifically the fatherly, neglect of feminine maturation in eighteenth-century Germany, from which all three of the women can be shown to have suffered.

The story of the beautiful soul opens with an erasure: "Bis in mein achtes Jahr war ich ein ganz gesundes Kind, weiß mich aber von dieser Zeit so wenig zu erinnern als von dem Tage meiner Geburt" (I was quite a healthy child until my eighth year, but I remember as little about that period as I do about the day I was born [*WML*, p. 358]). The passage refers to what Freud would later term "infantile amnesia," which occurs sometime between the ages of six and eight. The child forgets its own early experiences of sexuality, that is, it forgets nearly everything from its first years, with the possible exception of certain "screen memories" (*Deckerinnerungen*), which for the beautiful soul consist in unspecified recollections that she was not a completely

---

of Mignon: Object Relations, Abandonment, Abuse, and Narrative Structure," *Goethe Yearbook*, 7 (forthcoming).

7 In addition to Wilhelm, the figures who are shown to be acquainted with the "Confessions" are the doctor, Aurelie, and Natalie. Wilhelm is the only figure to whom Therese recounts her story.

healthy child. Infantile amnesia marks the transition between the Oedipal phase (roughly ages three to five or six) and the period of "latency" that lasts until the rearousal of the child's sexuality during puberty. During this period the child unconsciously carries forward the Oedipal wishes that have already been developed. The experiences recounted by the beautiful soul therefore recapitulate and extend her earlier sexual fantasies. By commencing the narration during a time when previous Oedipal desire is both potent and forgotten, Goethe establishes unconscious repetition as the dominant psychic structure for the beautiful soul. Her life will be informed by a continuous reenactment of her primary, originating erotic encounter with her father.

In the usual course of feminine psychosexual development, daughters both identify with their mothers and become enraged toward them.[8] Identification with the mother predates the Oedipal phase; it is present almost from birth, because the female child naturally views her parent of the same sex as being like herself. During the pre-Oedipal period, the mother is the daughter's primary object of love, just as she is for little boys. Infants of both sexes live in a state of erotic symbiosis with the mother. The daughter's sexual attachment to her mother shifts in the Oedipal phase as the father becomes her love object, but the identification with the mother, which may still contain pre-Oedipal erotic elements, remains. (Little boys stay attached to the love object, mother, but their identification shifts to the father.) As the daughter develops the desire for exclusive possession of her father's love, she becomes enviously aware of her inferior position within the Oedipal

8 Sigmund Freud, *The Standard Edition of the Complete Psychological Works*, trans. and ed. James Strachey and Anna Freud, 24 vols. (London: Hogarth, 1962). I have drawn primarily on the following essays: "Three Essays on Sexuality" (vol. 7); "The Sexual Life of Human Beings," "The Development of the Libido and the Sexual Organizations," "Some Thoughts on Development and Regression—Aetiology," and "The Libido Theory and Narcissism" (vol. 16); and "Anxiety and Instinctual Life" and "Femininity" (vol. 22). My reading of Freud has been aided by Erik H. Erikson, *Childhood and Society* (New York: Norton, 1950), esp. chaps. 2, 7; Juliet Mitchell, *Psychoanalysis and Feminism* (New York: Vintage, 1975); Nancy Chodorow, *The Reproduction of Mothering: Psychoanalysis and the Sociology of Gender* (Berkeley: University of California Press, 1978); and Chodorow, *Feminism and Psychoanalytic Theory* (New Haven, Conn.: Yale University Press, 1989). I am also grateful to Jane K. Brown and especially to Ursula R. Mahlendorf for their reactions to my thoughts over the last few years as this essay has taken form.

triad and feels rage toward her mother as a result. Moreover, she is terrified of being punished should her desire for her father and her angry aggression toward her mother be discovered. Under favorable circumstances, daughters eventually resolve their ambivalence toward the mother as they develop erotic relationships with male peers.[9] But feminine identification with the mother is, Goethe suggests, pathologically complicated in the patriarchy of late-eighteenth-century Germany, especially for those daughters, like the beautiful soul, who have intellectual potential.

After mentioning her amnesia, the beautiful soul (who never receives a name because her story is a generic one) describes what happened in her bedroom when she was eight years old. The most significant visitor to sit on her bed was her father, who entertains her with all manner of natural objects from his "Kabinett" (cabinet, i.e, where his collection is held [*WML*, p. 358]). She seems almost to enjoy her illness and convalescence because in this *nine-month* period her father is drawn more frequently to her bed than he might otherwise have been. She says of this time, "Ich litt und liebte" (I suffered and loved [p. 358]). Because her mother has only told her Bible stories, leaving the narration of romances and fairy tales to an aunt, the beautiful soul knows that she cannot confide in her mother her erotically charged conversations with her father. She therefore creates a surrogate: her invisible friend (also called "das unsichtbare Wesen" [the invisible Being]), whose versified, and therefore "disciplined," conversations (p. 359) she does feel safe in dictating to her mother. She has learned that her erotic attachment to Father is unacceptable to Mother.

Shortly after her illness, she gives up dolls. "Ich verlangte nach Wesen, die meine Liebe erwiderten" (I had a desire for beings who would return my love [p. 359]). With the help of the aunt's fairy tales, she is able to fantasize that she is a princess who marries a "verwünschter Prinz" (a prince who was bewitched), who had previously been a

9 This highly schematic explanation of feminine ambivalence cannot do justice to the complexities of interaction between individual mothers and daughters. Furthermore, ambivalence is probably not confined to the Oedipal phase but appears to begin much earlier. Freud takes note of some special possibilities for "disturbance" in feminine development at the end of his essay "Femininity," pp. 131–35; see also Chodorow, *Reproduction*, chap. 6.

"Schäfchen" (lamb).[10] The beautiful soul says that she derives a lot of pleasure from her father's various animals (p. 359), and she associates them with her magical lamb, which stands also for the Lamb of God, or the invisible Being, or Father. She soon discovers, however, that she might never acquire what she calls "einen so köstlichen Besitz" (such a precious possession [p. 359]). She then consoles herself with the fascinating love stories she finds in books. And she believes that her surrogate friend will compensate her for the love she actually wants from her lamb (cf. pp. 359–60).

When her mother has her father take her books away, the father secretly returns them. The mother engages in a prohibition vis-à-vis the daughter just as the father tries to deny Wilhelm his visits to the theater. The beautiful soul knows that she and Father are deceiving Mother. The mother eventually realizes her weak position in the triad and allows her daughter to read again, but she tries to channel her reading by denying her seductive works ("verführerische Bücher" [p. 360]). The child, however, merely circumvents the mother and informs herself about sex from the Bible's "bedenkliche Stellen" (questionable passages [p. 360]).

The same sexual curiosity that had motivated her attentive study of the Bible, ("diese Wißbegierde" [p. 360]), eventually leads her into the art of cooking, where she will learn from her mother how animals, that is to say, how women, are cut open and prepared for consumption by men. The child uses these occasions, which she always refers to as "ein Fest" (festival, party [p. 360]), to play with and display to her father animal intestines ("Eingeweide" [p. 360]), which she views as sexual organs. He responds to this kind of play activity by conversing with her as if she were a young student and by calling her his "mißratener Sohn" (misbegotten son [p. 360]). In its context this means the following: "I wish you wouldn't display yourself as my potential sexual partner. I wish you were a boy." Because desire can never be eradicated but only transformed, the beautiful soul takes her father's response to mean: "If I am to fulfill his desire and possess his love, I

---

10 My interpretation at this point, where the prince is taken to represent Father, assumes that fairy tales are or can be expressions of the child's sexual wishes, as Bruno Bettelheim has argued in his now-classic study *The Uses of Enchantment: The Meaning and Importance of Fairy Tales* (New York: Knopf, 1976).

must identify with him. I must be a boy." From this point on, all of her potentially erotic encounters are necessarily identificatory: Damon, Narziß, and Philo.

In her thirteenth year, for example, the beautiful soul compares her soul to a mirror, which is a familiar Neoplatonic image. She is subsequently attracted to Narziß (Narcissus), whose primary mythic activity is looking at his own reflection. In Narziß she finds her own identity, which is that of a person in love with his or her own reflection. The identification is underlined in their first private moment together: he has a nosebleed, reminiscent of her own "Blutsturz" (coughing up of blood [p. 358]) at the beginning of her remembered life. Later on, after his blood from an injury is washed from her body, she stands gazing at herself in a mirror and acknowledging her own beauty. Still later she meets a man to whom she gives the name Philo, which with respect to sound is the masculine form of the name Phyllis that she gave herself in early adolescence. And Philo had, she says, "im ganzen eine entfernte Ähnlichkeit mit Narzissen" (on the whole a distant similarity to Narcissus [p. 391]).

In her three major encounters with men as partners, the beautiful soul seeks intellectual companionship (which she sometimes receives and sometimes does not) because she believes that it will ultimately result in the fulfillment of her Oedipal wishes for her father. Only in Damon does she believe that she has found her "gewünschtes Schäfchen" (desired lamb [p. 362]). But Damon is a double figure. He has a younger brother who, like Damon himself and like the beautiful soul, is ill. This doubling represents the parental dyad: the older boy, like the father, encourages the identificatory bond with the child, while the younger brother, like the mother, wants to destroy it. This fact did not escape the beautiful soul, who now points out that "die Eifersucht des Jüngeren machte den Roman vollkommen" (the jealousy of the younger boy added the finishing touch to our novel [i.e., love story] [p. 362]). "Phyllis," as she called herself during the affair, can forget the death of both brothers so easily (p. 363), despite her intense involvement with them because she incorporates them. Her independence, both sexual and intellectual, follows from this and prevents her from ever marrying.

Hence neither Narziß nor Philo, nor the many other men the beau-

tiful soul meets—she has many suitors (cf. p. 382)—can compete with
her invisible friend, with whom she eventually "consummates" her love
in an out-of-body experience, which is the logical conclusion of her
desire to be a boy, that is, not to be a girl. The experience is set in
motion when Philo tells her of his many love affairs, which she associates with David's seduction of Bathsheba and murder of her husband
Uriah (cf. pp. 391–93). She fears that she could commit similar
crimes and worries about an ineradicable "Herrschaft der Neigung"
(primacy of inclination [p. 393]) within herself. The parallel she draws
to David suggests that she is frightened of her desire for illicit sex with
the female and elimination of the male competitor, for which she
would be punished: These are the Oedipal fantasies of a little boy, but
in the beautiful soul they have a somewhat different significance. The
"sin" she finds so difficult to conquer is her continuing, unconscious
erotic attachment to Mother, which interferes with her relationship to
God the Father and places her in a state of perpetual anxiety. Because
her father had conveyed to her as a child that her feminine eroticism
toward him was unwelcome, the beautiful soul tries throughout her
life to cast off her identification with her mother, which is grounded
in a powerful pre-Oedipal sexual bond. Her attempts at this explain
her lifelong unwillingness to cultivate female friends. At the same time,
she is unconsciously enraged at her father for asking her to give up her
attachment to her mother and wishes therefore to kill him. When her
father finally dies, she says she enjoys "die größte Freiheit" (the greatest freedom [p. 414]). The intense ambivalence she feels toward
her father—desire for his love along with hatred for him because he
will not accept her as a female lover—is eventually overcome, but not
resolved, with a compromise. In an ecstatic mystical union with "einem
abwesenden Geliebten" (an absent lover [p. 394]), she feels herself to
be without her body. She has chosen to repress her feminine identity
even at the physical level in a sacrificial merging with Christ on the
Cross (p. 394).[11]

11   The three other criminals with whom the beautiful soul identifies during her
spiritual crisis following Philo's revelations all reflect her ambivalence toward her
father. Without the Father's "unsichtbare Hand" (invisible hand [*WML*, p. 392]) to
hold her in check, that is, to block her eroticism, she believes that she could have
been responsible for the seduction of a female child by its father confessor, that she

Later we find the beautiful soul tending, in a motherly fashion, her sick and elderly father. When her uncle describes her long canceled engagement to Narziß as an "Aufopferung" (sacrifice), she replies that she was "gern und willig" (happy) to sacrifice her "geliebtes Schaf" (beloved lamb) in favor of the "Gesundheit eines verehrten Vaters" (the health of her dearly respected father [p. 406]). Her refusal to marry has allowed her now to assume, finally, her deceased mother's position. When one of her sisters, who acts as Mother by virtue of her role as the head of the household that they share with their father, dies of a "Brustkrankheit" (chest infection [p. 412]), the beautiful soul cannot attend the funeral because she herself suffers from "der alte Schaden auf meiner Brust" (the old wound and damage to my chest [p. 412]). Her psychosomatic identification with her sibling indicates that she no longer wishes to identify with her father, but with her mother, whose imago has been displaced onto her sister. Her original, unresolved wish to occupy Mother's place is manifested in her desire to care for her other sister's children. But her uncle bars her from them, and the beautiful soul consequently suffers the deepest anguish of her life precisely when she would be Mother's most appropriate surrogate.

Patriarchal societies like the one in which the beautiful soul grows to maturity reserve the category of development (*Bildung*) for men. Mothers have been co-opted by the patriarchy because they have internalized the restrictive values of their fathers.[12] Hence mothers are threatened by their daughters' intellectual curiosity, which the patriarchy has banished from the mother's character, for curiosity allows the daughter secret communion with her father. The idea of this com-

---

could have been a thief (i.e, could have stolen her father from her mother), and that she could have attempted to assassinate the king (her father).

12 Barbara Becker-Cantarino ("'Die Bekenntnisse einer schönen Seele': Zur Ausgrenzung und Vereinnahmung des Weiblichen in der patriarchalen Utopie von 'Wilhelm Meisters Lehrjahren,'" in *Verantwortung und Utopie*, ed. Wolfgang Wittkowski [Tübingen: Niemeyer, 1988], pp. 70–86) offers the best discussion to date of patriarchal structures in the *Lehrjahre*. Her argument that the beautiful soul receives her socialization only through men (p. 73), however, overlooks the complicity of the mother in the socialization of the daughter. Becker-Cantarino locates the first appearance of the invisible friend in the Narziß episode, when in fact the invisible friend is a bedroom strategy devised by the child to cope with the prohibitions of the mother.

munion is threatening for the mother because it reanimates her own unresolved wish for exclusive communion with *her* father. Thus, rather than participate in and enjoy the daughter's intellectual pursuits, the mother seeks to control them in a futile attempt to eliminate a competitor for her husband's (i.e., her "father's") attention.[13] Because the mother cannot identify with her daughter's intellectual inclinations and refuses to let her daughter identify with her as her husband's other lover, the daughter has no choice but to introject the father. She believes that doing so will guarantee her both eros and logos, but she is sorely mistaken. Her father is not threatened by her intellectuality per se, because he is not tempted to identify with his female child. But he *is* threatened by her erotic desire for him, because, paradoxically, it is accompanied by intellectual interests that he cannot share with her mother.

Thus little girls are "shortchanged" in comparison to little boys. For while the mother is able and willing to accept, indeed to arouse, her son's desire as an aspect of his intellectual development (as Kittler and Kaiser have argued in their perceptive but androcentric study of the *Lehrjahre*), fathers in this patriarchy refuse to do the same for their daughters. Sons therefore eventually resolve their Oedipal conflicts by transferring their eroticism onto peer partners. Daughters, on the other hand, are never allowed to work through and disengage from their Oedipal fantasies, because neither parent will acknowledge to them the acceptability of such childhood desires.

Several recent interpretations of the "Confessions" posit the independence of the beautiful soul as an absolute value in itself and castigate the men who seek to hinder its development and expression.[14]

13 As I have already suggested, mothers in a patriarchy, who are of course also daughters, suffer (like their daughters) from unresolved or unresolvable Oedipal fantasies. The mother's competitiveness with and envy for her daughter mean that she has displaced her own mother's imago onto her daughter, a devastating burden for any child to carry.

14 In addition to the studies cited at the end of note 4, see Marianne Hirsch, "Spiritual *Bildung*: The Beautiful Soul as Paradigm," in *The Voyage In: Fictions of Female Development*, ed. Elizabeth Abel, Marianne Hirsch, and Elizabeth Langland (Hanover, N.H.: University Press of New England, 1983), pp. 23–48; and Ulrike Prokop, *Die Illusion vom Großen Paar*, vol. 1 of *Weibliche Lebensentwürfe im deutschen Bildungsbürgertum, 1750–1770* (Frankfurt am Main: Fischer, 1991), pp. 106–99. Prokop states in her foreword that this book is a psychoanalytic study of three representative female lives:

But they ignore the cultural-historical and personal-historical origins of independence in the context of the familial Oedipal configuration. Hence they deny the importance, even the existence, of sexual desire in little girls. Such approaches cannot address, and may even unwittingly reproduce, the patriarchal attitudes represented in the "Confessions." In particular, the repression of unbounded female sexuality is accompanied by life-threatening consequences for women such as Mariane, the Countess, Mignon, and Mignon's mother who experience desire outside the domestic setting. Aurelie, to whom the "Confessions" are read as a form of psychotherapy meant to help her deal with a traumatic sexual rejection and the disintegrating experience of all-consuming desire, does not receive the therapeutic benefit predicted by the doctor. In fact, the story's message of hopelessness kills her. In reviewing the life of a woman who learned to live with unfulfilled or vicariously fulfilled desire, Aurelie is overwhelmed by the patriarchal hostility toward feminine eroticism, which she herself refuses to view as bad or wrong. The history of the beautiful soul, whose Oedipal wishes have not been harmoniously resolved, shows her how harmful it is for a woman to compromise her sexuality, and she dies rather than do so herself.

The secondary literature on the *Lehrjahre* often gives one the impression that critics have not really known what to make of the story of the beautiful soul. Interpretations range from the primitive biographical (the beautiful soul is a depiction of Susanna von Klettenberg), to the formalist-technical (book 6 functions as a moment of retardation in the plot), to the social-historical (the beautiful soul represents the conflicts between marriage and independence that women faced in the late eighteenth century). Yet most studies do not show, except in the most superficial way, how book 6 is related to the rest of the novel. It

Goethe's mother, his sister Cornelia, and Susanna von Klettenberg. Her treatment of the material is not, however, psychoanalytic but sociological in orientation. Thus she carefully and vividly describes the intellectual, economic, and emotional isolation of these women within the German patriarchy, but she does not provide a psychodynamic investigation of their character. In the case of the "Confessions," which she reductively views as a biography of Klettenberg, Prokop only briefly mentions the early childhood of the beautiful soul (p. 124). My colleague Ehrhard Bahr kindly drew my attention to Prokop's work.

has even been argued that book 6 cannot or should not be integrated into the entire text (Zantop, esp. pp. 87–8). However, as a pedagogical reflection provided to Aurelie and Natalie, who is so often viewed as the ideal of womanhood in the *Lehrjahre*, book 6 must be taken as a paradigm of feminine development. Examining the paradigmatic status of the "Confessions" more closely will help us understand the relationship between Natalie and her aunt as more than a vague "harmony" of their souls.

People like the beautiful soul, Natalie tells Wilhelm, resemble ideals that are "nicht zum Nachahmen, sondern zum Nachstreben" (not to be imitated but rather emulated [*WML,* p. 518]). It has never been noticed that Natalie employs terms fundamental to Karl Philipp Moritz's analysis of imitation in the opening pages of his essay "Über die bildende Nachahmung des Schönen" (1788), written while he and Goethe were together in Rome.[15] Because Natalie, following Moritz, prefers the sublime process of emulation to the base act of imitation (Moritz's word is "nachäffen" [to ape]), she is not interested in replicating the activities of the woman she both resembles and does not resemble in appearance. For example, she does not spend hours in the company of books as her aunt had done; she does not engage in disputations over aesthetics such as her aunt had conducted with the uncle; and she is not given to her aunt's dependence on "das unsichtbare Wesen." As we shall see, the last fact reflects Natalie's different feelings for and relationship to *her* father.

From her earliest years, however, Natalie does pursue what she believes is a creative emulation of the general virtue that she discerns in her aunt's life. The beautiful soul reports that Natalie, as a little girl, liked to appropriate and tailor her aunt's clothing—we could say her aunt's persona—for little girls in need of clothing, which is to say for little girls like herself who were developing a persona. When we encounter Natalie as an adult in book 8, we find her still caring for little girls and displaying her habit by dressing up Mignon. While femininist social historians might see in Natalie's activity merely the static role of the nurturing female, I view her continuing interest in the welfare of little girls as an indication of her development (*Bildung*). From

15 See *Moritz: Werke in zwei Bänden* (Berlin: Aufbau, 1973), 2:255–6.

her model Natalie thinks she has learned, first of all, that she can occupy the place of Mother without having to develop a sexual bond to a peer partner, and second, that her autonomy is grounded in her asexual existence. When Wilhelm, standing with her before the portrait of the beautiful soul, praises her aunt's "Reinlichkeit des Daseins" (purity of existence) and the "Selbständigkeit ihrer Natur" (her independence of character)—epithets perfectly appropriate for the Virgin Mother—Natalie agrees. She then observes that "jeder gebildete Mensch weiß, wie sehr er an sich und andern mit einer gewissen Roheit zu kämpfen hat" (every well-developed person knows how much he has to battle a certain crudeness in himself and in others [*WML*, p. 518]). Like the beautiful soul, she has a deep awareness of the danger of desire; we recall her aunt's reference to the "Ungeheuer in jedem menschlichen Busen" (monster in every human breast [p. 420]).

Natalie believes that she has learned how to be an asexual mother from her aunt; but one's gender identity is fixed in a much more fundamental way than through occasional interaction with an aunt in one's youth (i.e., during latency or preadolescence). Natalie may well identify with the beautiful soul, but the cause of her identification almost certainly lies in her much earlier relationship to her parents. The story of her childhood, however, does not exist as a cohesive first-person narrative such as we have in Wilhelm's monologue to Mariane, Therese's report to Wilhelm about her early years, or the beautiful soul's narrative. Natalie's childhood is recounted in the third person because she herself, like Mignon, was so traumatized by the events of her early life that she can neither speak nor write about them. She cannot be conscious of the catastrophe resulting from the death of her parents because it is hidden behind the veil of infantile amnesia; she experienced her loss sometime between the ages of three and five, precisely when she was undergoing the most crucial phase of gender identity formation.

The recollections of her aunt about her own sister's family (*WML*, pp. 412–20) provide us with the most important body of facts about Natalie's early experience.[16] The beautiful soul tells us that Natalie's

---

16 In this section of my interpretation, I am indebted to John Bowlby, *Loss: Sadness and Depression*, vol. 3 of *Attachment and Loss* (New York: Basic Books, 1980); Bowlby, "Pathological Mourning and Childhood Mourning," *Journal of the American Psychoan-*

father and mother were not happily married and quarreled often. Natalie's mother felt so guilty about it that she asked her sister not to tell their father. Natalie's mother seems to have suffered severe anxiety about the potential loss of love from her own father and thus of his ability to protect her. When he fell seriously ill during her first pregnancy, for example, she suffered a miscarriage. At the time of her husband's death in a riding accident, her daughter Natalie was in the Oedipal phase and still carried a pre-Oedipal identification with her mother. Through her identification Natalie would have absorbed and replicated her mother's anxiety over the loss of her father, Natalie's grandfather, which then actually came to pass when her own father was killed. Natalie's already considerable fears of separation from the father and her feelings of helplessness could only have been intensified as a result.

To make matters worse, Natalie's father had been angry at the birth of his two daughters, according to the beautiful soul; he had hoped instead for sons who could eventually help him administer the family estate. Children perceive the death of a parent as abandonment; Natalie ascribed it—not illogically, given her father's preferences—to the fact that she was not a boy. Furthermore, she assumed that her infantile anger toward her father for preferring boys to girls would cause her father to punish her by dying and leaving her. Natalie's interpretation of her father's death is one important source of what would become her lifelong shame over her feminine identity; it explains, for example, why she wears her great-uncle's cape, in which she first appears to us. With the cape she assures herself of the protection of a significant male caregiver, and she is able to hide or deny her female body underneath it.[17]

---

alytic Association, 11 (1963): 500–541; see also Sol Altschul, ed., *Childhood Bereavement and Its Aftermath* (Madison, Wis.: International Universities Press, 1988). Although Natalie is born into an aristocratic family, her parents appear to have been her primary caregivers, inasmuch as Goethe does not mention any others and wants, moreover, to depict an aristocracy moving toward certain middle-class behavioral patterns.

17 Given the crucial psychological significance of the cape for Natalie, one wonders how she was able to give it up to Wilhelm when he was injured. A sensible answer to this question has been given by Hans-Jürgen Schings ("Wilhelm Meisters schöne Amazone," *Jahrbuch der Deutschen Schillergesellschaft*, 29 [1985]: 141–206), who

Her father's rejection of her female identity prior to his death is not the only reason for Natalie's refusal to view herself as a woman. When on the heels of his death her mother also dies after giving birth to Friedrich, Natalie sees firsthand the dangers that await her as a mature woman. But more important than this insight is the issue of her Oedipal guilt. During the Oedipal state of identification with the mother, little girls may wish for the death of the mother in order to occupy her place with the father; they also fear that their aggressive desire vis-à-vis the mother will be found out and punished. When the mother actually dies, the daughter naturally concludes that her wishing has brought it about and that she is being punished by the mother for having had the wish in the first place. Natalie, already in a state of high anxiety and feeling helpless because of the loss of her father, now must cope with the loss of her mother, her last remaining caregiver, and must deal with the fantasy that the death was her fault.

To atone for this horrible crime, which is after all a crime primarily against herself, and to overcome the helplessness that she has introduced into her life, Natalie adopts two strategies. First, she denies her helplessness by becoming utterly self-reliant and self-sufficient. Her aunt reports: "Sie war keinen Augenblick ihres Lebens unbeschäftigt, und jedes Geschäft ward unter ihren Händen zur würdigen Handlung. . . . und ebenso konnte sie ruhig, ohne Ungeduld, bleiben, wenn sich nichts zu tun fand. Diese Tätigkeit ohne Bedürfnis einer Beschäftigung habe ich in meinem Leben nicht wieder gesehen" (She was never idle for a moment, and every task was ennobled by her hands. . . . yet she could also be patiently still if there was nothing to do. I have never in my life seen such industry that was not driven by need [*WML*, pp. 417–8]). Second, Natalie projects her helplessness onto other children and then spends the rest of her life as a compulsive caregiver.

Let us observe how Natalie's shame, guilt, and subsequent caregiving express themselves in her interaction with one of her charges, Mignon. The girls have heard from peasant children living nearby that angels sometimes visit children in order to punish the bad ones and to pre-

---

reminds us that one of Natalie's main activities is to clothe children or others in need (pp. 203–4).

sent gifts to the good ones. Natalie decides to use the impending birth-
day of twin girls—the doubling suggests the secret link between
Natalie and Mignon—as an occasion to teach the little girls that angels
do not really exist. Symbolically, Natalie wants to do away with a magical method of telling who is good and who is bad. Her psychological
investment in this process is a reflection of her ambivalence toward
herself. She knows that she is bad for having "killed" her mother, but
she does not want to be found out; she is afraid that an omniscient
force might identify and punish her. So Natalie reverts to her childhood custom of dressing up a little girl, this time as an angel. When
Mignon finally appears, holding her lily of purity, the other girls are
entertained by the fiction, which they immediately penetrate. But
Natalie herself is "überrascht" (surprised [p. 515]) at how angelic
Mignon seems. In fact, her astonishment stems from her unacknowledged wish to herself be an angel. Natalie then decides to let Mignon
keep her angel's dress and to provide her with similarly feminine clothing. Natalie achieves here a pseudoresolution of her Oedipal guilt and
a vicarious acceptance of her "shameful" female identity by projecting
the entire complex onto Mignon. Mignon, with whom she unconsciously identifies, becomes the angelic woman whom Natalie cannot
find within herself.[18]

   Although Natalie's dedication to the children is universally praised
by the figures in the novel, the narrator has a different opinion. When
Natalie is busy telling Wilhelm about all the wonderful things she has
done for the little girls, the narrator ironically interrupts her: "Einen
umständlichern Bericht, wie Natalie mit ihren Kindern verfuhr, ver-
sparen wir auf eine andere Gelegenheit" (We shall present a more circumstantial report of how Natalie treated her children on another

---

18 Mignon's song on this occasion (*WML*, pp. 515–6) applies just as well to
Natalie's inner life as to her own. For example, the line "Zieht mir das weiße Kleid
nicht aus!" (Do not take off my white dress!) expresses Natalie's wish to be free of guilt;
the reference to "jene himmlischen Gestalten, / Sie fragen nicht nach Mann und
Weib" (those heavenly forms / do not ask whether male or female) captures Natalie's
fantasy about a place that would be heavenly because she would not be punished for
her sex; "Vor Kummer altert' ich zu frühe" (By worrying I grew old too early) tells us
that her "mature" but defensive self-sufficiency damaged her natural growth from
child into adult; "Macht mich auf ewig wieder jung!" (Make me eternally young
again!) conveys her desire to be a child, which means to be dependent on others.

occasion [p. 528]). That the occasion never returns is not an oversight on Goethe's part. Natalie's caregiving is the displacement onto other children of her own unacknowledged and therefore unresolvable desire to be taken care of. Because she does not understand that she wants care, attention, and safety, she is not opposed to Wilhelm's abandoning her after their dispassionate engagement.[19]

In 1953 Karl Schlechta went against the grain of traditional views of Natalie by suggesting that "she has no drives [*Triebe*] or passions, no desire or memory"; she only partakes of a "lifeless nature."[20] Hans-Jürgen Schings, responding in 1986 to Schlechta's criticism, tells us that perfect characters are always subjected to the harshest criticism and that in fact Natalie is the embodiment of Spinoza's concept of absolute love. She knows no desire because she is completely unselfish ("vollkommen uneigennützig").[21] While Schlechta's interpretation obviously comes closer to what I have proposed than Schings's, their readings of the text have an important feature in common. Caught in the irrelevant, indeed unaskable, question of whether Natalie is a good or a bad person, neither critic examines the role of Natalie as a literary construct within the text. Although Schlechta is mystified by Philine, who he says gives up her eroticism ("kapituliert") in an opaque ("nicht ganz überschaubar" [p. 226]) way, clearly her domestication goes hand in hand with the stories of the beautiful soul and her niece the "beautiful amazon." Schings for his part overlooks the fact that by equating sexual desire with selfishness, he celebrates Natalie's guilt. At issue is not a character but an idea: the fate of female sexuality in Goethe's novel.

The women in the *Lehrjahre* who have known intense desire are either killed off (Mariane, Sperata, Mignon, Aurelie) or domesticated (Philine, Lydie); only women who have repressed their sexuality eventually find a role in the Tower Society.[22] Although the question of the novel's utopian dimension has historically been treated in terms of

19 The physically distant quality of their relationship has been well described by Eichner (p. 188 n. 56).

20 *Goethes Wilhelm Meister* (Frankfurt am Main: Klostermann, 1953), p. 57.

21 "Goethes 'Wilhelm Meister' und Spinoza," in Wittkowski, pp. 57–69, esp. pp. 64–65.

22 This grouping of the women in the *Lehrjahre* was first suggested to me by Mahlendorf, "The Mystery of Mignon."

relations among the social classes or in terms of the individual's relationship to the community, it could now also be approached from the standpoint of gender roles.[23] The patriarchal world of the *Lehrjahre* seems to include desexualization of its women as a utopian expression of a generalized male wish. Compromised feminine sexuality therefore functions in the novel as the primary virtue of Therese, who will become the consort of the patriarch in the new world created by the Tower Society.

Like Natalie and the beautiful soul, Therese is given a detailed history, which she recounts to Wilhelm as they sit together one day under an oak tree. The first thing Therese mentions about her early years is how much she respected her father and how much she disliked her mother for not appreciating how wonderful her father was. (We learn at the end of the novel, of course, that Therese's mother is *not* her mother. While this fact helps to explain, for example, Therese's observation that her mother did not love her, the question of her biological origin is not relevant to Therese's early feelings about the woman she thought was her mother.) Therese's statement to Wilhelm is a clear and rather typical formulation of an Oedipal conflict: she believes that she would have made her father a much better partner than her mother did. The pathology of Therese's childhood is rooted in the fact that her father agrees with her.

Following the breakdown of an initially happy marriage, Therese's mother seeks amusement outside the home with her artistic friends. Seizing the chance to displace her mother, Therese takes over many household duties in an attempt to please her father. Like the beautiful soul, she finds that working with her father allows her to enjoy more of his companionship: "Ich wuchs heran, mit den Jahren vermehrte sich meine Tätigkeit und die Liebe meines Vaters zu mir" (I was growing up, and as the years passed my activities increased, as did my father's love for me [*WML*, p. 447]). Because Therese is the daughter of a

23 Wilhelm Voßkamp ("Utopie und Utopiekritik in Goethes Romanen *Wilhelm Meisters Lehrjahren* und *Wilhelm Meisters Wanderjahren*," in *Utopieforschung*, ed. Wilhelm Voßkamp [Baden-Baden: Suhrkamp, 1985], 3:227–49) discusses the problematic nature of the concept "utopia" in the novel and also provides additional useful bibliography on the topic. Becker-Cantarino offers an approach to the novel's "utopianism" in terms of gender that is slightly different from my own.

woman to whom her father had been passionately attached and who had capably managed the entire household, we need not view Therese's observation as merely a fantasy about her father's love. She did indeed receive more love as she came to carry out more of the duties that her real mother had assumed (and as she physically matured). In other words, rather than simply accept his daughter's erotically charged feelings for him, Therese's father actively encouraged them, because he was exploiting his child as the replacement for her real mother, whose death soon after Therese's birth he had never accepted (he was "trostlos" [disconsolate] [p. 561]) and with whom he was still in love.[24]

The attention that Therese receives from her father enhances and solidifies her identification with him. "Ich glich meinem Vater an Gestalt und Gesinnungen" (I resembled my father in appearance and attitude [p. 447]), she says, but only after telling Wilhelm of her hostility toward her mother. The identification with the father is most significantly an aspect of Oedipal aggression toward her mother, in which her father unconsciously and inappropriately participates. When Therese's mother and competitor finally leaves the household, she and her father rejoice: "Wir waren nun frei und lebten wie im Himmel" (Now we were free and lived as if in paradise [p. 449]). But Therese's real Oedipal triumph is relatively short-lived. Her father dies, and Therese is left without an inheritance because of a bargain he and his wife had struck before her birth that she knew nothing about. Friends encourage her to contest the will. She refuses because she idealizes her father: "Ich verehrte das Andenken meines Vaters zu sehr" (I respected my father's memory too much [p. 451]).

The idealization is, however, a rationalization. Therese's reluctance to assert her financial rights is based on her unconscious guilt over her relationship with her father. Unlike most daughters, Therese has expe-

24   To avoid misunderstanding, I stress that Therese's father indulges his own fantasies that his daughter could be his lover; I am not suggesting that incest occurred between them. That fathers have fantasies in the Oedipal situation was generally overlooked by Freud: "In the case of fathers and daughters, Freud claims to distinguish between a daughter's fantasies of seduction and actual seduction by her father, but he ignores the reciprocal possibility—that absence of actual paternal seduction is not the same thing as absence of seductive fantasies toward a daughter or behavior which expresses such a fantasy" (Chodorow, *Reproduction*, p. 160).

rienced the fulfillment of her Oedipal fantasies: she has acquired exclusive possession of her father's love. But her success in taking something that she is not supposed to own only arouses in her the most intense terror that she will be devastatingly punished by the mother. Punishment is swift; the father dies. Therese interprets his abandonment of her as the price she must pay for having so grievously transgressed against the mother. Her remorse is infinite.

In reality, Therese never won, but rather lost, the Oedipal battle in a more serious way than any daughter should. She does not know that her father's financial arrangement with his wife reflects his decision to enjoy Therese's mother under the condition that he not provide for his daughter. Hence Therese feels a need to atone for what her father had led her to believe was an Oedipal victory. She becomes compulsively self-sufficient. Her organizational skills are legendary; her household is always in perfect order. And her psyche functions just as smoothly as her home; it is never disrupted by anger, most notably when she is abandoned once again, by Lothario, for abandonment by the male is equivalent in Therese's mind to punishment, which she feels she deserves.[25]

Goethe recapitulates Therese's Oedipal conflicts in the subplot of Lothario's affairs with Lydie and with Therese's mother, using a considerable amount of narrative irony that would be comic were Therese's predicament not so tragic. The original engagement between Lothario and Therese was formed not because they had fallen in love but because both parties shared a devotion to the successful functioning of an estate. Therese is excited by the possibility of such a marriage because it would allow her to reenact, on a much grander scale than before, her relationship with her father. Moreover, she appears to have won out over Lydie, another competitor for Lothario's affection, just as she had earlier displaced her mother in her father's life.

Lydie, who was raised in Therese's family, acts as a surrogate sister to Therese. Ironically, Therese and Lydie have a more symmetrical relationship than they know in that neither of them has a biological link to Therese's supposed mother. From the beginning, Therese is aware

25 At the two points in the text where Therese is shown crying over the loss of Lothario, she dismisses one episode (*WML*, p. 443) as the result of an eye infection; the second (p. 458) she cuts short, refusing to give herself over to grief.

of and threatened by Lydie as a sibling competitor for her father's love; hence she easily associates her with her mother. The ever-practical Therese notes that Lydie is "reizend" (charming [p. 448; cf. p. 454]), that she has what Therese views as her mother's frivolous attachment to "Romane" (novels, love stories [p. 460]), and that she became involved not only in her mother's theatrical pursuits but also with her mother's lovers (p. 449). When the mother leaves the home to conduct her libertine activities elsewhere, Lydie accompanies her (p. 451). Finally, just when Therese has lost her father and directly prior to her meeting Lothario, Lydie suddenly and hauntingly reappears, like the ghost of her mother. Similarly, when the engagement between Therese and Lothario is announced, Lydie mysteriously disappears.

Lothario for his part is horrified to discover, soon after his engagement to Therese, that he has had a prior affair with her mother, who lives away from her husband and daughter under the assumed name "Frau von Saint Alban." In the wake of a casual conversation with Therese, during which she unwittingly reveals the identity of Frau von Saint Alban, Lothario suddenly leaves her house, apparently never to return. Because he, like Therese, does not know that his former lover is not Therese's natural mother, he is quick to assume that continuing the engagement would amount to incest.[26] Therese then concludes that her mother has somehow caused Lothario's departure, that she has lost him to her or because of her. Lothario's subsequent diversion with Lydie, who in the meantime has returned, only reinforces Therese's Oedipal anxiety. She responds to Lothario's "unfaithfulness" just as she responded to her father's before: she assumes that she is

26 Lothario's terror of a relationship that is even symbolically incestuous is intimately linked to his promiscuity. Like his sister Natalie, he is a troubled survivor of childhood bereavement. As the oldest of four children, he was probably well into latency or even early adolescence at the time of his parents' death. During this period he would have felt intense ambivalence toward his father that he may not have had an opportunity to resolve. The alternating identification with and fear of his father produce Lothario's ambivalence toward women: his many love affairs are with surrogates for Mother in that Lothario only ever views them as temporarily available to him. He assumes Father's position vis-à-vis the women, and then retreats out of guilt or fear for having done so. When he is confronted "in reality" with the fact that he has slept with "Mother," he bolts.

being punished and atones for her crime by withdrawing into her obsessive perfectionism in the management of her household.

   Therese's guilt does not eliminate her desire for her father. Instead, it inspires her to discover a way to possess him that also allows her to hide their relationship. She therefore intensifies her identification with him, for example, by preferring male clothing. She appears to use "defensive identification," in which the bereaved person attempts to deny the loss, and the pain it evokes, by incorporating the personality of the deceased, who then is felt to live on within the bereaved. Having frozen her father's persona inside her, Therese would treat Lothario just as her father had treated his wife: had they married, she says, she would have tolerated his affairs "wenn es nur ihre häusliche Ordnung nicht gestört hätte" (as long as it did not disrupt her domestic order [p. 461]). Her tolerance, far from being an expression of understanding toward Lothario, exemplifies Therese's expectation that she will be continually rejected even as she pursues an essentially narcissistic bond with her father. She is incapable of responding to a man as an autonomous other, as a human being with a sexual identity and boundaries to the self that are distinct from her own. Therese's eventual marriage to Lothario is an asexual merging with a partner who she believes is like her father and therefore exactly like herself.

The beautiful soul, Natalie, and Therese represent three prismatic aspects of feminine character in *Wilhelm Meisters Lehrjahre*. While the representation of these desexualized women may open Goethe to the charge of misogyny, I believe that something else is at stake in the novel. In the histories of these women we are given graphic depictions of the failure of the German patriarchy to provide the conditions under which little girls might resolve their conflicts over gender identity. With true psychoanalytic skill, Goethe reveals that growing up female in the eighteenth century had a pathological side with origins in the failure of fathers to understand or accept the needs and desires of their young daughters, who then carried the failure forward by internalizing their fathers' attitudes. All of the women I have discussed unconsciously participate in their own desexualization because, for individual reasons, they paradoxically believe that it will make them more acceptable to their fathers and more likely to triumph in their

Oedipal conflict with their mothers. They then rationalize their desexualization by acting out an apparent autonomy that allows them to
deny their attachment to their father and their wish for his approval.
The pathology is most profound and therefore most tragic for Natalie,
whom Schiller and countless readers after him have viewed as the most
perfect of these idealized women, because in her sexual purity she
affirms her father's perverse patriarchal wish that she had not been
born female at all.

Hans Eichner has argued that *Wilhelm Meisters Lehrjahre* presents a
view of the world that runs counter to the optimism of the Enlightenment. Mastery or maturity ("Meisterschaft") in this world is marked by
insight into limitation: some things can be achieved only at the cost of
others (esp. pp. 186–92).[27] The figure who best illustrates this principle for Eichner is Natalie: as the embodiment ("Verkörperung") of car-
itas she cannot have the erotic vitality of a Philine. Eichner is virtually
alone among critics in having recognized the compensatory nature of
Natalie's character, but he does not understand its cause. Moreover, he
does not distinguish between those figures in the novel who learn to
understand, even imperfectly, their limitation and those who simply
live out its consequences unconsciously.

Wilhelm's psychosexual maturation is overtly thematized with the
Hamlet motif and with the painting of the "kranker Königssohn" (the
king's son who is ill). The characters in the novel participate in his
(imperfect) growth by discussing with him his relationship (or lack
thereof) to Hamlet's predicament, or by referring to the existence of
the painting and to what it might mean to him. But the sexual development of Natalie, Therese, and the beautiful soul is buried in narratives of early childhood experience whose significance none of the figures in the novel, including the women themselves, appear to have
grasped. These women occupy positions of great respect within the
Tower Society (despite the uncle's reservations about the beautiful soul
or the occasional ironic remarks we hear, for example, from the impish
Friedrich about his sister [cf. *WML*, p. 565]). The beautiful soul is the
spiritual *grande dame* of the group; Therese is the faithful and knowl-

27 Quite inexplicably, Eichner's interpretation at this point studiously avoids any
mention of, though it deals with, the Goethean concept of *Entsagung* (renunciation).

edgeable administrator of a soon-to-be extended household; Natalie single-handedly provides the society's primary emotional support system. Together, their functions are those of an ideal mother. The esteem in which they are held effectively distracts them from (supports their continuing denial of) the compromises they have made with their fathers, on which their apparently satisfying roles in the society are based. They have no knowledge of the early childhood conflicts that so severely damaged them and hence no desire to resolve them or possibility of doing so. These idealized women therefore acquire the dubious honor of incarnating the fundamental, irrevocable loss of eroticism that Freud would later describe as "das Unbehagen in der Kultur" (civilization and its discontents).

Goethe's decision to kill off or domesticate the erotically sensitive women in his novel and to populate the Tower Society with asexual, or rather desexualized, types accounts for every female character in the *Lehrjahre* except one: Margarete, the tenant farmer's daughter. She is presented to us in the context of a fairy tale recounted by Lothario to Jarno and Wilhelm over dinner one evening. An analysis of this patri-archal narrative provides a final insight into the representation of female sexuality in the work.

Margarete was a former lover of Lothario's to whom he had been especially attached. Now she is unavailable to him because she is "weit weg verheiratet" (married and living far away [*WML*, p. 464]). One day Lothario hears that she is visiting her father, who still lives nearby, and decides to seek her out. As he rides away from his estate, he travels through an idyllic natural setting reminiscent of their first meeting, finally reaching the "Zauberwelt" (magical world [p. 465]) where he hopes to find her. Like so many fairy tales, the story is laden with Oedi-pal themes, but what we especially note is Lothario's reaction. Nor-mally hypersensitive, as we have seen, to the very possibility of incestu-ous affairs, he is unconcerned about them as he moves through this magical sphere. He becomes immediately fascinated with Margarete's "Muhme" (niece, cousin [p. 466]), who resembles his former lover and whom he first meets instead of her. She is ten years younger than Margarete and thus evokes the image of the woman he remembers. On his first foray into the "Zauberwelt," Lothario is enchanted with multiplying female presences, but he fails to find Margarete herself.

Lothario ends his account at this point, and the other men contribute their own stories of erotic adventure, which the narrator compares to "Gespenstergeschichten" (ghost stories [p. 466]). Lothario then offers the opinion that his marriage to Therese, now apparently impossible, would have been a "Himmel" (paradise), but not one of "schwärmerischen Glücks" (ecstasy [p. 467]). Instead he could have counted on the solid happiness that comes from an ordered life. The interpolation is important because it anticipates the outcome of the fairy tale.

A few days later, Lothario tries a second time to visit Margarete at her father's home, and on this occasion he succeeds. Here again he finds Margarete's "Ebenbild" (likeness [p. 470]), now sitting behind an unambiguously feminine symbol, the spinning wheel, where his lover herself used to sit. Among Margarete's several young children assembled with her is a little daughter who clearly resembles her mother. Lothario later says that in seeing these multiple generations of women, all so charming and similar in appearance, he was cast into a timeless, organic realm where, as if in an orange grove, blossoms and fruit seemed to exist side by side (cf. pp. 470–71).

The considerable pathos of Lothario's encounter with Margarete and their brief conversation (p. 471) lies in their mutual recognition of an intense desire that is alive but not livable. A man of Lothario's social standing would not have married a woman like Margarete, but this is not Goethe's point in this complex symbolic episode. Lothario can find Margarete only in the "unreal" matriarchal world of vegetative magic and fairy tales. The real patriarchal world to which he returns is one of erotically sterile unions, for which daughters are carefully prepared.

Mary Robinson and

the Myth of Sappho

Jerome McGann

Describing the scope of her *Fictions of Sappho, 1546–1937*, Joan DeJean points out that the French dominated the reception history of the Greek poet until the eighteenth century, when "the English and the Germans really began to play a role."[1] These facts explain why DeJean focuses on French traditions. But she then adds: "Once other traditions become active, I refer to all the major contributions to the composite portrait of Sappho that originate outside of France. I dwell especially on those foreign traditions when they create original fictions that subsequently serve as models for French authors" (4). However, the single most important English contribution to the Sapphic tradition is never mentioned in DeJean's study: Mary Robinson's *Sappho and Phaon* (1796).[2]

Far more is at issue here than filling an omission in an important scholarly study. Robinson's work had little influence on subsequent treatments of Sappho in any language, so we can understand why DeJean overlooked it. To say that *Sappho and Phaon* is a central document in the

---

1 DeJean, *Fictions of Sappho, 1546–1937* (Chicago: University of Chicago Press, 1989), 4.

2 One other signal contribution, Swinburne's, is treated rather perfunctorily, as if it were simply a footnote to Baudelaire (DeJean, 272). But Swinburne's is a highly original contribution to the tradition (see Jerome McGann, *Swinburne: An Experiment in Criticism* [Chicago: University of Chicago Press, 1972], esp. 112–7).

114

poetry of sensibility—which it is—already hints at the problem. The literature of sensibility has been, as we say these days, securely marginalized. And the poetry of sensibility has long been virtually invisible. Of course the impact of the great original writings of sensibility, both prose and verse, has scarcely been negligible. Touchstone writers in the tradition—Rousseau and Sterne, Goethe and Richardson, or the "major romantic poets"—are canonical figures. But tradition and the profession of letters have not preserved their work *because of its sentimentality*. Their cultural value is judged by other measures, with their sentimentalism being viewed in neutralized "historical" terms.

As a result, the literatures of sensibility tend to be read through categories that exclude the (aesthetic) value of sensibility as a mode of expression. Though the styles and the culture of sensibility permeate Western society to the present day, they typically function in low cultural and social registers: popular music, pulp fiction, and the movies. More fastidious souls—often splendid enough, in their own way—look with judgmental eyes on figures like Marianne Dashwood and Mary Robinson. Sometimes these looks are censorious, sometimes condescending, occasionally sympathetic. They are nearly always conscious of their superiority.

Sappho and Phaon is not itself lowbrow; on the contrary, it is a learned production fully aware of the major works serving the tradition it interprets. Robinson gives special prominence to Ovid's culminant epistle in the *Heroides* and Barthélemy's *Voyage du jeune Anacharsis en Grèce* (1788), and her handling of both tells us much about the distinctive features of her work. Indeed, contemporary readers of *Sappho and Phaon* were most disturbed by its serious and radical philosophical pretensions. Most reactionary critics in the 1790s lacked the intellectual tools to combat the imaginative forms of these pretensions—for example, in Della Cruscan poetry—so the attacks came as invective, travesty, ridicule. The prominent antagonists were Gifford, Polwhele, Matthias, and the anti-Jacobin writers, though only the latter achieved true poetic distinction. A major figure of reaction would soon emerge in the person of "the later Coleridge," himself a lapsed Della Cruscan poet.[3]

One needs to recall this history to revise it radically. The all-but-

3 See his poetry of 1792–94, in particular "Kisses," "The Sigh," and "The Kiss."

complete excision of Della Cruscan poetry from the history of English writing has been a cultural disaster, not because the work of the original English Della Cruscans was in itself a major poetic achievement, though they certainly have their impressive moments, but because

1 it provides an invaluable corpus for studying the conventions of the poetry of sensibility;
2 understanding those conventions gives greater access to the work of the major poets who worked in the first phase of the tradition, that is, in the years 1760–1840;
3 understanding the poetry of sensibility in that period opens new avenues for (re)reading the poetry that succeeded it.

To date we possess virtually no studies of the formal and rhetorical conventions of the kind of verse that Mary Robinson cultivated. How then can we read with any confidence the poetry of Robert Merry, Charlotte Smith, or Ann Batten Cristall, much less the work of Felicia Hemans or Laetitia Elizabeth Landon? Or how evaluate what we may read? Much of the writing is currently under historical recovery through the efforts of cultural historians, feminist and otherwise. But such readers tend to ignore the art of this writing, and instead interrogate it for social, moral, or ideological significance.[4]

We can scarcely manage distinctions between sentimental poetry, poetry of sensibility, and romantic verse. As for the latter, which we pretend to understand, its conventions are widely misunderstood or ignored. The fact that romantic poetry operates with conventions of sincerity—that the famous "true voice of feeling" is an artful construction—remains widely unappreciated. Poe and Wilde have provided brilliant guides for studying such work, but neither one is taken seriously as a poet, and their criticism of poetry remains to this day badly misunderstood. (We have yet to plumb the depth of Poe's serious joking in "The Raven" and "The Philosophy of Composition" or the profound inconsequence of Wilde's various elucidations and critiques of

4 In his good study *Radical Sensibility: Literature and Ideas in the 1790s* (New York: Routledge, 1993), Chris Jones has "used the two terms interchangeably, as much from a conviction of their continuity as from the inconvenient absence of an adjectival form for 'sensibility'" (5). His move is common and seems symptomatic of a wholly inadequate critical procedure—and all the more inadequate if, as he believes, there is a "continuity" between the terms. (For "continuity" I would myself put "close relation.")

romanticism and sincerity—for example, in *The Importance of Being Earnest.*)

Though the ultimate issues here are aesthetic ones—and sociopolitical to the extent that we can appreciate the sociopolitical dimensions of aesthetic action—the immediate problems are critical. We want to elucidate the rhetorics of sentimentalism, sensibility, and sincerity in a way that might correspond to the early twentieth century's critical exploration of the metaphysicals and their Augustan inheritors. To do so demands a return to formal analysis and close reading. But in the present case the acts will have to be self-consciously (re)historicized, so that the classicist histories (and evaluations) established through the discourse of modernism can be fundamentally relativized. If you demand of "poetry" what can be followed through Pound or Eliot or Yeats or Stevens, you will have great difficulty understanding, much less appreciating, most of the poetry written between 1760 and 1900, and you will work hard to exorcise a poet like Stein, the chief modernist inheritor of those traditions. You will also select those writers who can be shown to have broken with—in fact "romanticized"—the original spirits of sentimentalism and sensibility.

Here is the context in which one wants to reread Robinson's *Sappho and Phaon*. The book was written as a comprehensive manifesto for poetry (that is to say, for poetry of a certain kind—for a poetry of sensibility). It is in this respect a polemic for "modern" poetry (that is to say, for verse that was understood at the time to be new and innovative, or—in the rhetoric of its hostile critics—dangerous and newfangled). The manifesto comes at once as a theory and a practice, with the two moves formally marked in the work's prose and verse sections. Indeed, one key (dialectical) argument of *Sappho and Phaon* is that a proper poetical practice ought to be fully "theorized" (self-conscious, philosophical, and in Schiller's sense "sentimental"), just as an adequate theory of poetry would have to establish feeling and emotion as intellectual and philosophical grounds.

Robinson's Myth of Sappho: General Theory

Robinson's manifesto—like the more celebrated ones of Wordsworth, Percy Shelley, and others—directly engages current poetical theory and practice. Most important, *Sappho and Phaon* follows eighteenth-century theory in taking "sensibility" and "feeling" as distinguishing marks of poetical writing. From Edward Young's "Discourse of Lyric Poetry" (1728) through Dugald Stewart's *Elements of the Philosophy of the Human Mind* (1792–1827), poetry is associated with a feminized "feeling" and "imagination" and is opposed to the sober and practical "masculine power[s] of the mind."[5] The opposition is codified as a distinction between reason and imagination. Like later romantic writers, Robinson contests the invidious judgment often implied in the comparison.

Her argument, both as theory and as practice, is specifically gendered female, not simply because of her sex, but—more crucially—because the substance of the argument demands it. She assumes—as everyone else at the time did—that sensibility is a feminized "experience." She is equally aware, however, that the philosophical discourse of sensibility has been dominantly masculine. Robinson's work proceeds to turn this cultural limit to her polemical advantage. If sensibility (in theory) is to have a discursive form, it will have to be an "experiential" one, that is, a poetic (aesthetic) form.

This context of thought explains Robinson's purposes in *Sappho and Phaon*. First, she will elucidate her perceived contradiction between the discourse of poetry and that of philosophy. Second, she will argue the philosophical case of poetry *in the discourse of poetry* (and implicitly critique the relevance or effectiveness of any philosophical discourse that eschews the practice of sensibility and what she takes as its chief discursive vehicle, poetry). Her position contradicts the two dominant (and masculinist) theories of poetry articulated in the volatile 1790s, the one reactionary, the other revisionist. As one target of Gifford's anti–Della Cruscan satire *The Baviad* (1791), Robinson means to disestablish a "dead but sceptred" view of poetry that clung to its authority in face of the many bold new writing ventures of the later eighteenth century. On the other hand, her book of sonnets constructs its positive interpretation (or myth) of the new poetical scene. In this respect her argument anticipates Wordsworth's defense of poetry against the emerg-

---

5 *The Works of Mary Wollstonecraft*, ed. Janet Todd and Marilyn Butler, 7 vols. (London: William Pickering, 1989), 1:146.

ing cultural claims of science and philosophy. As a specifically Della Cruscan myth, however, Robinson's approach would be undermined in Wordsworth's revisionist preface to *Lyrical Ballads* (1800), which seeks to restore poetry—including the poetry of feeling and imagination—to its "manly" heritage.

Sappho and Phaon perfectly illustrates Schiller's theoretical dialectic of naive versus sentimental poetry. Robinson's work is fully sentimental exactly because it (imaginatively) constructs a naive body of Sapphic writing. The construction draws a running parallel between a model of ancient cultural "enlightenment" and the contemporary world (Europe in general, but England in particular).[6] The prose shape of the argument is set forth in Robinson's "Preface," address "To the Reader," and "Account of Sappho," all of which introduce the sonnet sequence.

Robinson's Sappho is first of all a model of the passionate "naive" poet, whose poems are "the genuine effusions of a supremely enlightened soul" (25). "Distinguished by the title of the tenth Muse," Sappho's "fame . . . spread even to the remotest parts of the earth" (21, 22). Again and again Robinson associates Sappho with cultural enlightenment: "For it is known, that poetry was, at the period in which she lived, held in the most sacred veneration; and that those who were gifted with that divine inspiration, were ranked as the first class of human beings" (18). In the consciousness of the golden age of Greek civilization, Sappho and her work embodied the highest values available to a civilized culture, and "the most competent judges" of later ages "esteemed" her work "as the standard for the pathetic, the glowing, and the amatory" (24).

In associating cultural enlightenment with poetry, and in (implicitly) proposing a poetry of sensibility as a touchstone of poetical work, Robinson does two important things at once. First, she feminizes the Schillerian dialectic by replacing Homer with Sappho as the paradigmatic naive writer of ancient Greece. In contemporary terms, Robinson is accepting eighteenth-century sentimentality and sensibility as (the) distinctive features of poetical expression. That acceptance, how-

---

6 Robinson stresses the term *enlightened*, its various cognates, and related words (like *lustre*). For eighteenth-century thinkers the term was an all-purpose figure for advanced and liberal thought. As early as 1732 Berkeley refers to "the select spirits of this enlightened age" (*Alciphron*, 1.9).

ever, does not lead her to neglect the more broadly social functions and responsibilities of the poet. On the contrary, in fact. The move to Sappho is part of a general argument on behalf of the enlightenment powers of "pathetic . . . glowing [and] amatory" verse. A "lustre of intellectual light" (10) inheres in this poetry and diffuses throughout every enlightened society. Robinson explicitly associates it with the entire movement of progressive cultural views that men like Polwhele and Gifford in the 1790s so deplored.

> It is the interest of the ignorant and powerful to suppress the effusions of enlightened minds: when only monks could write, and nobles read, authority rose triumphant over right; and the slave, spell-bound in ignorance, hugged his fetters without repining. It was then that the best powers of reason lay buried like the gem in the dark mine; by a slow and tedious progress they have been drawn forth, and must, ere long, diffuse an universal lustre; for that era is rapidly advancing, when talents will tower like an unperishable column, while the globe will be strewed with the wrecks of superstition. (14–5)

But "that era" of full enlightenment is not yet come, even (!) in 1796, and Robinson's Sappho also functions as the exponent of an unripened historical evolution.

In this last respect Robinson's Sappho is at once the index of a current (inadequate) condition and the prophet of a future day. Though herself "supremely enlightened," Sappho's very sensibility—her greatest virtue—became through circumstance a defect or error: "That Sappho was not herself insensible to the feelings she so well described is evident in her writings; but it was scarcely possible, that a mind so exquisitely tender, so sublimely gifted, should escape those fascinations" (24). In Robinson's myth, Sappho's love for Phaon appears a madness because he proves unworthy of her devotion. The explanation comes in the sonnets proper rather than in the prefatory prose documents, although in the latter it is sketched in the theme of Sappho's detractors. Following Rousseau and Goethe, Robinson turns Sappho's apparent madness into a psychological sign of a general social dysfunction. In this way Robinson argues that Sappho's love is *prophetic,* that is, it forecasts a time when a Phaon might come who would be worthy of her love. In the meantime Sappho exhibits a soul tortured by the failures of time and circumstance.

This is to express Robinson's myth in interpersonal terms and perhaps to recall the less happy events of her personal experience. As such it courts a view probably quite far removed from Robinson's specific intentions, which are clearly much more social and even—in their own way—Wollstonecraftian. The more broadly cultural purposes of Robinson's myth of Sappho are clear in the following key passages:

> Addison was of the opinion, that the writings of Sappho were replete with such fascinating beauties, and adorned with such a vivid glow of sensibility, that, probably, had they been preserved entire, it would have been dangerous to have perused them. They possessed none of the artificial decorations of a feigned passion; they were the genuine effusions of a supremely enlightened soul, labouring to subdue a fatal enchantment; and vainly opposing the conscious pride of illustrious fame, against the warm susceptibility of a generous bosom. (24–5)

> If her writings were, in some instances, too glowing for the fastidious refinement of modern times; let it be her excuse, and the honour of her country, that the liberal education of the Greeks was such, as inspired them with an unprejudiced enthusiasm for the works of genius; and that when they paid adoration to Sappho, they idolized the MUSE, and not the WOMAN. (27)

In her critical presentation Robinson is not prepared to say that Sappho's poetry is ever censurable as such. Sappho's writings constitute the essence ("the MUSE") of poetry. That they might appear terrible, excessive, even frightening can be admitted and should be said, but those qualities result from unripened conditions. Addison's limited and "fastidious" admiration for Sappho signifies that his soul is not as enlightened as it might be. In this respect he embodies Phaon. Addison's position in Robinson's argument is important because he shows how "enlightenment" is never uniformly distributed, either across history or within a particular epoch. Robinson's critical myth of Sappho, finally addressed to her "enlightened" contemporaries, demonstrates that the differences between ancient Greek civilization and the more "fastidious" society of late-eighteenth-century England can be regressive ones.

When stressing Sappho's prophetic importance, Robinson is thinking in these historical terms. "Sappho . . . knew that she was writing for future ages" (26), and the remark applies as well to Robinson herself in writing *Sappho and Phaon*. For the epoch forecast by Sappho's work is not yet come ("that era is rapidly advancing"), as Robinson knows because of the persistent "neglect . . . of literary merit" (16) in the present—a neglect foreshadowed, Robinson repeatedly argues, in Sappho's own neglect by her later detractors who envied her fame. *Sappho and Phaon* comes therefore to history as a song before the sunrise of that new day whose advent clearly appears in the prophetic signs of the present: "I cannot conclude these opinions without paying tribute to the talents of my illustrious countrywomen; who, unpatronized by courts, and unprotected by the powerful, persevere in the paths of literature, and ennoble themselves by the unperishable lustre of MENTAL PRE-EMINENCE!" (16). Here Robinson's basic argument is being summarized and repeated at the level of a strong rhetorical address. At the end of the preface Robinson comes out as "a woman speaking to women" about feminized sources of poetical power. With Sappho as their progenitor, Robinson's "illustrious countrywomen" have entirely restructured the philosophy of literature in terms of the feelings and the passions. Here sensibility is being represented as a preeminent intellectual force, and the emblem of whatever social and philosophical advancement the present age can claim for itself. Well might Wordsworth, in face of such a consciously feminized prophecy, step slightly back and try to reestablish poetry as the discourse of "a man speaking to men."

The Myth as Poetical Technique

The sonnets of *Sappho and Phaon* reread, and rewrite, their sources, in particular Ovid's famous epistle "Sappho to Phaon." Historicizing her materials in the prefatory prose texts, Robinson develops a general interpretive rationale to undermine the commonplace and narrower focus. In the latter Sappho emblemizes a mind deranged by excessive love; she serves future generations as a monitory sign of the danger of ungoverned passion. In Robinson's work Sappho becomes a Promethean figure who will inaugurate a new age of enlightenment and higher "Reason."

To understand Robinson's poetical method we have to stay a while with her prose preface, particularly the opening section where she conducts a technical discussion of poetry. The text forces us to reflect upon the poetical form of Robinson's re-creative verse. Robinson's Sappho speaks (in 1796) in the most finished of verse forms, the "legitimate sonnet." The choice of form sharply distinguishes Robinson's Sappho from how Ovid (and Pope) represent her. In the latter the epistolary form emblematizes the extinction of Sappho's poetic gift, as Sappho herself famously declares in Ovid's text: "Flendus amor meus est, elegeia flebile carmen; / Non facit ad lacrimas barbitos ulla meas."[7] Robinson places this very epigraph at the head of her sonnet sequence, along with Pope's translation: "Love taught my Tears in sadder Notes to flow, / And tun'd my Heart to Elegies of Woe" ("Sappho to Phaon," 7–8). The startling form adopted by Robinson for her retelling of Sappho's story suggests the exact opposite of what Ovid wants to intimate when he has Sappho discuss her abandonment of the Sapphic for the elegiac measure, "cum lyricis sim magis apta modis" (since I am more apt with lyric measures [6]). In Robinson the Italian sonnet —a sign of a firmly self-conscious artistic intelligence—argues that Sappho's poetical genius must be seen to persist even during her silence and apparent derangement. Ovid's elegiacs misrepresent Sappho and her love for Phaon.

This subject merits further attention, not least because Robinson herself spends a substantial part of the preface discussing her chosen verse form, the Italian (Petrarchan, or "legitimate") sonnet. Her remarks explicitly relate the form and Sappho via Milton's sonnet to the nightingale, which Robinson reads as an address to Sappho.[8] Robinson stresses the technical skill required to work in the form to reinforce the Sapphic connection. Ovid's elegiacs are an index of Sappho's poetic desuetude: "Nec mihi, dispositis quae iungam carmina nervis, / Proveniunt,

---

7 Ovid, *Amores, epistulae, de medicamine, artis amatoriae, remediorum amoris*, ed. Rudolphi Merkelii (Leipzig: Teubneri, 1852), ll. 7–8.

8 The most ancient traditions associate Sappho with the nightingale.

vacuae carmina mentis opus" (Songs no longer come for me to compose on harmonizing strings, songs that are the works of an untroubled mind) (13–4). In Robinson, however, Sappho's emotional condition does not affect her art of poetry.

The "legitimate sonnet"—which is Robinson's shrewdly chosen term—explicitly represents not merely a sure artistic control but "a chaste and elegant model" (3n) of poetic style. The terms all reflect upon the image of Sappho that Robinson is building. When Robinson considers the current craze for sonnet writing, she observes a mélange of "non-descript ephemera from the heated brains of self-important poetasters" (10). The "legitimate sonnet" thus stands for the possibility of a strongly passionate and emotional poetry that yet preserves its artistic power and integrity.

The entire discussion of the sonnet, which opens Robinson's preface, grounds the argument of her general manifesto for poetry. Being "an enthusiastic votary of the Muse," Robinson is writing to prevent the "chaos of dissipated pursuits which has too long been growing like an overwhelming shadow, and menacing the lustre of intellectual light, should, aided by the idleness of some, and the profligacy of others, at last obscure the finer mental powers, and reduce the dignity of talents to the lowest degradation" (10). This is at once brilliant and pointed: brilliant, because Robinson's wit has stolen the language of the enemies of the new poetry of sensibility and thrown it back at them; and pointed, because she simultaneously recurs to her central subject, the need to promote the "intellectual light" of poetry and its relation to "the finer mental powers" of the soul.

The emergence of the authority of sensibility tended to narrow poetry's authority to the field of personal or interpersonal emotions. While Robinson by no means wants to undermine this culture of sensibility, she is intent upon arguing its largest philosophical and social claims. So she begins by declaring that "the LEGITIMATE SONNET, may be carried on in a series of sketches, composing, in parts, one historical or imaginary subject, and forming in the whole a complete and connected story" (5). With good reason Robinson chooses Milton to authorize her resort to the Italian sonnet. Her claim here establishes the importance of "major form," a poetic vehicle capable of dealing with transcendent matters.[9] Robinson concludes her discussion by expanding upon the significance of forming "in the whole a complete and connected story." Clearly anticipating Wordsworth's and Percy Shelley's later arguments, Robinson asserts the power of "grand and harmonious compositions" to "look beyond the surface of events" (11). Such works are prophetic and historically visionary, and she concludes by aligning *Sappho and Phaon* with the claims made by perhaps the most admired poet of the day, William Cowper:

> So when remote futurity is brought
> Before the keen inquiry of her thought,
> A terrible sagacity informs
> The Poet's heart, he looks to distant storms,
> He hears the thunder e'er the tempest lowers,
> And, arm'd with strength surpassing human pow'rs,
> Seizes events as yet unknown to man,
> And darts his soul into the dawning plan. ("Table Talk," 492–99)

Once again we are struck by the extremity of Robinson's wit. An "enlightened" mind reads Cowper's text in complex contemporary terms, as the shrewd use of the feminine pronoun in the second quoted line shows. The word literally refers to "the MUSE" (just mentioned in the previous prose text), but of course in the context of Robinson's work it carries several more pointed references: to Sappho, to Robinson, and (generally) to the "MENTAL PRE-EMINENCE" of those "illustrious countrywomen" whom Robinson finally determines to celebrate (16).

Though never explicitly named, Mary Wollstonecraft is the most important one, not only because of her general celebrity, or her friendship with Robinson, but more especially because *Sappho and Phaon* clearly steps away from certain key Wollstonecraftian positions. How does *Sappho and Phaon* relate, for example, to the following? "Women subjected by ignorance to their sensations, and only taught to look for happiness in love, refine on sensual feelings, and adopt

---

9 The legitimate sonnet, according to Robinson, has the power to generate "a complete and connected story" because of its formal structure. In this it is unlike "the modern sonnet [which concludes] with two lines, winding up the sentiment of the whole [and confining] the poet's fancy" (5).

metaphysical notions respecting that passion, which lead them shamefully to neglect the duties of life, and frequently in the midst of these sublime refinements they plump into actual vice" (*Works* 5:255). In certain (obvious) ways, *Sappho and Phaon* might be taken as a perfect illustration of Wollstonecraft's complaint: its central subject is love, it scrutinizes "sensual feelings," it works up an elaborate philosophical rationale for itself, it tells the story of a suicide. And behind it all stands the notorious figure of "Perdita" Robinson, whose personal life was a scandal.

Another famous passage from the *Vindication* can help to clarify the issues:

> Novels, music, poetry, and gallantry, all tend to make women the creatures of sensation. . . . This overstretched sensibility naturally relaxes the other powers of the mind, and prevents intellect from attaining that sovereignty which it ought to attain to render a rational creature useful to others . . . : for the exercise of the understanding, as life advances, is the only method pointed out by nature to calm the passions. (130)

In this context one can see that Robinson wants to argue with Wollstonecraft about the social, philosophical, and intellectual power of "sensibility." Robinson does not disagree about the terms or issues at stake; what she contests is Wollstonecraft's recurrent tendency to denigrate the importance of "passion," "love," and the philosophy of sensibility that underpins those ideas and experiences.

Wollstonecraft's personal life regularly defied her public positions, as her many detractors liked to point out. The contradiction is important for Robinson, since it draws certain telling parallels between Robinson and Wollstonecraft and—most salient—Sappho. Like Sappho (and Robinson), Wollstonecraft is a prophetic soul, and her contradictions are an index of her historical position and significance. Furthermore— and this is the most crucial point of all—Wollstonecraft's philosophical work (as opposed to her personal history) replicates the contradictions of her life. The theorist who regularly argues down the passions is not in fact unaware of their power and importance: "They . . . who complain of the delusions of passion, do not recollect that they are exclaiming against a strong proof of the immortality of the soul" (143). Wollstonecraft is not an atheist, so that her remark here introduces an important qualification to the paragraph of arguments against the pursuit of love and happiness that this sentence finishes. And the next short paragraph elaborates the point: "But leaving superior minds to correct themselves, and pay dearly for their experience, it is necessary to observe, that it is not against strong, persevering passions; but romantic wavering feelings that I wish to guard the female heart by exercising the understanding: for these paradisiacal reveries are oftener the effect of idleness than of a lively fancy" (143). Here is exactly where *Sappho and Phaon* enters Wollstonecraft's argument. Like Wollstonecraft, Sappho is one of those "superior minds" who—to borrow and adapt Percy Shelley's splendid later description of Byron as the emblematic poet—"learn in suffering what they teach in song." *Sappho and Phaon* is Robinson's explication of the "strong, persevering passion" that Wollstonecraft must finally defend.

The Myth in Poetical Practice

The sonnets provide a new answer to the traditional question re-posed by Robinson at the outset of the narrative:[10]

> Why, when I gaze on Phaon's beauteous eyes,
>   Why does each thought in wild disorder stray?
>   Why does each fainting faculty decay,
> And my chill'd breast in throbbing tumults rise?
> Mute, on the ground my Lyre neglected lies,
>   The Muse forgot, and lost the melting lay;
>
>   (1–6)

As Robinson's retold story develops, we realize that the answer to these initial questions comes through a more broadly based, less "prejudiced" study of the situation and materials. *Sappho and Phaon* as a whole does this. When Ovid's "Sappho *to* Phaon" becomes Robinson's *Sappho and Phaon*, the changed middle term signals an important

---

10 The fourth sonnet of the sequence begins the narrative proper of the events in Sappho's story. Sonnets 1–3 are not "spoken" by Sappho at all; sonnet 1 is introductory, and sonnets 2 and 3 set the allegorical terms within which the Sapphic events will be explained.

change of attention. Sappho is placed in a larger context of under-standing, as Robinson's prose materials emphasize, and the widening includes a closer investigation of Phaon.

Robinson's work underscores the relevance of the investigation, for Sappho's beloved is a highly problematic figure. Most importantly, he has proved himself faithless to their love devotions. He exhibits the very opposite of Wollstonecraft's (and Sappho's) "strong, persevering passion." At the narrative level, Robinson represents his corruption by first associating him with the pursuit of dark pleasures, love hidden away or practiced at night (see for example sonnet 9). Then, in his (traditional) departure from Greece to Sicily he is represented as for-saking Sappho for lesser lovers. In each instance his debasement signi-fies a retreat from "enlightenment," the meaning of his Sicilian adven-tures appearing through a contrast of mortal and immortal fires, Aetna and the maidens of Sicily versus Apollo and Sappho. "Ah! think, that while on Aetna's shores you stray, / A fire, more fierce than Aetna's, fills my breast" (23.9–10). That fire is explicitly poetical and Apollo-nian. When it pours and focuses upon Phaon ("Oft o'er that form, enamour'd have I hung" [10.5]), it brings him to a new and higher (poetical) life:

> So, on the modest lily's leaves of snow
> The proud Sun revels in resplendent rays!
>   Warm as his beams this sensate heart shall glow,
> Till life's last hour, with Phaon's self decays.
>   (10.11–4)

The figure here startles because of its gender reversals (Sappho as the sun, Phaon as the lily) and the explicit equation of Sappho's love and poetry with the sun/Apollo's natural heat and ideal inspiration. "Sen-sate heart" is a particularly fine epithet, echoing the diction of Della Cruscan verse and its wellspring, the poetry of sensibility. Its function here is metaphysical: to argue (in poetic figuration) that a certain movement in modern writing (sensibility) most fully represents the tra-dition and "original genius" of poetry.

Sappho and Phaon will therefore repeatedly explore the ambiguous significance of passion and reason, chastity and pleasure, feeling and thought. Robinson introduces Sappho's dramatic monologue of son-nets with an allegorical pair (sonnets 2 and 3) that set the terms of what will follow. One describes the Temple of "Chastity divine" (1.3), the other a "vale beneath" "the bow'r of Pleasure" (2.1, 4). The Temple, though "rear'd by immortal pow'rs" (1.2), appears cold and inhuman—its promise of "celestial joys" (1.8) marred by the forms in which those promises are carried:

> On the frozen floor
> Studded with tear-drops, petrified by scorn
> Pale vestals kneel the Goddess to adore.
>
> (1.11–3)

The contrast with the "bow'r of Pleasure" is explicit: "There witching beauty greets the ravish'd sight," and "birds breathe bliss! light zephyrs kiss the ground" (3.6, 9). Nonetheless, the bower's limitations are also clearly marked, not least in the figural fact that its "tangled shade / Excludes the blazing torch of noon-day light" (3.1–2). In a work where the sun/Apollo represents an "enlightened" norm, both Temple and Bower suffer from its diminished presence. The text maintains Chastity and Pleasure as ideal forms, but equally as forms operating under constraint and limitation.

As a prophetic instrument, Robinson's Sappho expresses the topics raised by the text. Like the mythic creatures in Blake's prophetic books, she is transacted by everything her texts reveal. The derangement of her mind and heart enacts an incompetent social and philosophical situation, which is itself figured in Robinson's work as the unbalanced relations of thought and passion, pleasure and chastity. As a consequence, spiritual absolutes like "Love" and "Reason" become, along with Sappho, disordered, and (literally) lose their identities—as we see with special clarity in sonnet 5, for example:

> O! How can Love exulting Reason quell!
>   How fades each nobler passion from his gaze!
>   E'en Fame, that cherishes the Poet's lays,
> That Fame, ill-fated Sappho lov'd so well.
> Lost is the wretch, who in his fatal spell
>   Wastes the short Summer of delicious days,
>   And from the tranquil path of wisdom strays,
> In passion's thorny wild, forlorn to dwell.
>
> (5.1–8)

The initial ambiguous syntax operates through the entire poem, which represents with fine poetic exactitude a confusion of heart and mind in a soul committed to fully realizing the virtues of both. Hence Sappho addresses "Reason" in despair, for in her quotidian experience "Reason"—Sappho's commitment to full and conscious awareness of herself and the meaning of her desires—comes only in demonic form: "Around thy throne destructive tumults rise, / And hell-fraught jealousies" (11.11–2). Hence too her despair when her ideal quest is experienced as the commitment to Love: "Ah! why is rapture so allied to pain?" (18.14). Perfection is clearly defined in the sonnets as "endless rapture" (37.12), but in the immediate event the rapture grows debased by circumstance. Both heart and mind, Love and Reason get confused and overthrown: a "potent mischief riots in the brain," and "in the heart [a] Tyrant lives enshrin'd" (17.6, 8).

Robinson's Sappho does not advocate an ordinary balance of head and heart, or reason and feeling. In the traditional (masculine) version of an ideal of balance, order is established at a literally undesirable level. The apothegm "Moderation in all things" governs the terms by which thought and feeling get measured.[11] On the contrary, this new Sappho is imagined as finally realizing the exalted demands upon heart and head that the Greek poetess originally, if ineffectually, sought. What is required is a balance of raptures, according to the analogous Blakean proverb of hell: "The road of excess leads to the palace of wisdom."[12]

In this frame of reference, Sappho's love for Phaon is not only explicable but emblematically appropriate. Phaon is for Sappho an ideal form of both mind and heart exactly because he is masculine. Cultural tradition has to this point regularly cast that ideal form in masculine terms; indeed, even idealized female figures, like Richardson's Clarissa or the Venus de Milo, are masculine forms of expression, "emanations"—to borrow Blake's Neoplatonic term—of the "human

---

11 To the degree that Wollstonecraft adheres to such a view, to that extent Robinson is critiquing her work. Wollstonecraft draws her adherence to a philosophy of moderation from dissenting traditions, whereas aristocratic contexts dominate Robinson's life and imagination.

12 Blake, *The Marriage of Heaven and Hell,* introduction and commentary by Sir Geoffrey Keynes (New York: Oxford University Press, 1975), pl. 7.

imagination" (that is, the *male* imagination). Robinson's work moves upon this context to transpose its terms, though not its (ultimate) values of an enlightened heart and head.

A Sapphic perspective perceives Phaon not as a figure of heterosexual promise but as a traditional sign of the exalted power of thought and liberated pleasure. Phaon-as-ideal is to be transformed through the passion and desire of Sappho, whose love is determined to strip him of his corruptions. Her love is committed to *this* Phaon, whose ideal form (literally) is at once glimpsed in and betrayed by the "historical" Phaon pursued by Sappho. Phaon's own sexual wanderings therefore become yet another figural representation of Sappho's own desire and pursuit of the whole—even more particularly, her desire and pursuit of the whole in the ideal immediacy of a mortal and historical existence. The ideal demands made by Robinson's work are thus revolutionary ones in a social and political sense. At the time they would be (and were) seen as Jacobinical.[13]

Robinson's way with Phaon is brilliantly illustrated in sonnet 12, which her index titles "Previous to her Interview with Phaon." The heading is important.

> Now, o'er the tessellated pavement strew
>   Fresh saffron, steep'd in essence of the rose
>   While down yon agate column gently flows
> A glitt'ring streamlet of ambrosial dew!
> My Phaon smiles! the rich carnation's hue,
>   On his flush'd cheek in conscious lustre glows,
>   While o'er his breast enamour'd Venus throws
> Her starry mantle of celestial blue!
>   Breathe soft, ye dulcet flutes, among the trees
>   Where clust'ring bows with golden citron twine;
>   While slow vibrations, dying on the breeze,

---

13 When Richard Polwhele deplores the "Philosophism" of Robinson's writings, he is in effect labeling the work "Jacobin" (see *The Unsex'd Females* [1798], l. 93n). In the same critique he appears to be thinking specifically of *Sappho and Phaon* when he urges Robinson "to dismiss the gloomy phantom of annihilation; to think seriously of a future retribution; and to communicate to the world, a recantation of errors that originated in levity, and have been nurs'd by pleasure."

> Shall soothe his soul with harmony divine!
> Then let my form his yielding fancy seize,
> And all his fondest wishes blend with mine.

The sonnet invokes an absent and imagined Phaon, an ideal figure with idealized desires that match Sappho's own. Their ecstatic union is an imagined "harmony divine" achieved within the orbit of the planet of (Sappho's) love. It is crucial to see that this union is sexual, even as it is being literally cast in ideal erotic terms. The ideal thus summons its full achievement by arousing an as yet unfulfilled reality, which is itself figured as the absent Phaon. The splendid double meaning worked into the syntax of the final two lines emphasizes the character of Sappho's desire, which imagines a perfect equality between lovers.

The desired conjunction (and hence the actual disjunction) of real and ideal orders is replicated at various subordinate textual levels—for example, in the first appearance of the imagined Phaon in the sonnet: "My Phaon smiles! the rich carnation's hue, / On his flush'd cheek in conscious lustre glows" (5–6). The complex figuration ultimately stands for the whole "meaning" of Phaon. The imaginary blush has been created through the erotic conjuring of lines 1–4, to which Phaon responds—indeed, within which he is literally brought to life, like a male Galatea ("*My* Phaon"). The blush's "conscious lustre" locates a key metaphysical moment. A traditional figure of involuntary desire is being imagined at a higher level, as it were—as an embodied consciousness, the very image of Sappho's own desire (of a fully conscious eroticism, a complete integration of the highest desires of the head and of the heart).[14]

That the sonnet situates all these events at the level of Sappho's fantasy and desire provides the (modern) reader with a perspective that fully answers to the "conscious lustre" imaged on Phaon's face. Phaon registers his desire at the most primitive level, as a blush; Sappho registers hers in the prophetic figuration she gives to this blush, the text's "conscious lustre"; finally, Robinson frames both events in a contem-

---

14 For good discussions of the crucial term *conscious* see Jean H. Hagstrum, *Eros and Vision: The Restoration to Romanticism* (Evanston, Ill.: Northwestern University Press, 1989), chap. 1.

porary context that explicates their prophetic truth. A recurrent and central figure in the writing of sensibility, the blush signifies the body's instinctive knowledge of good and evil, a knowledge no longer judged by dark biblical norms; on the contrary. In Robinson's text Sappho refigures Phaon's blush in enlightened terms. The phrase "conscious lustre" raises up the body's knowledge from its low estate by asserting its powers of intelligence. As a figure for blushing, the phrase is a virtual emblem of enlightened sensibility, a fact underscored by the term *lustre*, which the sonnet sequence explicitly associates with poetry and Apollo, the "Lord of Lustre" (9.7). The phrase is therefore at once Sappho's prophecy on the body of Phaon and Robinson's hymn to the intellectual beauty of her enlightened ideal of the fully liberated body and mind, and their harmonious union.

The opening sonnet, in the sestet especially, nicely articulates the sequence's fundamental argument:

> For thou, blest POESY! with godlike pow'rs
> To calm the misery of man wert given;
>   When passion rends, and hopeless love devours,
> By mem'ry goaded, and by frenzy driv'n,
>   'Tis thine to guide him 'midst Elysian bow'rs,
> And shew his fainting soul,—a glimpse of Heav'n.
>
> (9–14)

The tradition of erotic poetry establishes the sexual import of the figures in the last two lines. Equally, the tradition of masculinist ideology establishes a privileged meaning for the term *man*, so that the blessings and powers of POESY are especially secured for *men* rather than *women*. In this text, however, Robinson works a transvaluation of these values by playing that privileged term *man* off against the pronouns *him* and *his* (in ll. 12–3). In the context of a work dealing with the loves of Sappho and Phaon, where the latter's frustrations and failures in love are exposed through the poetic sufferings of Sappho, those pronouns acquire a particular reference. The passage is another (at this narrative point, a secret) prophecy that Sappho's poetry will liberate Phaon from his frustrated condition. The hidden meaning takes Phaon as a figure of *man*, and thus prophesies that Sappho's POESY will ultimately redeem *his* condition.

The meaning of all this is patent. Robinson is the avatar of Sappho, and through her POESY the benighted condition of *man* will be redeemed. In literal terms, the verse exposes the ideological freight concealed in the term *man*, and proposes a new standard of POESY to be re-imagined through a female, a specifically Sapphic, perspective. So despite its ostensible subject (personal and erotic love) and form (poetic), Robinson's is finally a political and republican work. Indeed, its most cherished positions are probably (*a*) "the personal is the political" and (*b*) "poets are the unacknowledged legislators of the world."

Robinson does not conceal the politics of her work, as we see from her prefatory prose materials, the final section of which comprises an extended quotation from "the learned and enlightened ABBE BARTHELMI" (27). With this text Robinson fairly labels her work "republican." Nevertheless, her treatment of Barthélemy's celebrated *Voyage* is subtle and indirect and very much in keeping with her poetical commitments. Quoting the *Voyage* for a culminant "vindication and eulogy of the Grecian Poetess" (27) might even be expected, given the well-known views of both Robinson and Barthélemy. More to the point, one startling feature of the *Voyage* is its new and specifically political interpretation of Sappho's life. According to Barthélemy, Sappho's move from Lesbos to Sicily is a political act, a flight from a society corrupted (like eighteenth-century Paris) by luxury and license.[15]

Robinson's long quotation from the *Voyage* is notable, however, precisely because it betrays no reference whatsoever to any of these matters. On the contrary, the quoted texts all focus on the "sensibility" of Sappho, as well as her great influence in maintaining a culture of "sensibility":

> Sappho undertook to inspire the Lesbian women with a taste for literature; many of them received instructions from her, and foreign women increased the number of her disciples. She loved them to excess, because it was impossible for her to love otherwise; and she expressed her tenderness in all the violence of passion: your surprize at this will cease, when you are acquainted with the extreme sensibility of the Greeks. (28)

15 The historical effect of this new interpretation was notable. "In Barthelemy's wake, Sappho was enshrined as a political exile, a revolutionary who had fought alongside Alceus to overthrow tyranny. This reading won acceptance despite the fact that Sappho's poetry, unlike Alceus's, is resolutely apolitical" (DeJean, 160).

This (current) politics of sensibility is a feminized equivalent of Sade's politics of pornography. Where Sade is outrageous, however, Robinson is nuanced. In the first place, she invokes political issues with a cool presence-by-absence technique. Beyond that, she elaborates a subtle politicized critique of all those, whether on the right or on the left, who uncouple a social and political consciousness from "extreme sensibility." Sappho's detractors have regularly deplored the sensual excess of her loves, but Robinson wants not merely to defend the poet on these counts, she wants to defend the politics of the poet. So "to this hatred" that her life and writings provoked, Sappho "replied by truths and irony, which completely exasperated her enemies" (28–9).

Robinson's quotation reveals a remarkable self-reflexiveness and wit. Not only does she transform the political significance of Barthélemy's Sappho, she does so by verbatim quotation of his own commentary. This is to reply "by truths and irony" indeed, with those "finer mental powers" (10) that Robinson attributes to the poets. The subtlety of her technique seems especially fine when we register the text's autobiographical motifs. Throughout *Sappho and Phaon* Robinson builds a shrewd retort to the facile slanders regularly directed at her. Robinson's and Sappho's histories reflect each other because (and as) their poetries are made reflective through *Sappho and Phaon*. The poetic sensibility exposes the relations, according to Robinson, and the poetry of sensibility puts them into most effective (social) action. Not that the more polemical views and approaches of Barthélemy (or Wollstonecraft) are unimportant or ineffective. But for Robinson the poet is especially favored with the power to wed the longest philosophical view ("the whole" [5]) with full, intense, and immediate awareness ("passion").

Reading the Moment and the Moment of Reading in Graffigny's

Lettres d'une péruvienne

Thomas M. Kavanagh

Few works reveal more about the convoluted relations between experience and expression, reading and writing, reception and cultural history, and the vagaries of canon formation than Françoise de Graffigny's *Lettres d'une péruvienne*. First published in 1747, this novel consists of letters written by Zilia, an Inca virgin of the Temple of the Sun, to Aza, the Inca prince she was to marry on the very day the Spanish conquistadors invaded Cuzco and carried her off as their prisoner. An overwhelming sense of the chance-laden, irreversible "moment" at work pervades both the writing and successive readings of this fascinating story. I would like to examine how abrupt percussions of the moment structure the novel's setting, which itself intensified the author's own most crucial experience of the moment. The agendas of distinct historical moments—1751, 1871, and the late 1980s—have produced vastly different readings of a text that, first constructed as Inca knotted cords, or quipus, ultimately embraces an aesthetics of the moment as the dominant form of its heroine's greatest suffering and most intense happiness.

The term "moment" designates a particular intensity of the unexpected and unpredictable, of an event creating a chasm between the past and the future. By abolishing what preceded while allowing no anticipation of what will follow, the moment is experienced as an instance of pure chance. It fractures any continuity allowing the subject to understand and control what has so drastically happened and announces itself as an end to any previously secure sense of a symbolic order declaring itself the equivalent of law and nature. Deprived of any coherence between past and future, the subject experiences the moment as a reshaping of consciousness, an inexplicable event redefining both the rule of law and the pull of desire. The chance moment, traumatic or ecstatic, transforms a previously calm perception of sustaining continuities into an uncomprehending bewilderment at the jagged shape of the instant's tear in the careful weave of life narratives.

In *Lettres d'une péruvienne*, Zilia's voice reverberates as a writing consciousness shattered by the impact of a moment that has abolished the law of her religion, the narrative of her love, and the sense of her identity. "Since the terrible moment which should have been snatched out of the chain of time and replunged into the eternal ideas, since the moment of horror when these impious savages bore me away from the worship of the Sun, from myself, from thy love, I experience only the effects of misfortune, without being able to discover their cause."[1] "Since the moment," obsessively repeated, summarizes Zilia's reaction to the Spaniards' sacking of Cuzco as they obliterated a civilization unable to resist. Few scenes from world history capture as sharply the calamity of that moment when two cultures clashed in such a way that for one, the Inca, their future of defeat and enslavement will be unlike anything their previous experience had prepared them for. It was very much by chance that, in 1531, after several earlier unproductive expeditions, a small band of less than two hundred Spaniards wandering on an unexplored continent came upon and, in only a few days, defeated the Inca empire.

Graffigny's presentation of this event (which she freely transposes two hundred years into the future so that Zilia can arrive in eighteenth-century France) emphasizes how the Inca, with devastating results,

1 Graffigny, *Lettres d'une péruvienne*, in *Lettres portugaises, Lettres d'une péruvienne, et autres romans d'amour par lettres*, ed. Bernard Bray and Isabelle Landy-Houillon (Paris: Garnier-Flammarion, 1983), 257. The English translations are mine. I have often followed the 1758 translation that appeared in London of the 1747 (and therefore incomplete in relation to the 1752 edition) version of the novel: *Letters Written by a Peruvian Princesse* (New York: Garland, 1974) in the Flowering of the Novel reprint series.

translated this moment of chance into a series of ominous continuities with their preexisting worldview. Being part of a culture means accepting the power of its sustaining symbolic order to explain reality, to find within what happens not the haphazard fruits of chance but the working of understood causalities. This misplaced epistemological confidence led to some fatal "mistranslations" of the Spaniards' irruption into the Incan order: an ancient oracle had announced that men unlike any they had ever seen before would invade their empire and destroy their religion; astrologers had detected three sinister circles around the moon; and augurs had seen an eagle pursued by other birds. All these signs convinced the Inca that the Spaniards were in fact the sons of the dreaded Viracocha, the prince of destruction who had been the subject of a nightmare by an earlier emperor. The Inca's tragic refusal of chance and their insistence on translating the Spaniards in terms of Inca culture only consolidated the catastrophe. Spanish gunpowder and muskets became a sign of protection by the thunder god of justice, Yalpor. The metal bits in the mouths of Spanish horses persuaded the Inca that these "eaters of metal" might be mollified by gold and silver presents—a gesture that only intensified the conquistadors' rapaciousness.

For Zilia, the tragic and profoundly misunderstood moment of the Spaniards' arrival stands in opposition to and draws its meaning from an earlier and equally intense experience of the moment: her discovery that the son of the Capa-Inca, prince Aza, shared the love she felt for him. Now a prisoner of the Spanish, Zilia's thoughts return compulsively to what she describes as "this first moment of my happiness" (263) when, as a sacred virgin confined to the Temple of the Sun, she saw for the first time prince Aza. Her memory of his unexpected appearance in the temple concentrates the force of that event within a moment introducing an entirely new dimension of her experience: "You appeared in the midst of us like a rising sun, whose tender light prepares the serenity of a fine day . . . astonishment and silence reigned on every side. . . . For the first time I felt at the same time upset, anxiety, and pleasure" [du trouble, de l'inquiétude, et cependant du plaisir] (263).

Beginning in a moment's tragedy made all the more palpable by its opposition to that earlier moment of love's discovery, Zilia's story after the fall becomes that of a forced sea voyage. Ripped away from the ordered world of the temple, Zilia is a prisoner adrift on what, for the eighteenth century, was the realm of chance par excellence. Unforeseeable storms, fires, wrecks, and sea battles were only a few of the aleatory moments punctuating life at sea and waiting to redefine the situation. One morning, she is suddenly awakened by explosions so intense that they seem to signal the very destruction of nature. In fact, a French ship, captained by the gallant Déterville, has stormed the galleon on which she is a prisoner. That moment, too, will change entirely the shape of what lies before Zilia.

Torn away from the Inca culture that formerly defined her past and future, Zilia experiences the new world of the sea and what lies beyond it as a series of chance-driven moments occurring with an abruptness so intense that, in trying to understand what is happening to her, she can say only that "each moment destroys the opinion an earlier moment had given me" (271). Lost in a world with no constancy of law, no coherence provided by a comprehensible symbolic order, Zilia's experience of the moment's abruptness becomes the abiding modality of all she will discover in exile. Déterville may prove to be the best intentioned of captors, but Zilia's response to his attentions will always be limited by her insistence that "it is chance alone that brought us together" (312). Later, after many more changes, as her story draws to a close, Zilia will propose to Déterville a happiness defined not by the continuities of marriage but by an intensified awareness of existence as a momentary plenitude bringing with it what she has learned to be the only happiness life might provide.

For the eighteenth century, the Spanish conquest of the Inca was the most momentous and calamitous collision of cultures in recorded history. Writers like Garcilaso de la Vega and Bartolomé de Las Casas— translated, frequently reedited, and widely read in France—told clearly and vividly the terrifying tale of how a small army of Spaniards had, in little more than a moment, determined the sad fate of a New World culture whose population numbered in the millions. The abrupt fall of entire empires and the unimaginable sufferings of their dispersed and exploited inhabitants provided examples of horror surpassing anything previously available to the European imagination. And speak to that imagination they did.

If Graffigny chose this most lurid example of political rapacity and human suffering as the background for her story of a woman's shattered love, it was because that setting eloquently expressed an experience of the moment's reversal of which she herself had been the chosen victim. Born in 1695 within the nobility of the then independent duchy of Lorraine, Françoise d'Issembourg d'Happoncourt became an influential member of the Lorraine court through her marriage in 1711 to Huguet de Graffigny, the court chamberlain and *exempt des gardes du corps*. After financially exploiting and physically abusing her throughout their unhappy marriage, her husband at least had the discretion to die in 1725. At the age of thirty-one, Graffigny was left with the freedom and security of a widow close to and protected by Madame, the duchesse de Lorraine and former regent. During this period Graffigny began a long and intense liaison with a young cavalry officer, Léopold Desmarest. The Treaty of Vienna in 1736 shattered Graffigny's social and affective security, however, and redefined the fortunes of the fragile duchy as a function of complex political forces acting from far beyond its borders. Lorraine fell into the hands of Stanislas Leszcynski, who had become the king of Poland in 1733 thanks to the support he had received from Louis XV, who was married to his daughter, Marie. Leszcynski's second reign as king of Poland (he had previously ruled 1704–9) came, however, to an abrupt end when the Russians expelled him and imposed Frederick Augustus, the Elector of Saxony, as the new king. Ever the faithful protector, Louis XV obtained the duchy of Lorraine as a compensation for Stanislas with, for himself, the added advantage that, upon Stanislas's death, the duchy would become a possession of France. The Treaty's game of musical chairs awarded the duchy of Tuscany as a parallel compensation to the then twenty-eight-year-old duc de Lorraine.

For Graffigny there was no consolation prize. Part of the disbanded court of the now-deposed duc, she suddenly found herself an all-but-penniless refugee forced to live by borrowing and expediency. Her reversal of fortune at the age of forty-one put her in straits that would well prepare her to re-create, a decade later, that abrupt separation from homeland and beloved under the hyperbolic guise of an Inca princess. After two years of travel during which she relied on the dubious comfort of strangers, Graffigny's long visit to Madame de Châtelet

and Voltaire at Cirey during the winter of 1738–39 ended in recrimi-
nation when Madame de Châtelet, systematically steaming open her
guests' letters, accused Graffigny of having risked Voltaire's arrest by
communicating to one of her correspondents an entire *canto* from the
incendiary *La Pucelle.* Forced to leave at a moment's notice, Graffigny
headed for Paris with only two hundred francs. Once there, only the
help of the duchesse de Richelieu kept her from financial ruin. The
final prod to the creation of Zilia's voice came in 1743 when Graffigny
was abandoned by her beloved but absent Desmarest, who finally
broke off what by then had become only an epistolary affair. Three
years later, *Lettres d'une péruvienne* would tell the story of that terrible
moment of 1531 in a voice very much inflected by Graffigny's own
experience of the political and dynastic reversals in the Lunéville court
of 1736. If she transposed events of the sixteenth century into the
eighteenth, it was not by error or oversight. Responding to what she
saw as a mutual attraction between the moments of 1531 and 1736,
Graffigny's story of the Inca princess became a metaphor of everything
her own present had become.

The version of the *Lettres d'une péruvienne* we read today dates from
1752. Deeply disappointed that the original 1747 version, published
anonymously and, like all novels of the period, without a *permission,*
had, in spite of its tremendous popularity, brought her only three hundred livres, Graffigny was anxious to find a better arrangement. In
1751, with the help of Malesherbes, she at last obtained a *permission* for
her novel and published under her name a corrected and augmented
version with Duchêne for which she received three thousand livres.[2]
As Graffigny prepared that second edition of forty-one rather than
thirty-eight letters, she sought counsel from her circle of friends on
revising the original text. One important indication of how Graffigny's
contemporaries responded to her novel can be found in a letter to her
of 1751 from the then unknown Turgot—who, some twenty years
later, would, as *contrôleur général des finances,* become the last but quickly
dashed hope of the philosophes for an effective reform of ancien

2 For an extensive discussion of the *Lettres'* publication history, see English Showalter, "*Les Lettres d'une péruvienne:* composition, publication, suites," *Archives et Biblio-
thèque de Belgique* 54 (1983): 14–28.

régime economic policies. Only twenty-four at the time he wrote to the fifty-six-year-old Graffigny, Turgot was concerned that Zilia's story be made more relevant to the specific moment of French society at mid-century.[3]

Reading Turgot's counsels to Graffigny, one has the strong sense that the person in fact being addressed is Rousseau, whose *Discourse on the Arts and Sciences* had just been crowned by the Dijon Academy. Profoundly disturbed by Rousseau's blanket rejection of the arts and sciences, of everything associated with the nascent *lumières* of the philosophes, Turgot insists that Graffigny's task should be to "show Zilia as a Frenchwoman, after having shown her as a Peruvian."[4] To accomplish this Graffigny must provide in her revised novel some positive balance to the negative portrait of French society presented in the letters of social criticism.[5] Turgot feels that there must be a "French Zilia" because portraying her only as a Peruvian, limiting her voice to observations heavy with primitivism and naive idealism, confines her to an exoticism all too easily interpreted as arguing in the same direction as Rousseau. A French Zilia, whose reading and experience have allowed her to understand how and why European society must be different from the Inca world, would possess a true objectivity. Rather than looking at French society only through Inca eyes, the new Zilia would understand that every encounter with a different society provides an all-too fertile ground for ethnocentric prejudices. Turgot's Zilia would, to the contrary, have reached a point where, recognizing this, she can "compare her prejudices with our own" (459) rather than presenting the assumptions of her Inca culture as one with fact and nature.

A French Zilia would understand why what Turgot calls the "distri-

---

3 For a discussion of other contemporary reactions to Graffigny's novel by Abbé Raynal, Pierre Clément, Elie Fréron, and Joseph de La Porte, see Janet Gurkin Altman, "A Woman's Place in the Enlightenment Sun: The Case of F. de Graffigny," *Romance Quarterly* 83 (1991): 261–73.

4 Turgot to Mme de Graffigny, cited in *Lettres d'une péruvienne*, ed. Gianni Nicoletti (Bari: Adriatica, 1967), 459.

5 Pierre Hartmann argues convincingly that Turgot was responding not to the 1747 version of Graffigny's novel but to her manuscript for the augmented version of 1752 that contained far more explicit criticism of French society. See "Turgot lecteur de Mme de Grafigny" in *Vierge du soleil/fille des lumières: La Péruvienne de Mme de Graffigny et ses suites* (Strasbourg: Presses Universitaires de Strasbourg, 1989), 121.

bution des conditions" is necessary and inevitable. Zilia's primitivist espousal of a self-sufficient agrarian society where all live on what they produce might hold some abstract interest as an exercise in exoticism. It is, however, an ideal Turgot sees as dangerously ambiguous. Uncannily anticipating and setting out to refute what, three years later, will be the central argument of *Rousseau's Discourse on the Origin of Inequality*, Turgot argues that such an ideal implies a society reduced to a subsistence level where all grow their own food, produce their own implements and clothing, and remain cut off from the advantages of an organized and integrated economy. As Turgot sees it, inequality between individuals is inevitable. People have different degrees of physical strength, mental genius, technical skill, and commercial prowess. Not only must society reflect those differences if it is to exist as something other than totalitarian leveling, but society's division of labor, specialization, and economies of scale, while they produce disparities, allow for the overcoming of far more destructive evils. "What would provide an income to those living in infertile areas? Who would transport products from one region to another? The poorest peasant today enjoys a plethora of goods imported from distant regions. . . . The distribution of professions leads necessarily to some inequality of conditions. Without it, who would strive to perfect the useful arts? Who would spread enlightened ideas? . . . Who would hold in check the ferocity of some and aid the weakness of others?" (461). Challenging what he saw as Graffigny's too-facile idealism, Turgot's posture of cold-eyed realism leads him to question even the most revered shibboleths of the day: "Liberty! . . . I say it with a sigh, men are not always worthy of you!— Equality! . . . We ardently long for you, but can we ever attain you!" (461). Given Graffigny's identification with her heroine, it is hardly surprising that she chose to ignore the young Turgot's suggestions. It was unlikely that Zilia should justify the very forces of which she saw herself as the chosen victim.

The next moment to be examined in the history of how Graffigny's novel has been read came as a highly curious response to questions raised by another moment of social cataclysm, by another empire's fall. Writing in the *Revue des deux mondes* of mid-July 1871, only six weeks after the carnage of the "Semaine sanglante" tragically ended the revolutionary government of the Paris Commune (itself the final chapter in the fall of the Second Empire), the conservative Louis Etienne ironically suggests that only the present moment in France's political history allows readers to appreciate Graffigny's novel at its true value. If Etienne chooses to write about what was then an all-but-forgotten text, it is not, he makes clear, out of any sympathy for "the charm she exercised on our great-grandmothers."[6]

As though correcting Turgot's criticism that Graffigny's heroine was not sufficiently French, Etienne claims that "Zilia is far more French and European than she seems" (461). For him the *Lettres'* "Frenchness" emanates from their unvarnished portrayal of the real threat to the creation of a truly republican government, free from the taint of France's monarchical heritage. For Etienne, Zilia and her Inca perspective brought to eighteenth-century France one of the first flickers of what has since become the burning political question of contemporary Europe. "It was reserved to Mme de Graffigny to be the first to hazard a series of paradoxes concerning private property. The most striking aspect of her work can only be described, for want of a better word, as socialist" (459). If Etienne feels the rereading of this forgotten eighteenth-century novel is relevant to a Parisian audience still surrounded by the ruins of their failed revolution, it is on the basis of what in fact is a relatively minor theme in Graffigny's novel. In letter 20, Zilia observes that "rather than being like the Capa-Inca who provides for the welfare of his people, the sovereigns of Europe draw their own from the labors of their subjects" (303). Zilia, as Etienne reads her, recommends to France the Inca model of a centralized state for which all must work and by which all will be supported. If Etienne attributes such considerable importance to Graffigny's passing espousal of a centralized state providing universal welfare, it is because he sees that ideal as synonymous with everything that has gone wrong in France's difficult and delayed transformation from monarchy into republic.

The argument informing Etienne's reading of Graffigny turns on what he calls "parasitism." That word, Etienne points out, in the context of the 1870s' political vocabulary, only refers to the monarchy. Par-

6 Louis Etienne, "Un Roman socialiste d'autrefois," *Revue des deux mondes* 94 (15 July 1871), 454. This article is also reproduced as an appendix to Nicoletti's 1967 edition of the *Lettres*.

asitism describes how, a century ago, monarchy functioned through an elaborate system of royal stipends consisting of pensions for the nobility, alms for the poor, and countless offices in the service of the centralized state for the bourgeoisie. If France's attempts at a new and truly republican form of government have so clearly failed, Etienne insists, it is because the social changes effected by her revolutions have not been accompanied by any real change in the people's mentality, by any real rejection of a parasitism that has survived all changes of government. Sounding like a Reagan republican, Etienne states that "before 1789 it was thought shameful to receive charity from individuals, but charity from the prince was an envied privilege. Today it is still shameful to ask one's fellow citizens for a handout, but it seems perfectly natural to beg from the Republic a livelihood eliminating any real obligation to work" (462–3). Parasitism, Etienne concludes, did not die with the monarchy. It has survived and multiplied under such new names as "socialism, solidarity, collectivity, and the organization of labor" (463).

By allowing parasitism to continue, French republicanism has embraced a practice betraying every attempt to leave the abuses of monarchy behind. Under the patriarchal model of monarchy, the king ruled as the often tyrannical father of his people, taxing as he wished, because "people believed that all wealth within the state ultimately belonged to him" (463). While the state may now call itself a republic, it will in fact re-create all the evils of monarchy so long as it accords itself the same patriarchal privileges over individual wealth. The true republic must be imagined neither as tyrannical father nor as nourishing mother. Instead, Etienne claims, the Republic must be an "emancipated family all of whose members are brothers owing each other fraternal support" (463). Without a king or a father free to spoil his favored children, the older brothers will aid the younger, and they in turn will "earn their place on the basis of merit and labor" (463). In denouncing Graffigny's utopian socialism as parasitism, Etienne rehearses a tenet of conservative thought going back to Edmund Burke: that the unlimited powers of the state at the heart of the socialist vision would, no matter how generous its social and economic programs, create a new court and courtier class of state agents who will only perpetuate and intensify the very class divisions they claim to abolish. For Etienne, a socialist republic can only become another Versailles, drawing to its service an unlimited corps of officeholders all too anxious to profit from its overzealous administration.

As a novelist, Etienne continues, Graffigny presents a socialism different in one crucial way from that at work in 1871. Rather than offering any "full-blown social theory for changing the world," she needed only to "expatiate on her reveries of inconsequential utopias" (462). The product of an unfettered imagination untroubled by reality, the *Lettres* could propose Zilia's ideals as pure nostalgia for a lost homeland outside any obligation to enunciate a plan for making them a political reality. In writing a novel rather than a treatise, Graffigny had, as Etienne sees it, the wisdom to choose what will always be the most appropriate vehicle for socialist thought. "If it is true that socialism is the search for an honest and effective way of attenuating the distinctions between what is yours and what is mine [le tien et le mien], that search is always more convincing when carried out with frivolity rather than with scientific method" (459–60). Free to dream, the novel can present its visions of a golden age, communal ownership of property, and generously opened purses with utter disregard for how these ideals would work in the reality of contemporary French society. Zilia, having spent her entire life in an Inca temple, need never trouble herself with the difficult questions that would surface so brutally in 1871— "why those at the bottom, with their pittance, should not demand to be at the top with all its advantages" (462). As an exercise of pure imagination remembering a faraway country, the novel can ignore the violence and bloodshed so sadly concomitant with every transition from the is to the ought.

After Etienne's tendentious rereading through the embers of the Commune, *Lettres d'une péruvienne* returned to the placid precincts of literary history. Whereas it was reedited, reprinted, and translated over 130 times between 1747 and 1835, there were only two small French editions during the rest of the nineteenth century and none at all in the first two-thirds of the twentieth.[7] The first book-length study of Graf-

7 See David Smith, "The Popularity of Mme de Graffigny's *Lettres d'une Péruvienne*: The Bibliographical Evidence," *Eighteenth-Century Fiction* 3 (1990): 1–20. While Smith hazards no explanation for the novel's fall from popularity after 1835, Janet Gurkin

figny's work was not published until 1913 by Georges Noel. Hardly positive in tone, it expanded on Etienne's negative reading and took as its title *Une Primitive oubliée de l'école des cœurs sensibles*. After yet another half-century the American scholar, English Showalter, following the time-honored tradition of devoting one's doctoral thesis to the major work of a minor author, brought new attention to Graffigny's pages with his dissertation titled *An Eighteenth-Century Bestseller* (1964). These works had little effect, however, on the overwhelmingly negative consensus concerning the novel's value and importance. In England, Vivienne Mylne conceded that, if the *Lettres* is hardly mentioned in most histories of literature, it is "with good reason."[8] On the other side of the Channel, Henri Coulet's *Roman jusqu'à la Révolution* (1967) presents the *Lettres* as little more than an interesting variant on what Montesquieu had done better before her and what Rousseau would do more eloquently after her. The seeds of the *Lettres'* real resurrection came in 1983 when Bernard Bray and Isabelle Landy-Houillon included Graffigny's *Lettres* in a collection of five love-letter novels published in the large-printing Garnier-Flammarion paperback series.[9] Even as they edited it, however, Bray and Landy-Houillon felt obliged to point out that, thematically and philosophically, the novel was of far less interest than the two works most often cited as its sources, Guilleragues's *Lettres portugaises* or Montesquieu's *Lettres persanes*.

Two centuries of obscurity for Zilia (Etienne's 1871 diatribe hardly brought new readers to the work) ended, appropriately enough, because of developments in the New World. By the mid-1980s the culture wars being waged in American universities over the proper repre-

Altman offers the only partially satisfying hypothesis that the French could hardly be sympathetic readers of Zilia's story when, simultaneously, they were beginning the construction of their colonial empire in Algeria and the first generation of women raised under the patriarchal Napoleonic code was coming of age. This hypothesis neglects mid-eighteenth-century France's considerable if frustrated colonial ambitions in North America and says little of the drop in the number of translations published outside France after 1835.

8 Mylne, *The Eighteenth-Century French Novel* (Manchester: Manchester University Press, 1965), 148.

9 One earlier edition, Gianni Nicoletti's (see n. 4), had appeared in 1967 from a small Italian press and at least made the novel available outside the rare book rooms of research libraries.

sentation of women and minorities in the curriculum had made it egregiously reactionary to introduce the eighteenth-century French novel via reading lists that usually included only such writers as Marivaux, Prévost, Crébillon, Voltaire, Diderot, Rousseau, and Laclos—all of whom, whatever their virtues, fell squarely into the dubious category of Dead White European Males. Riccoboni, Tencin, Charrière, La Guesnerie, and Beaumont were among the important female novelists from the period, but, with the possible exception of Riccoboni, none had generated a significant body of scholarship—perhaps another confirmation of the academy's gender bias. Of greater practical importance, however, none of these women's texts were available for class use in inexpensive editions. The one exception, thanks to Bray and Landy-Houillon, was Graffigny's *Lettres d'une péruvienne*. It had other advantages as well. Not only was it written by a woman, but Zilia, its main character and exclusive narrative focus, was also a woman. Graffigny's novel also had the significant virtue of being a relatively short novel at a time when asking undergraduates to read a work of the dimensions of *La Nouvelle Héloïse* had become pure folly.

In addition to the work's physical availability, the new perspectives of feminist scholarship began to contribute significantly to a Graffigny renaissance. Nancy K. Miller, in her *Heroine's Text* of 1980, and even more so in her two 1988 articles on Graffigny, argued eloquently for the crucial importance of the *Lettres d'une péruvienne* as an exception to the period's implicit law of novelistic production—that female characters must always either marry and submit to the laws of patriarchy or die.[10] For Miller, the real significance of Graffigny's novel lay not so much in its representation of a conflict between European and New World cultures as in its implicit deconstruction of socially imposed gender roles and distinctions. Far more than a foreigner suffering forced integration into French society, Zilia became a symbol of everywoman struggling against patriarchy and finally accepting a place within it only

10 See Miller, *The Heroine's Text: Readings in the French and English Novel, 1722– 1782* (New York: Columbia University Press, 1980); "The Knot, the Letter, and the Book: Graffigny's *Peruvian Letters*" in *Subject to Change: Reading Feminist Writing* (New York: Columbia University Press, 1988), 125–61; and "Men's Reading, Women's Writing: Gender and the Rise of the Novel," *Yale French Studies*, no. 75 (1988): 40–55. See also Jack Undank's "Grafigny's Room of Her Own," *French Forum* 13 (1988): 297–318.

on her own terms. After well over a century with only the most limited readership, *Lettres d'une péruvienne*, freshly interpreted, became the one text sure to appear on the syllabus of every eighteenth-century French course taught in North America. While even as late as 1989 a Euro-centric critic like Pierre Hartmann could, oblivious to what was happening across the ocean, claim that Graffigny's novel was hardly known even by specialists,[11] the American momentum behind the work's rise to the highest ranks of the domestic French canon culminated in the simultaneous publication, in inexpensive classroom editions, of both the French original and a new English translation among the inaugural volumes of the Modern Language Association's new Texts and Translations series.

Other more tenuous options were also exercised for attuning Graffigny to the dictates of the politically appropriate. Playing the culture rather than the gender card, Janet Gurkin Altman argued that Zilia should be read as a "Third-World intellectual heroine" whose plea for "the respect of cultural difference" establishes her as the spokesperson for a long-neglected "Third-World enlightenment (be it fact or fable)."[12] Altman's parenthetical caveat, "be it fact or fable," does have its role to play because, as it has been understood from the eighteenth century to the present, the reality of the Inca culture from which Zilia was to derive her enlightenment did have its darker side. The short entry under "Inca" in Diderot and d'Alembert's *Encyclopédie*, for instance, lingers far longer over practices evoking oriental despotism than over Enlightenment ideals. "Should someone have offended the king in the slightest way, the city from which he came would be demolished or ruined" or, as concerns their funeral rites, "the wives and servants of the dead king were sacrificed as part of his funeral rites. They were burned at the same moment as his body and on the same pyre."[13] Scholarship has, if anything, been even less enthusiastic about an Inca

11 Pierre Hartmann, "*Les Lettres d'une péruvienne* dans l'histoire du roman épisto-laire," in *Vierge du soleil/fille des lumières*, 93.

12 Altman, "Graffigny's Epistemology and the Emergence of Third-World Ideol-ogy," in *Writing the Female Voice: Essays on Epistolary Fiction*, ed. Elizabeth C. Goldsmith (Boston, Mass.: Northeastern University Press, 1989), 172, 194, 198.

13 Denis Diderot and Jean d'Alembert, *Encylopédie, ou Dictionnaire raisonné des sci-ences, des arts et des métiers* (1751–57; rpt. [17 vols. plus pls. and supp. in 5 vols.], New York: Readex Microprint, 1969), 2:44.

Enlightenment. Arnold Toynbee, in his foreword to Livermore's English translation of Garcilaso's *Royal Commentaries* (the same work whose French translation served as the principal source for Graffigny's local color), describes the Inca state as "authoritarian, bureaucratic, and socialistic to a degree that has perhaps not been approached by any other state at any other time or place. . . . The Inca imperial government dictated to its subjects, in detail, the locality in which they were to live, the kind of work they were to do there, and the use that was to be made of the product of their labour."[14] If Enlightenment there was, it came with a dubiously Stalinist hue.

Graffigny's novel, its composition as well as the multiplicity of its interpretations, well illustrates the force of the moment as it reshapes the cultural context through which writing and reading begin. This dialectic of the continuous and the momentary is inscribed at the core of the *Lettres d'une péruvienne* in the Inca artifact defining the work's status as text: the quipus or knotted string constructions in which, the novel claims, the first seventeen of Zilia's letters were originally composed.

The material status of the letters as quipus points, however, to a dilemma. The first mention of quipus in letter 1 is accompanied by a note defining this central symbol of Inca culture as "strings of different colors which the Indians use, for want of writing, in counting the payment of their troops and the number of their people. Some authors claim that they also use them to transmit to posterity the memorable deeds of the Incas" (258). Referring to the quipus as a counting device, as a stringing together of cords and knots representing only the quantitative, numeric counts of persons and sums, questions their ability to serve as the material basis of the text we are reading. Quipus are like the isolated numbers of a balance sheet, markers lacking any inherent reference to the identity of the objects they enumerate.

The same ambiguity of the quipus' status as a writing system can be found in Graffigny's principal source on Inca culture, Garcilaso's *Royal Commentaries.* Born in 1539, only a few years after the arrival of the first Spaniards in Peru, Garcilaso was himself an incarnation of the troubled communication between these two cultures. The disinherited

14 Garcilaso de la Vega (El Inca), *Royal Commentaries of the Incas and General History of Peru*, trans. Harold V. Livermore (Austin: University of Texas Press, 1966), xi.

mixed-blooded son of one of Pizarro's original conquistadors and the Inca princess Nusta Chimpu Ocllo (herself a second cousin to the last Inca king), Garcilaso had the difficult task of explaining each side of his ancestry to the other. He too states that the quipus were essentially an accounting device, an artifact central to the Inca empire because they made possible the minute inventories of everything countable by its rulers and administrators. Chapter 14 of book 5 opens with an almost Borgesian list of the people, animals, grains, trees, objects, and land configurations that were inventoried and reported back to the emperor upon the conquest of any new territory. Updated annually with even more thoroughness, the counts allowed centralized control of the distribution of goods and peoples throughout the empire. Garcilaso makes scattered references to other functions served by the quipus: keeping historical annals, recording the speeches of emperors and dignitaries, and composing poems—all of which seem to imply that the quipus functioned as a written language as well as a counting device. These references are, however, usually attributed to Spanish travelers describing phenomena they did not entirely understand.

The explanation of this ambiguity (and perhaps also of why Graffigny dropped the quipus as letters actually exchanged between Zilia and Aza after letter 2) comes in Garcilaso's most extensive statement on quipus. He begins chapter 9 of book 6, "What they recorded in their accounts, and how they were read" (331) by stating that the Inca recorded with their knots "everything that could be counted, even mentioning battles and fights, all the embassies that had come to visit the Inca, and all the speeches and arguments the king had uttered" (331). Garcilaso seems to suggest that the quipus were used for purposes previously described as incompatible with their physical structure. Resolving this apparent contradiction requires understanding precisely how they were used. The "reading" of quipus was confined to a specialized group, the *quipucamayus* (those who have charge of the knots), who supplemented the knotted strings they used as mnemonic devices with what Garcilaso describes as "speeches preserved by memory in a summarized form of a few words [which] were committed to memory and taught by tradition to their successors and descendants from father to son" (332). To a visitor from outside the culture, these *quipucamayus* certainly appeared to be "reading" a quipu. In fact, however, the quipu as a document was legible only to that *quipucamayu* who had memorized the verbal discourse the knots would prod him to recall. Garcilaso concludes that "the Incas had no system of writing," but would "preserve the tradition of their deeds by means of the knots, strings, and colored threads, using their stories and poems as an aid" (332).[15] We are not far from Ray Bradbury and François Truffaut's *Fahrenheit 451*, where, in a future totalitarian state that forbids books, an underground organization of Book People memorize whole volumes of the classics and, before dying, teach them to younger members who will continue on as living repositories of the texts. The best contemporary study, *The Code of the Quipu*, coauthored by an anthropologist and a mathematician, argues that the quipus should be seen as embodying the anthropological "insistence" of Inca culture: they summarize, by reason of their structure and cultural function, the very essence of that civilization as an obsessive counting and centralized control of goods and peoples made possible by the quipus as the instruments of an almost Weberian bureaucracy.[16]

On the basis of the anthropological evidence, then, the message of Zilia's quipus is necessarily ambiguous. They speak as they do only for Zilia at the moment she knots them. She is the single possible reader able to use their mnemonic structure as a prod to speech. Woven

15 The quipus' intersection of the materially numeric and a memorized discourse could become problematic, especially when, in the wake of the Spanish conquest, they were used to represent concepts from the other culture. Referring to an explanation of the Christian doctrine of the Trinity, Garcilaso recounts how "instead of God three in one, he said God three and one makes four, adding the numbers in order to make himself understood" (682).

16 Martha Ascher and Robert Ascher, *The Code of the Quipu* (Ann Arbor: University of Michigan Press, 1981). As eminent an anthropologist of pre-Columbian cultures as John R. Swanton could not, even in 1943, resist the same leap of faith we find in Graffigny's assumptions about the quipus' nature. Deciding that the physical evidence must be incomplete and Garcilaso wrong, Swanton argues that the Inca's considerable accomplishments in agriculture, medicine, and statecraft make it unthinkable that they did not have a writing system: "Something of the kind [i.e., a writing system] is called for by the accomplishments in other fields of the people who employed it. It is demanded by the very splendor of the Andean civilization as a whole." See Swanton, "The Quipu and Peruvian Civilization," in *Anthropological Papers*, no. 26 (Washington, D.C.: Smithsonian Institution, Bureau of American Ethnology, 1943), 596. The Ascher study makes it clear, however, that that demand cannot be met.

within a context of loss and exile, they resurrect through memory a past self with which she no longer fully coincides at the moment of their eventual translation. To transcribe the quipus only she can read into French is to transcribe a past moment of consciousness now redefined by her apprenticeship to an entirely different symbolic system. Her letters exist as an idiolect: what at the moment of the quipus' knotting was readable only by the bereaved self remains, in spite of its translation into French, fully legible only for that single consciousness torn between a memory of the text's earlier moment as quipu and its later and different moment as French.

The paradox of the *Lettres d'une péruvienne* as legible idiolect should not surprise. The functions of these letters first as quipus and later as written French are entirely different. The first seventeen letters, as quipus, neither had nor sought any audience other than Zilia. If the fiction of an impossible reply from Aza is dropped after its single appearance, it is because Zilia's knotting of the quipus remains a purely self-directed gesture. They have, beyond Zilia as their single reader, no more permanence than her cries that "like a morning vapor, float off and are dissipated before they arrive in thy presence" (257). If Zilia continues to devote every free moment to the knotting of quipus that can neither be sent to nor read by their intended recipient, it is because they alone keep alive her allegiance to the Inca culture from which she has been so brutally sundered. The quipus become for Zilia the single instrument of her struggle to instill within the chaos of her captivity some semblance of order and meaning. Weaving the quipus transforms despair into hope and becomes her one expression of a contact with Aza and her Inca past, shutting out the alien present of everything she is forced to experience. "When a single object unites all our thoughts, my dear Aza, we interest ourselves no further in events than as we find them assimilated to our own situation. If thou wast not the sole mover of my soul, could I have passed, as I have just done, from the horror of despair to the most flattering hope?" (276).

In letter 17, as Zilia's supply of cord runs out, she realizes her quipus can no longer serve to anchor the single meaning she would find in the chaos of experience. Her monomania, now recognized as the illusion it must become, yields to a universe without meaning, a world punctuated only by the random succession of discrete moments that disappear with no trace. "Illusion quits me, frightful truth takes her place; my wandering thoughts, bewildered in the immense void of absence, will hereafter be annihilated with the same rapidity as time" (299). The depletion of Zilia's quipus symbolizes the threat her compulsive weaving strives to exorcise. More than anything else, the presence, invasiveness, and eventual seduction of France will, as a language and a culture, first force and then draw her away from the conviction that all meaning must refer back to the world she has left behind. A subtle evolution of the novel's form parallels, by a change in the function of the letters comprising it, the transformation of Zilia's mental universe. Woven into a monologue sustained by the fictive presence of Aza as the only audience, the first letters read as a cloistral prayer addressed to the single god of the absent beloved. Zilia seeks to shut out the debased reality of a world populated only by lesser creatures, to reduce experience to thoughts of Aza and the pain of his absence. As the voyage continues, however, her eyes are forced to open to what is happening around her. The monologic dialogue with Aza begins to include references to the man she calls the "cacique" of her "floating room." The letters become perplexed descriptions of persons and things outside the previously hermetic confines of the "I" and "You," herself and Aza. As she begins to understand French, progressively larger parts of her letters will be devoted to reproducing dialogues with and between third parties outside the couple.

The most important change occurs in the interval between letters 17 and 18, as the quipus run out and Zilia must complete her apprenticeship of French. To learn and use the language of the other brings with it an alienation from that earlier sense of self, defined exclusively through a native culture. Learning French has forced her to see that the Empire of the Sun is no longer an unfissured totality subject to the single rule of Aza's order. The sacred sun at the center of Inca culture shines, Zilia must recognize, on whole continents over which the Inca hold no sway and which will determine the remainder of their fate.

Zilia may continue to write only to Aza, but she does so in a language he cannot read. No longer centered on the intensity of her love for him, her letters describe the French society of which she finds herself becoming a part. Through the letters Zilia abandons the hoped-for resumption of her past happiness with Aza and instead prepares him to understand and find a place within the world of the French.

At this point Zilia perceives French society not as an alien observer for whom everything is chaos and chance but as someone who, while remaining other, both understands and can critique its coherence and rationales. The language of the French provides her with cognitive syntheses both enabling her to speak and constituting the audience to which she ultimately addresses herself. Zilia will continue to direct her letters to Aza, but the gesture has become little more than a lingering convention supporting a voice that speaks to a quite different audience. What she writes as letters to the single beloved reads as a diary ultimately addressed to the French.

Zilia's real drama turns less on her relation to Aza than on her achievement, within a new language and a new culture, of expressivity without complicity—on her resistance, as she uses French, to being redefined by it. She chooses not to marry Déterville because marriage to a Frenchman, no matter how devoted, would mean integration within a social order threatening to abolish her identity. Zilia's trajectory demands, however, that this choice not exist only as a rejection. In refusing Déterville, Zilia must embrace something positive, something of greater value to her than escaping the socially sanctioned convention of female destiny. At one level, her refusal to marry Déterville is explained as loyalty to the memory of Aza, as her insistence on a distinction between love and friendship. While the memory of Aza will remain as the unique object of a passionate love she wishes never again to experience in the present, Zilia's affection for Déterville will take the form of a friendship different from love, but of no lesser value. "Renounce those tumultuous sentiments, the imperceptible destroyers of our being. Come, and learn to know innocent and durable pleasures; come, and enjoy them with me [venez en jouir avec moi]. You will find in my heart, in my friendship, in my sentiments, all that is wanting to indemnify you for the loss of love" (362).

Reminiscent of the protective *repos* chosen by Lafayette's heroine at the end of *La Princesse de Clèves*, this choice is, however, accompanied within Graffigny's text by another ideal of happiness, one based on a resurgent ethos of the moment. Earlier, Zilia's exile from her Inca past transformed her consciousness into one of moments occurring outside any continuity or coherence. Zilia first experienced the horrors of captivity by the Spanish as a concatenation of purely present moments cut off from past and future. That same temporality of the moment will, as she is "saved" by Déterville and enters the more hospitable reality of his world, continue as the abiding mode of her perception. Her epistemological journey from one culture to another is, however, paralleled by her discovery of an equally momentary plenitude within pure sensation, of an intense joy at her contact with the natural world. Zilia will discover in Europe not only another symbolic order, but a self-contained and unmediated experience of physical nature.

In letter 12 Zilia describes her four-day trip from the French port where she has landed to Déterville's home in Paris. Having spent her entire life until the arrival of the Spanish within the Temple of the Sun, Zilia admits, after her coach trip through the French countryside, "I have tasted pleasures during this voyage that were before unknown to me" (286). She experiences these lush country scenes, "which ceaselessly change and renew themselves before my eyes," as a delicious evanescence of ever-changing moments, "which transport my soul as rapidly as we pass through them" (286). Rather than attempting to describe that nature, Zilia evokes instead its effect on her, the momentary sensations it provokes, what she qualifies as a "majestic disorder attracting our admiration till we forget ourselves" (286). What is so happily forgotten in these moments of pure sensation within nature is the other reality of human society, the world of appearances and disappointments that imprison her. Turning away from that world, lost in sensation, Zilia finds "a delicious calm penetrates our soul, and we take pleasure in the universe as though we were its sole proprietors" (286).

This experience of the moment occurs not as a threat to her fidelity to Aza but as the joyous affirmation of a purely sentient self independent of any symbolic order fashioned by men. Seen from this perspective, Zilia's refusal of marriage to Déterville is not so much an obstinate commitment to the memory of Aza as it is her allegiance to the experience of a beatific sensation limiting itself to the always momentary present. Her final proclamation, "The pleasure of being; that forgotten pleasure, ignored by so many blind humans; that thought so sweet, that happiness so pure, *I am, I live, I exist* [je suis, je vis, j'existe] alone can render us happy, if only we remember it, if only we take pleasure from it [si l'on en jouissait], if only we saw its value" (362), flows from her discovery of nature as an arena of momentary intensities lifting consciousness beyond the necessities of any marriage and of any symbolic order. Zilia's ideal of a present moment of sensation shared by the elected other of friendship shuts itself off from the hypocrisies of society. Living in the country house bought for her by Déterville with the Inca gold taken from the Spanish ship, Zilia's final happiness implies an accommodation to the symbolic order, but she accepts society's sway only so that, redefined by the momentary epiphanies of the moment, she might move beyond its constraints and expectations. Through no choice of her own, she has come to live within and understand French society. She does so, however, only as part of a trajectory taking her to the country house and away from society. There, as both captive and princess, as both indebted dependent yet mistress of her estate, Zilia transcends the contradictions of those identities within the aestheticized present that limits her existence to an utterly fulfilling experience of the moment.

Zilia's story, no less than the strange story of how that story has been read, speaks to literary historians of an inevitable caveat to our enterprise, of a necessary limit to the objectivity and scientificity we would claim for our endeavor. As historians, we feel that our attention must be turned toward continuities, toward sequences of causes and effects whose perception brings with them an understanding and mastery of how things have come to be as they are and to mean as they do. Story becomes history, or so we are told, as the narrative in question sets aside and moves beyond those haphazard facticities of circumstance and chance that might ever so easily have happened quite differently than they did. In their place, the discourse of literary history offers a perhaps intricate but ultimately rational intermeshing of causal agencies establishing us as the spokespersons of their necessity. Graffigny's newfound centrality within the canon of the eighteenth-century novel, much like Etienne's decidedly eccentric rereading of her tale in 1871, testifies to another dimension within the history we would chronicle: the abiding sway of the fortuitous moment and the chance event within the apparently necessary narratives of literary history. To acknowledge that dimension is not, as some might fear, to relinquish any claim to the status of our discourse as history. It is, on the contrary, to open ourselves to a more complete understanding of history, to a perception of our task without the systematic denegation of chance inherited from the determinism of nineteenth-century positivism. Chance, no longer a shameful synonym of human ignorance, provides instead a necessary accommodation to that freedom from necessity continually reborn within the unpredictable dynamics of the moment.

De-familiarizing the Family; or, Writing Family History from Literary Sources

Ruth Perry

> In some tragedies and romances we meet with many beautiful and interesting scenes, founded upon what is called the force of blood, or upon the wonderful affections which near relations are supposed to conceive for one another, even before they know that they have any such connection.
>
> —Adam Smith, *The Theory of Moral Sentiments* (1759)

After a series of adventures that prove his noble generosity and the world's duplicity, Smollett's Roderick Random arrives in Rio de la Plata near the end of the book in the company of his maternal uncle. Merchant partners, Random and his uncle have come to trade; they are co-owners of a vessel filled with a legal cargo of Guinea slaves and an illegal cargo of European bale goods. Their commodities are in great demand: they sell the people easily and profitably (they could have sold five times as many slaves at any price) and dispose of their smuggled manufactures too, "at great advantage." Once they have discharged their responsibilities to commerce, they are free to enjoy themselves and to look around. "Our ship being freed from the disagreeable lading of Negroes, to whom indeed I had been a miserable slave, since our leaving the coast of Guinea, I began to enjoy myself and breathe with pleasure the pure air of Paraguay."[1] No longer responsible for the maintenance and surveillance of these most "disagreeable" of commodities, they are at liberty to mingle socially with the local residents. Invited to the country villa of a local Spanish gentleman, they are joined by an expatriate Englishman who has lived in the region for fifteen or sixteen years. The stranger is tall, "remarkably well shaped, of a fine mien" and commanding appearance (411). Random tells us that he was "struck with a profound veneration for him at his first coming into the room." In the course of their conversation, the stranger "eyes" Random with "uncommon attachment" and our hero tells us he "felt a surprizing attraction towards him when he spoke . . . the dignity of his deportment filled me with affection and awe; in short, the emotions of my soul, in presence of this stranger, were strong and unaccountable" (412).

This was the "voice of blood" speaking, as any eighteenth-century reader could tell you. The mysterious stranger had to be intimately related to Roderick; such strong instinctual feelings always signaled consanguinity. Even when separated at birth, parents and children, brothers and sisters knew when they came into each others' presence that there was a mysterious bond between them, a primal, palpable link that no intervening worldly experience could undo. The eponymous heroine of Frances Burney's *Evelina* is drawn to her long-lost brother, Macartney, at first sight. Although they are strangers, their instantaneous interest in one another's welfare derives from their blood bond. In *Roderick Random*, the uncle verifies the maternal lineage of the hero for his rediscovered father. Testifying with masculine authority for the missing woman, the uncle also exemplifies, in his loving care of his sister's son Roderick, responsibility to one's family of origin and the fulfillment of consanguineous obligation. The shadowy backdrop of the slave trade dimly suggests the separation of families and the commodification of persons, twin effects of capitalism, evils that the newly discovered bond of blood remedies and opposes.

The scene of recognition and reunion like this one from Smollett, in which biological connection declares itself the unerring basis of human relationships, was a familiar topos from French classical

---

1 Tobias George Smollett, *The Adventures of Roderick Random*, ed. Paul-Gabriel Boucé (Oxford: Oxford University Press, 1979), 410.

tragedy. Ultimately derived from Greek novels (such as Heliodorus's *Aethiopica*) and found closer to the eighteenth century in Cervantes's exemplary novels, the *cri du sang*—a sudden and instinctive sympathy between strangers that signaled consanguinity—enabled family members in the tragicomedies of Alexandre Hardy and the tragedies of Corneille to recognize one another in time to avert betrayal, incest, and murder.[2] Occasionally characters in French drama confuse the force of blood with romantic love and mistake the magnetism of kinship for erotic attraction to someone who is really a sibling. Dryden uses the trope in this way in his tragicomedy, *The Spanish Fryar* (1680), and in his heroic tragedy, *Don Sebastian* (1689), where characters drawn from French and Spanish romances confuse sexual attraction with their instantaneous magnetism for one another—the pull of hidden siblinghood.[3] The voice of blood also occurs in French sentimental comedies and romanesque tragedies of the eighteenth century, notably in Crébillon and in Voltaire, who used it to prove the existence of natural law and the value of instinct as a moral principle.[4]

Despite the continuity of this topos in Continental drama, these mysterious urgings of the spirit in favor of a stranger who turns out to be from one's primary kin group disappear from English fiction for roughly the first fifty years of the eighteenth century. The device then reemerges with renewed force in the second half of the century.[5] Indeed, the plot in which biology asserts itself as intuition became so popular in the later eighteenth century that Jane Austen included it in

2 Clifton Cherpack, *The Call of Blood in French Classical Tragedy* (Baltimore, Md.: Johns Hopkins University Press, 1958), 3–28.

3 See Cherpack's reference to Crébillon's *Sémiramis* (1717) among other texts (98). This topos also appears in Mlle de La Roche Guilhem's *Almanzor and Almanzaida* (1674; trans. into English 1678). Thanks to Douglas Canfield for calling my attention to the use of the *cri du sang* in Dryden's plays.

4 Cherpack, 106–10.

5 W. Daniel Wilson's investigation of Enlightenment resistance to the incest taboo as "superstitious" or "socially constructed" and without biological basis lays out some of the complexities in English and Continental attitudes toward the voice of blood in fictional accounts of unwitting sibling incest ("Science, Natural Law, and Unwitting Sibling Incest in Eighteenth-Century Literature," *Studies in Eighteenth-Century Culture*, ed. O. M. Brack Jr., 13 [1984], 249–71). Wilson refers to an interesting example of sibling love in a German novel, Christoph Martin Wieland's *Agathon* (1766–67). Here the brother and sister's love remains pure and platonic and their instincts foreshadow the reconstruction of the family circle.

her 1790 send-up of sentimental fiction, *Love and Freindship*. The lovely young heroine Laura, who conducts her life as if it were a sentimental novel, perceives an older gentleman descending from a coroneted coach at an inn and reports to her interlocutor:

> At his first Appearance my Sensibility was wonderfully affected and e'er I had gazed at him a 2nd time, an instinctive Sympathy whispered to my Heart, that he was my Grandfather.

> Convinced that I could not be mistaken in my conjecture I instantly sprang from the Carriage I had just entered, and following the Venerable Stranger into the Room he had been shewn to, I threw myself on my knees before him and besought him to acknowledge me as his Grand Child. He started, and after having attentively examined my features, raised me from the Ground and throwing his Grand-fatherly arms around my Neck, exclaimed, "Acknowledge thee! Yes dear resemblance of my Laurina and my Laurina's Daughter, sweet image of my Claudia and my Claudia's Mother, I do acknowledge thee as the Daughter of the one and the Grandaughter of the other."[6]

Instantly Laura's bosom friend Sophia comes forward to be claimed as well, followed quickly by two beautiful young men who also represent themselves as the offspring of Laurina's other daughters. "But tell me," asks the old gentlemen "looking fearfully towards the Door," "have I other Grand-children in the House[?]" Assured that no other grandchildren are lurking about, he quickly doles out £50 banknotes to his newly discovered relatives and then exits, announcing that he has "done the Duty of a Grandfather" (92).

Announced by strong instinctual feeling and corroborated by familiar physiognomy, the consanguineal connection across generations in Austen's parody is ratified by financial generosity. As in Smollett's novels, generosity with money proves family feeling and family feeling is rewarded, in turn, by riches. This nexus of feeling and money testifies to the instantaneous power of blood relations to attach and instill reverence; but it also belies that power by commodifying it, by buying it off so to speak.

6 *The Collected Works of Jane Austen*, ed. Robert W. Chapman, 6 vols. (Oxford: Oxford University Press, 1954), 6:91.

Despite the popularity of this plot device in the late eighteenth century, great enough to provoke parody, one looks in vain for genuine
instances of it in early-eighteenth-century English fiction. Although
available in the European repertoire of plot devices used by Cervantes, Corneille, and Crébillon, the "voice of blood" topos was not
employed by English writers during the first half of the eighteenth
century. The rare exceptions—in fiction by Behn and Haywood—
function more to highlight the transgressive love between brothers
and sisters than to establish the indissolubility of blood kin ties. Aphra
Behn's *Dumb Virgin; or, The Force of Imagination* (1700), for example,
hinges on the confusion of family feeling and erotic love. Two sisters
fall in love with a naval hero who turns out to be their brother. Drawn
to him by "secret impulses of the Spirit" that mysteriously magnify his
attractions, they mistake the force of blood for erotic love, with tragic
results all around. But in Behn's text the sisters do not meet their
fated brother by chance. They purposely watch for him at a masquer-
ade because their uncle, the Admiral, has praised his skill and courage.
Indeed, so weak is the voice of blood that at first they mistake someone else for him in the general confusion of costumes and masks.
Eliza Haywood also portrays a young man and woman who do not
know that they are siblings and who love one another passionately.
But Felisinda and Ferdinando in *The Force of Nature; or, The Lucky Disappointment* (1724) were raised together in the same household, and
"they began to love each other, while they were both too innocent to
know what it was their Wishes aim'd at."[7] Although they later learn
that they are brother and sister, their fatal attraction can hardly be
said to illustrate the voice of blood, since they grew up together and
their love developed from deep and familiar knowledge of one
another rather than from mysterious, unseen forces. The examples
from Behn and Haywood of the *cri du sang* motif, central to each plot
without ever providing definitive proof of the instantaneous power of
kinship, come so close to the traditional use of the topos that their
subversive differences almost seem like denials of its force.

Nowhere is the utter disregard for the voice of blood in early-
eighteenth-century fiction more extravagantly illustrated than in *Moll*

7 Haywood, *The Force of Nature; or, The Lucky Disappointment* (London, 1724), 5.

Flanders (1722). Defoe represents Moll as marrying her own brother without any inkling of their relation, living happily with him and her own mother on a Virginia plantation and bearing two children without so much as a whisper from the voice of blood about their incestuous union. Only when she hears the story of her own consanguineal history told to her by her mother does she realize, with horror, what she has done. Even so, she continues in the marriage for another three years—although there are no more children. Neither drawn to her brother and mother nor repelled from them by supernatural prompt-ings, Moll's discomfort with her doubled relationships is intellectual, not visceral.

What does it mean that this old romanesque topos can be found in late-seventeenth-century English heroic drama, that it falls into disuse in the early eighteenth century, and that it returns with renewed force in the novels of the later part of the century? Does the reappearance of this plot device mean that biological lineal ties assumed a greater importance in English society during the second half of the eighteenth century? Or was the late-eighteenth-century emphasis compensatory, as blood ties lost importance? Were consanguineal relationships gain-ing strength, or were they weakening? What culture would produce an image of family members mysteriously drawn to one another: one that did or one that did not believe in the force of blood?

When one turns to historians studying the family with this question derived from literary evidence, one encounters a frustrating lack of fit between this question about the force of lineal ties and the kinds of arguments made about kin arrangements in the standard histo-ries of the family. Historians or anthropologists studying the family apparently find it difficult to cast off their twentieth-century biases and imagine compelling psychological configurations other than the famil-iar modern conjugal family. The advantage of literary evidence—as in this example of the historical patterning of the "voice of blood" topos—results from its potential to de-familiarize our unthinking assumptions about the family, suggesting other meanings to kin group-ings, other kin claims and interests, other emotional and psychological configurations, and other possibilities for subject positions within fam-ilies as they constitute society. While it is impossible to overcome entirely one's late-twentieth-century attitudes toward various social phenomena, critics who work with the novels of earlier periods have access to another means of assessing these matters, one with very different priorities, strategies, and logic from the historian's method.

Michael Anderson has distinguished among three historical approaches to the study of the European family—using demography, sentiments, and household economics. But all three, despite their differences, reveal a twentieth-century fixation on child-rearing. They all ask whether or not childhood was treated as a separate stage of life, whether children worked and what they did with their time, and what the attitudes were toward childhood sexuality. They ask whether the child was socialized severely and frequently punished or taught more gently. They ask whether parents bonded to their children and whether they could bear to make an emotional investment in the child, knowing that it would likely die before the age of five. The metaphor of investment no less than this child-centered treatment of the family and concern with love (what Lawrence Stone calls affective individualism) are questions of a post-Freudian culture interested in personal biography, social mobility, and self-fashioning.

After analyzing the ongoing decade-long debate between Peter Laslett and Lawrence Stone about the history of the family in England, Nancy Armstrong and Leonard Tennenhouse conclude in their analysis of family historians that both men, whatever their differences, are fixated on the conjugal bond in the nuclear family.[8] Asserting that Stone and Laslett's conclusions are based less "objectively" on information retrieved from the historical record than on "a set of modern metaphors that are deeply ingrained in the thinking of both men," Armstrong and Tennenhouse observe that these premier family historians are less interested in eighteenth-century differences from the modern family than in historical precedents for their own twentieth-century family formations.

> Ecclesiastical court records, county histories, the exhaustive demographic studies by Wrigley and Schofield; diaries; autobiographies; medical tracts on obstetrics, conception, and human anatomy; the

8 See the chapter "Family History," in *The Imaginary Puritan: Literature, Intellectual Labor, and the Origins of Personal Life,* by Armstrong and Tennenhouse (Berkeley: University of California Press, 1992), 69–88.

voluminous medical practice notes of a seventeenth-century astro-
logical physician; supplemented by accounts of disorder and its
treatment in coroner's inquests, court records, religious treatises,
and popular literature—all are distilled down to signs of the presence or absence of the emotions that bind individuals voluntarily
to their mates and to their immediate offspring. (Armstrong and
Tennenhouse, 82)

Stone's book *Broken Lives*, a study of broken marriages (and in some
cases mended lives) exemplifies the conjugal fixation.[9] Working with
"more or less verbatim" testimony offered by "dozens, or hundreds, of
persons, protagonists, witnesses, lawyers, and judges who gave evidence
or argued in a given case," collected from the archives of ecclesiastical
courts, Stone constructs his narratives of divorce, as he admits, by sort-
ing out contradictions, eliminating repetitions, and straightening out
chronologies (4). He extrapolates that "there is a peculiarly brutal and
exploitative quality about gender relations in the period 1680 to 1720.
. . . Violence, perjury, rape, and obsessive promiscuous sexuality are
the hallmark of this age, when gender relations were on the turn,
when women were at last beginning to assert themselves, and when
contractual theories were starting to spread even into domestic relations" (78). The country lost its "moral moorings" in this period, he
says, a "breakdown" visible in the plays of Shadwell, the novels of
Defoe, and "the popular literature of the age, especially in Mary de la
Riviere Manley's *New Atlantis* [*sic*] of 1714–20 [*sic*], and Mrs. Haywood's *Memoirs of a Certain Island* of 1725–6, both of which were best-
sellers" (28).[10]

Stone reads Shadwell, Defoe, Manley, and Haywood—together with
certain cases, notably *Calvert v. Calvert*—as psychopathically cold-
blooded, so as to corroborate his Whig history of the family. According
to his periodizing of this progressive historical narrative, the "compan-
ionate marriage" and affectionate and permissive styles of child-rearing
did not develop until later in the eighteenth century. So Stone affirms
that the world described "by these popular writers of the early years of

9 Stone, *Broken Lives: Separation and Divorce in England, 1660–1857* (Oxford:
Oxford University Press, 1993).

10 Delarivier Manley's *New Atalantis* was published in 1709.

the eighteenth century was a bleak one, dominated by avarice, lust, and duplicity," and adds that "this is exactly the same world as is revealed in the Calvert case" (29). As Stone tells it, the *Calvert* case was a tale of abject obedience, gratuitous cruelty, and profligate promiscuity—a cross between Richardson and de Sade—the sort of libertine excess that gave British aristocracy a bad name. With more brutality on the husband's part and more spite on the wife's in Stone's summary than was usually to be found in any single eighteenth-century fiction, the case reads like a composite of several novels. It seems at least as likely that fictional conventions of the day affected the way the Calverts and their witnesses narrated their stories as that their stories mirrored uninterpreted reality.

To a literary critic, aware of the cultural work that literature performs, the descriptions of sexual liaisons in the amatory fiction of Manley and Haywood represent not moral decay but the beginnings of cultural attention to—and regulation of—women's sexuality. Stone mistakenly assumes that those pages represented what happened in life, in the real world. But literary representation is never simply mimetic. According to Ros Ballaster and Melinda Rabb, for example, Manley must be read as a political satirist who represented Whig corruption as sexual scandal.[11] Undoubtedly, feelings about sexuality were very different in early-eighteenth-century England from what they are today. That difference is not easily inferred, however, from the erotic play depicted on the pages of Manley's scandalous novels, where honesty and dissimulation in sexual matters translate into the power politics of court life, filtered through the stylizations of heroic tragedy. When Stone reads these texts as evidence "of an abnormally cynical, mercenary, and predatory ruthlessness about human relationships" (27), he is not taking into account satiric exaggeration nor Manley's intention to expose particular individuals, nor the existing formal conventions of romance and tragedy that she is using.

Indeed, I have often suspected Stone (and certain other historians) of taking at face value the descriptions of society available in literary

11 See Ballaster, " 'A Genius for Love': Sex as Politics in Delarivier Manley's Scandal Fiction," in *Seductive Forms: Women's Amatory Fiction from 1684 to 1740* (Oxford: Clarendon, 1992), 114–52; Rabb presented part of her work in progress on Manley at the Center for Literary and Cultural Studies, Harvard University, December 1993.

texts, as if the historical age were transparently rendered by its contemporary authors and could be directly apprehended by twentieth-century readers, without the benefit of critical interpretation of idiosyncratic usages, literary conventions and traditions, or contextualized vocabularies. Literary critics then read these historians for their accounts of a distant age, convinced that the data of history are more "objective" than the highly interpreted evidence of their own discipline, and adopt formulations about earlier societies based on uninformed readings of texts that they, themselves, are better equipped to understand.

Trained to take into account formal conventions, pace, tone, juxtapositions, and sequence, no literary critic would read Defoe or Manley as describing the literal reality of their society. Defoe's contemporaries did not read his texts for everyday stories from daily life. Not intended to be realistic representations of the underclass, Defoe's tales of survival and surprising adventures, of class mobility and calculation, must be read, to some extent, in the context of the print culture of the day. In addition to what he saw around him, he drew upon what was already in print about rogues and outlaws, from ballads and folktales about highwaymen to newspaper accounts of castaways. Scholars interested in historical phenomena stand to learn a good deal from literary texts once they recognize that texts do not record behaviors but structures of feeling about social practices—as these are condensed into topoi and formulas with their own history of use, refinement, and parody.

"Structures of feeling," of course, is Raymond Williams's term for what literature records, "not feeling against thought, but thought as felt and feeling as thought: practical consciousness of a present kind, in a living and interrelating continuity."[12] Structures of feeling are the residues of lived experience and projections of emerging social formations, condensed and stored as forms in dialogue with other forms. His term is useful for thinking about the relation of literature to lived experience and to complex emerging cultural formations—a relationship that must concern anyone interested in cultural studies. Analyzed as a social practice within a market economy, literature consists of what people in a given period want to read about—constructed in familiar forms and conventions, consistent with other agents that socialize and

12 Williams, *Marxism and Literature* (Oxford: Oxford University Press, 1977), 132. Thanks to Curtis Perry for directing me to this passage.

constitute them as subjects within that culture. According to this way of thinking, art converts social consciousness into formal tropes that derive from lived experience but are not reducible to it. Thus textual evidence is not to be taken literally; especially when culled from so-called second-rate literature, textual evidence is too formulaic and two-dimensional to be taken as evidence of the ordinary lives of real people. But a literary critic trained to read these forms can try to interpret or unpack the structures of feeling, to make explicit the complex cultural attitudes that led to their formulation.[13] To make such judgments, the critic must understand how literary conventions are coded and how they are deployed—including how they comment on other literary conventions. In decoding the meaning of these forms and conventions, critics work with registers of feeling in texts, assessing intensities and qualities of tone used in writing about characters or incidents, in order to judge whether they are being mocked, celebrated, ironized, valorized, longed for, superstitiously repeated, denied, or flatly asserted. The advantage of literary evidence over, say, tax records, is that it permits a twentieth-century individual to briefly entertain the cultural attitudes of another era, to enter far enough into these moments of recorded consciousness or structures of feeling of another age to de-familiarize habitual responses to contemporary social formations and institutions.

But whose "structures of feeling" does the literary critic interpret, asks the historian? Are they the encoded collective unconscious of an entire society? Do writers serve, in this sense, as their cultures' amanuenses? Or are these structures of feeling the projections of individual geniuses, in dialogue with the values of their cultures? Pierre Macherey argues that the individual writer, shaped by society, uses artistry to manipulate figures and situations offered by the particular historical moment. Thus for Macherey, although a writer's representations of life are never transparently mimetic, the problematics of texts are always

13 Mary Poovey, describing the attempt to reconstruct the *mentalité* of another time, writes: "The object of my study is neither the individual text (of whatever kind) nor literary history, but something extrapolated from texts and reconstructed as the conditions of possibility for those texts—what I have called the symbolic economy or, more generally, the internal structure of ideology" (*Uneven Developments: The Ideological Work of Gender in Mid-Victorian England* [Chicago: University of Chicago Press, 1988], 15).

"precisely" given by that historical location and his culture. "The writer as the producer of the text, does not manufacture the materials with which he works."[14] That is not to say that the writer passively reflects already assimilated—already alienated—experience. Structures of feeling, as Williams points out, are "social experiences in solution" (133); those invented by writers often shape their culture's habits of thought and conceptions of life. Fiction understood this way becomes a strategy that writers—and readers—use to cope with the exigencies of life. Storytelling, like dreaming, is a means of rehearsing, predicting, denying, or validating human experience that is otherwise difficult to assimilate. Stories can function as magical thinking or wish fulfillment, catharsis, or theatrical staging, enabling an individual to confront powerful and inescapable realities. Literary critics assess these purposes by analyzing tonalities when interpreting the structures of feeling they find expressed in formal literary conventions and thus try to reconstruct contemporary attitudes toward social phenomena and human relations.

When eighteenth-century English authors of sentimental fiction retrieved from romanesque tragedy the voice of blood device in the mid to late eighteenth century, it probably did not mean that people were suddenly discovering long-lost relatives everywhere but rather that the reading public was moved by stories of recognition and reunion. What caused the renewed interest in the meaning of consanguinity requires further investigation. I believe that the recycling of this ancient topos in sentimental fiction may be a clue to profound changes in the practice and meaning of kinship in English eighteenth-century culture, changes brought about by new economic, political, and social practices, changes not apparent from parish records, demographic statistics, or even conduct manuals.

I have argued that literary evidence—of which the voice of blood topos is one small instance—reveals something about eighteenth-century attitudes toward the family that cannot be extrapolated from population statistics, rates and ages of marriage, patterns of inheritance, birth rates, or size and membership of households. Read in the

14 Macherey, *A Theory of Literary Production*, trans. Geoffrey Wall (1978; rpt. London: Routledge, 1989), 41.

changing tropes and formulas of popular fiction, literary evidence can inflect the archival sources of the historians by bringing to life attitudes about marriage, sexuality, and lineage that are very different from our own. Using art to reconstruct social history requires an understanding of formal conventions and current usages as well as of the material conditions under which artistic production occurred. Taking into account formal properties and contemporary usages, the critic can use literature to de-familiarize the family and suggest alternatives for the organization and meaning of human relations in the cultures that produced and consumed those texts.

The Anxiety of Change:

Reconfiguring

Family Relations in

Beaumarchais's Trilogy

Christie McDonald

Si j'étais professeur d'histoire de France, [dit l'histoire], et peut-être d'histoire du monde, je ferais lire [*La Mère coupable*] à mes élèves. . . . Je leur lirais d'abord les deux *comédies*; et ensuite je leur lirais le *drame*. . . . Rien ne permettrait autant de mesurer la différence de temps, la différence de ton, enfin ce qui fait proprement l'histoire et l'âge et l'événement d'un peuple et du monde. Je voudrais donner à mes élèves le goût même, la saveur pour ainsi dire physique de ce que c'était que 1775, 1784, 1792: je leur lirais simplement ces trois pièces.[1]—Histoire, in Péguy's *Clio*

I would like to frame what follows in the cross-current between literary, philosophical, and juridical discourses as they are worked out, not in systems but in the particularities of cases, experiences, and events (always textual) and in the transference among these discourses. In

1 If I were a professor of French history, says history, and perhaps of world history, I would have my students read *La Mère coupable*. . . . I would first read them the two comedies, then the drama. . . . There is no better measure of the difference in time, in tone, indeed in everything constituting the history, the period, and the incident[s] of a people and of the world. I would like to give my students the very taste, the physical sensation, as it were, of 1775, 1784, and 1792: I would simply read them these three plays (*Œuvres en prose complètes*, ed. Robert Burac, 3 vols. [Paris: Gallimard, 1992], 3:1072 [cited in *L'Autre Tartuffe, ou La Mère coupable, Comédie-Française* 183 (February 1990)]). Unless otherwise noted, all translations are mine.

the eighteenth century, the passage from rational to experimental philosophy saw an epistemological and ethical shift that allowed for reflection about the importance of the individual within the social order. In the twentieth century, following the exhaustion of European structuralism, which highlighted the systematic character of linguistic approaches, poststructuralism, especially in North America, refocused interest on the relationship of particulars to theory and systematic thought and on the change in character and conditions of thought. By considering the polemical and differential sides of thought, the singularity of texts and events, and their integration into a theory not founded upon reason alone, I hope to determine how the transference among discourses and disciplines effects a change in thought. This line of study presupposes that literature accompanies political, philosophical, and even juridical thought by evoking, investigating, or creating singular stories or cases that reveal the impasses and contradictions of rational discourse. The individual is subsumed into a discourse of singularity whose force goes beyond a single voice or position; both author and individual become part of a cultural identity that includes but is not limited to them. In Beaumarchais's three plays, *Le Barbier de Séville*, *Le Mariage de Figaro*, and *La Mère coupable*, one passes from individual discourse, in conflicting value systems, to a discourse that lays bare the premises of conceptual metaphors for reproductive and family relations. At issue also is the problem of how twentieth-century readers read eighteenth-century narratives.

Contemporary philosophical debates concerning the concept of Enlightenment are polarized between rationality and rational consensus found thought and life in society (Habermas) and that thought is at once constituted and questioned through rhetorical analyses of binary thought and writing as a performative act (Derrida). Questioning the primacy of reason has prompted some, like Lyotard, to situate disap-

I have written this essay with the help of a grant from the Social Sciences and Humanities Research Council of Canada. I would like to thank my assistants for their support and good cheer: Marie-Pierre Maybon and Ilhame El Himdy. I would also like to thank Michel Delon for his valuable suggestions in finding material; Mme Noëlle Guilbert, curator-archivist of the Library of the Comédie-Française; for her help in tracing the history of performance of *Le Mariage de Figaro*; Francis Duphil for finding a recording of Darius Milhaud's opera *La Mère coupable*; and my colleague, Walter Moser, for his critical reading of the essay.

pointed hopes of redemptive social discourse within a "story about the
death of a 'meta or master narrative'" taken to be that of the Enlightenment.[2] Those who have introduced gender centrally into the debate see
a fundamental transformation in Western culture. As Jane Flax suggests,
"[A] 'shape of life' is growing old. The demise of the old is being has-
tened by the end of colonialism, the uprising of women, the revolt of
other cultures against white Western hegemony, shifts in the balance of
economic and political power within the world economy, and a growing
awareness of the costs as well as the benefits of scientific and technolog-
ical 'progress'"(5). One of the most controversial issues is that of impartiality, a striving for consensus based on universal reason, and the ability
to speak in the name of a totality. Often a part (or a particular interest
group) represents the whole and is mistaken for it; the problem is that
any pretense to universality is always situated, contextual, and local.[3]

In eighteenth-century discussions concerning change, the effort to
comprehend and bring about cultural as well as political transformations
demanded, and was accompanied by, a questioning of the principles
upon which such transitions would be based. The Enlightenment was
more than the sum of any one thinker's philosophy, and certainly more
than the story of abstract thought alone, as Ernst Cassirer made clear: it
was the spontaneity of thought creating a new order.[4] But how that order
was to come about, where it could come from, how it could be legiti-
mated, and where it was going were problems rooted in the contemporary anxiety about change. To shed tutelage—defined by Kant as minority in both the chronological and juridical sense—means, in the texts to
which I will allude, reconfiguring the individual's relation to authority
through the family and its relationship to the sociopolitical context.

A critique of the past and of past assumptions connects the discourse
of the end of the eighteenth century with that of the late twentieth
century. Where these discourses perhaps differ most is on the meaning

2 Jane Flax, *Thinking Fragments: Psychoanalysis, Feminism, and Postmodernism in the Contemporary West* (Berkeley: University of California Press, 1990), 7.

3 "Much of the world seems to be seeking meaning in ethnic, national, and other traditions, and casting aspersions on the Enlightenment demand for impartiality" (Martha Nussbaum, "Justice for Women!" *New York Review of Books*, 8 October 1992, 44).

4 Cassirer, *The Philosophy of the Enlightenment*, trans. Fritz C. A. Koelln and James P. Pettegrove (Princeton, N.J.: Princeton University Press, 1951), 163.

of change and progress—whether any teleology is at work in the stories told.[5] The issues of legitimacy, dependence, and social transformation configured in them become at once fascinating and unnerving when one can no longer measure progress or regress from any model or fixed landmark in the tradition. "Tout est changé, et doit changer encore," wrote Abbé Raynal. "Mais les révolutions passées et celles qui doivent suivre ont-elles été, seront-elles *utiles* à la nature humaine? L'homme leur devra-t-il un jour plus de tranquillité, de bonheur et de plaisir? *Son état sera-t-il meilleur, ou ne fera-t-il que changer?*"[6] [Everything has changed, and will change again. Will past revolutions and those to follow prove useful to human nature? Will man enjoy greater tranquillity, happiness, and pleasure because of them? Will he be better off or will his circumstances simply go on changing?]

In his trilogy Beaumarchais steers an uncertain course on the high seas of political and cultural debate about what is now infamously referred to as "family values."[7] As a number of historians have shown, the eighteenth century constructs a family romance from its anxiety about change, in variants on Freud's familiar scenario. Calling upon the story of an "original social contract that would explain the genesis of 'the law of male sex-right,'" Lynn Hunt explains how with the death of the king the "break in the family model of politics" occurred in the passage from "deference and paternal authority" to a "new basis for political consent." "[T]he French had a kind of collective political unconscious that was structured by narratives of family relations."[8] Hunt reintroduces women into the equation to show how "[t]he

5 Flax states that her use of the word *transitional* or *transformative* is not "meant to imply that changes in Western culture are moving us in any particular preset (much less 'progressive') direction" (5).

6 Raynal, *Histoire philosophique et politique des deux Indes* (Paris: Maspero, 1981).

7 If the political inflation of this term wore out the patience of the American public during the 1992 presidential campaign, the detailed analyses of the problem in contemporary literary and historical terms began some time ago and must be continued through serious research and analysis, as Stephanie Coontz pointed out in "Let Scholars Bring Realism to the Debates on Family Values," *Chronicle of Higher Education*, 21 October, 1992, B1–B2.

8 Hunt, *The Family Romance of the French Revolution* (Berkeley: University of California Press, 1992), xiii. The family romance shows "the collective, unconscious images of the familial order that underlie revolutionary politics" (xiii). Hunt wants to find a middle way between Freudian and Girardian analyses of the foundation of society.

female figure occupied most of the symbolic space once taken by the father/king's body" (84). Carole Pateman discusses the conflict contained in the language of paternalism, as it harks "back to the traditional patriarchal model of the political order," in which patriarchy is understood as paternal power—"all rulers are like fathers"—and as contract theory. She puzzles over the "question of conjugal right and natural freedom and equality," in particular the "question of how the classic contract theorists began from premises that rendered illegitimate any claim to political right that appealed to nature, and then went on to construct the difference between men and women as the difference between natural freedom and natural subjection."[9]

The work of Hunt and Pateman testifies to the conflict between old status and rank and a new world of contractants, from which emerged a social reorganization that bore with it new anxieties about kinship lines. Rights that had been based on unequal social and economic status (rank, heredity, family) were now redistributed according to a social contract.[10] The ethical differences of reason and feeling were contested in the theater, where, prior to the killing of the father/monarch in the person of Louis XVI / Louis Capet, anxieties played themselves out in representations of changing family relations.

Serious drama encompassed the philosophical period of the 1750s and 1760s and, as a newly developing aesthetic, stimulated the debate around so-called family values through a mixed genre. During and prior to the Revolution intellectuals problematized in a discontinuous but productive fashion many of the issues still haunting us today: the

9 Pateman, *The Sexual Contract* (Stanford, Calif.: Stanford University Press, 1988), 54, 222. During the 1992 electoral campaign, Americans in search of a reason why their country was in such dire straits "hit on a new theory: 'the absent man.' Even before Dan Quayle gave the theory his official imprimatur, by berating a television heroine for choosing to bear a child out of wedlock, the Los Angeles riot had been blamed on a lack of responsible male authority-figures in the ghettos of America. Now the theory can be taken further. America itself is fatherless, struggling along under the wing of 'Granny' Barbara Bush, kid brother Quayle, and two households of feckless uncles bent on spending income they don't have. The man who should be shouldering his paternal responsibilities has become a deadbeat. Unless he pulls himself together the family may conclude it is better off without him" (*Economist*, 15 August 1992, 11–12).

10 Paul de Man contends that Rousseau misreads his text as a promise of political change largely because language dissociates cognition from act. See "Promises," in *Allegories of Reading* (New Haven, Conn.: Yale University Press, 1979) 246–78.

relation of the individual to the collectivity in the family and society, as well as the "sexual contract" between women, men, and children. How did the family model furnish both the basis of a harmonious contractual life in society and the narratives of conflict that showed how very fragile any consensus was to be?

Only the *drame bourgeois*, also called the *genre sérieux*, the *tragédie bourgeoise*, and simply the *drame*, seemed able to accommodate the two. Theorizing began with Diderot's *Entretiens sur le Fils naturel* (1757), *De la poésie dramatique* (1758), and *Eloge de Richardson* (1762); Beaumarchais followed up in *Essai sur le genre dramatique sérieux* (the preface to *Eugénie* [1767]) and the prefaces to his trilogy; and Mercier continued with his essay *Du théâtre ou nouvel essai sur l'art dramatique* (1773).[11] The new genre, in which virtue and goodness triumph without recourse to a foundational truth, repositioned the function of individuals within the family and seemed to offer, beyond any explicit moral schematization, the possibility of an ethical practice of fiction.

Beaumarchais's criticism is in some ways the strongest articulation of the *drame bourgeois*. He claims to write serious drama, which he situates between heroic tragedy and light comedy, in order to persuade the audience through feeling or sentiment, not reason, and to substitute the example for the precept or abstraction.[12] The human heart, rather than the faculty of reason, is his model. Because feeling grounds the particulars of the action, the reader or spectator—so goes the argument—will empathize or commiserate with the character.[13]

11 The *drame bourgeois* created a stir from 1757 to 1771. Its defenders were Mme d'Epinay, Grimm, and Voltaire; its enemies were Fréron, Pallisot, and Collé. The great success of Sedaine's *Philosophe sans le savoir* (1765) anticipated that of Diderot's *Père de famille* (1769).

12 Beaumarchais, *Œuvres*, ed. Pierre Larthomas, with Jacqueline Larthomas (Paris: Gallimard, 1988), 119. All quotations from Beaumarchais refer to this edition. Here Beaumarchais follows the *Eloge de Richardson*, in which Diderot praises Richardson for putting into action what Montaigne, La Rochefoucauld, and others left in maxims: "Une maxime est une règle abstraite et générale de conduite dont on nous laisse l'application à faire. Elle n'imprime par elle-même aucune image sensible dans notre esprit." [A maxim is a general abstract rule of conduct whose application is up to us. It does not imprint any sensory image on our mind] (*Œuvres esthétiques*, ed. Paul Vernière [Paris: Garnier, 1965], 29).

13 Diderot asserts that the world is divided into those who take pleasure in life and those who suffer; he identifies only with those who suffer (*Eloge*, 33). About truth and

While Diderot viewed sensibility as an "affection sociale," Rousseau argued that *pitié* (identification between sentient beings) was an innate social virtue prior to reason, and was, paradoxically, the only natural faculty to allow for the equalizing of social relationships. The stories of individuals, which considered the unexceptional and mundane, were meant to serve as models for moral judgment and conduct. Yet the models applied only if everyone was conceived as fundamentally alike. They presented idealized social relationships, but they could not account for the particulars of life and circumstance. Generalizing a life story became a problem analogous to that of the social contract: how, in Diderot's terms, to generalize the ungeneralizable, or, in Rousseau's, to voluntarily submit individual desire to a social order for the collective good. The ability to "feel with" ordinary people transfers Rousseau's social principle of *pitié* to the theater.

Beaumarchais acknowledges Diderot as his model, pointing to the strength and vigorous male tone of one of Diderot's plays, *Le père de famille*, and suggests that through the connection between the characters and the spectator, serious drama offers moral standards more directly than heroic tragedy.[14] Oedipus and Orestes might inspire terror, for example, but as blind instruments of the gods' anger or fancy they frighten rather than touch by their destiny. Instead, Beaumarchais seeks to provoke a reaction to an event so "real" that one might mistake it for reality and experience the desired emotional effect. Repre-

---

lies he writes: "O Richardson! j'oserai dire que l'histoire la plus vraie est pleine de mensonges, et que ton roman est plein de vérités. L'histoire peint quelques individus; tu peins l'espèce humaine: l'histoire attribue à quelques individus ce qu'ils n'ont ni dit, ni fait; tout ce que tu attribues à l'homme, il l'a dit et fait. . . . Le cœur humain, qui a été, est et sera toujours le même, est le modèle d'après lequel tu copies" ["O Richardson! I daresay the truest history has many lies and your novel many truths. History portrays individuals; you portray the human species. History attributes to a few individuals what they have neither said nor done; everything that you attribute to man he has said and done. . . . The human heart, which has been and always will be the same, is the model from which you copy] (39–40).

14 "Vouloir arrêter les efforts du génie dans la création d'un nouveau genre de spectacle, ou dans l'extension de ceux qu'il connaît déjà, est un attentat contre ses droits, une entreprise contre ses plaisirs" [To attempt to stop a genius in the act of creating a new kind of entertainment or developing one already known is an attack on his rights, a venture against his pleasure] (*Essai*, 121).

sentation of what happens in the world demands a faithful picture of real objects, by which Beaumarchais meant ordinary people rather than kings or nobles.[15] Identification through feeling "sert de base à ce principe certain de l'Art, qu'il n'y a moralité ni intérêt au théâtre sans un secret rapport du sujet dramatique à nous" [underlies the basic principle of art: there can be neither morality nor interest in theater without a secret relationship between the dramatic subject and ourselves] (*Essai*, 126). Feeling transferred by analogy touches and thereby changes the spectator.[16]

Beaumarchais asks whether dramatic force arises from character or from civil status. He then answers that nature imbues ordinary people with as much character as princes, and that serious drama should have the same impact as heroic tragedy (*Essai*, 129–32). Bourgeois drama was tragedy brought down into the everyday, domestic realm, whereas tragedy relied on extraordinary individuals and comedy on types.[17]

Two images emerge from the conception of identification in theater; both are drawn from the family constellation. The first, paternal image indicates authority and comprehends not only fathers and husbands within the plays but the very act of writing. In a letter concerning *Les Deux amis*, Beaumarchais compares himself and the actors at the Comédie-Française to adoptive parents with shared paternal responsibilities: "Par la nouvelle adoption que vous venez d'en faire . . . vous partagerez désormais avec moi tous les soucis de la paternité" [With the new adoption that you have just undertaken (with my play) . . . you

15 "Le véritable intérêt du cœur, sa vraie relation, est donc toujours d'un homme à un homme, et non d'un homme à un roi. . . . Plus l'homme qui pâtit est d'un état qui se rapproche du mien, et plus son malheur a de prise sur mon âme." [The true interest of the heart, its true connection, is always from man to man, not man to king. The closer a suffering man comes to my condition, the greater hold his misfortune has on my soul] (*Essai*, 125).

16 "Tout objet trop neuf pour présenter en soi des règles positives de discussion se juge par analogie à des objets de même nature, mais plus connus" [Any object too new to introduce its own positive rules of discussion is judged by analogy to objects of the same kind, but better-known] (*Essai*, 129).

17 Diderot, *Entretiens sur le Fils naturel*, Classiques Larousse (Paris: Librairie Larousse, 1975), 159, 171; *Le Drame bourgeois. Fiction 2*, ed. Jaques Chouillet and Anne-Marie Chouillet (Paris: Hermann, 1980), 129–46.

share all the worries of paternity with me] (*Œuvres*, 1272).[18] Louis-Sébastien Mercier adds that the poet resembles a legislator who, because of his exquisite sensibility, would expand the moral code and judge not according to written laws but according to those imprinted within the structure of consciousness.[19]

Beaumarchais also likens himself to a mother when he describes theatrical works as "concus avec volupté, menés à terme avec fatigue, enfantés avec douleur et vivant rarement assez pour payer les parents de leurs soins, ils coûtent plus de chagrins qu'il ne donnent de plaisirs" [conceived in sensuality, brought to term with fatigue, borne with pain, and rarely alive long enough to repay their parents for their care; they cost more in grief than they return in pleasure] (272). The masculine creator therefore co-opts not only a paternal but a maternal role to legitimate the autonomy of his creation.[20] This second, maternal image becomes for others a quasi-transcendental concept.

Diderot, asserting that what he calls a *tableau* is the presentation of a state of mind, cites Iphigénie's mother in Racine's play. Her importance is not that she is queen of Argos and wife of the Greek general; rather, she embodies "le tableau de l'amour maternel dans toute sa vérité" [the picture of maternal love in all its truth] (Diderot, *Entretiens*, 118). Clytemnestra is also a model, because her grief is common to all mothers. Within the bourgeois drama, as Peter Szondi points out, the notions of woman and mother come not out of the bourgeoisie but out of an antique, mythologized Greek nature.[21] The inherited sense of maternal feeling then undergoes an intensification leading to the concepts of justice and equality.

Critics agree that the theater of the *drame bourgeois* was unsuccessful, but no consensus exists on the importance of this mostly forgotten

18 "La part que nous avons à cet enfant commun a cela de différent que je l'ai conçu avec plaisir dans le silence, et qu'il y a tout à craindre que vous ne l'enfantiez avec douleur parmis les cris et le tapage" [The share that each of us has in this common child is different in that I conceived it with pleasure in silence, and there is every reason to fear that you may deliver it in pain amidst shouting and uproar] (*Les Deux amis*, 1272).

19 Mercier, *Du théâtre, ou nouvel essai sur l'art dramatique* (Geneva: Slatkine, 1970), 152–3.

20 I would like to thank Walter Moser for his remarks to this effect.

21 Szondi, "Tableau et coup de théâtre," *Poétique* 9 (1972): 3.

genre. I suggest that the attempt at a "moral" genre not only conveys the revolutionary changes implicit in the theory and practice of the plays but tells us something about the recent need for ethical guides within criticism today. Tragedy and comedy had failed in their depictions of ordinary people because Diderot wished to focus on *conditions* rather than character: "Pour peu que le caractère fût chargé, un spectateur pouvait se dire à lui-même, ce n'est pas moi. Mais il ne peut se cacher que l'état qu'on joue devant lui, ne soit le sien" [So long as the character was exaggerated, a spectator could still say, this is not me. Yet he could not fail to see that the condition before him was his own] (*Entretiens*, 144). To the insistence on conditions Beaumarchais added the representation of choice and plurality, which brings this distant genre closer to contemporary preoccupations.

The discourses on family and state were interconnected and more than rhetorically bound in the eighteenth century: they were interchangeable at the level of language, belief, and daily experience. Just how they were related concerned philosophers, especially Diderot and Rousseau, in search of a model for society. Both had attempted to write narratives of the origin and the development of the family and society: *Le Supplément au voyage de Bougainville* and *Le Discours sur les origines et les fondements de l'inégalité parmi les hommes*. The distinction between natural law and the conventions of culture permeated the fictional status of any such narrative. For Diderot, no natural hierarchical order confers the right to command others; the only natural authority is paternal. He distinguishes clearly between the family and society, however, in the concept of a social contract.[22] In the *Fragments politiques*, he writes that a father may be king in the family, but no king (not even a good one) can be a father of society—the king is only a steward.[23] Rousseau, pondering the relationship between the family and society, at one point eliminated the family altogether only to restore it as the primary model for society in *Du contrat social*. The philosophical questions concerning the foundation of society and the development of the family were not questions of fact; they were hypothetical, and the

22 See Diderot, "Autorité politique," *Encyclopédie 1*, vol. 5, ed. John Lough and Jacques Proust (Paris: Hermann, 1976), 540.

23 Diderot, "Pensées détachées ou fragments politiques échappés du portefeuille d'un philosophe," *œuvres complètes* 10:74−5.

arguments about natural right and natural law laid down the basis for the social contract. Yet the portrayals of individuals in the family pitted the particulars of life stories against a long-standing tradition of marriage and family and began to effect a transformation.

The article "Mariage," listed under theology in the *Encyclopédie*, evokes in the marital relationship a natural contract, a civil contract, and a sacrament.[24] Basic Christian doctrine concerning the governance of the family is found in *Ephesians*: women, children, and servants must obey the master of the house in the same way that Christians obey God (5.22, 6.9). Historian of the family Jean-Louis Flandrin adds that "[f]rom the very beginning of Christianity the family was considered as the monarchy of divine right."[25] The authority of the father of the family and that of God legitimate not only each other but all other authority. Here the *genre bourgeois* must contend with what hap-

---

24 "Mariage considéré en lui-même et quant à sa simple étymologie, signifie obligation, devoir, charge et fonction d'une mère. . . . A le prendre dans son sens théologique et naturel, il désigne l'union volontaire et maritale d'un homme et d'une femme contractée par des personnes libres pour avoir des enfants. . . . Une union volontaire, parce que tout contrat suppose par sa propre nature le consentement mutuel des parties contractantes. . . . Autrefois les esclaves ne pouvaient se marier sans le consentement de leurs maîtres, et aujourd'hui, dans les états bien policés, les enfants ne peuvent se marier sans le consentement de leurs parents ou tuteurs, s'ils sont mineurs. . . . La naissance des enfants est le but et la fin du mariage" [Marriage considered in itself and with respect to etymology alone signifies obligation, duty, burden and function of the mother. . . . Taking it in its theological and natural sense, it designates the voluntary marital union of a man and a woman contracted by free persons in order to have children. . . . [It is] a voluntary union because all contracts presuppose by their very nature the mutual consent of the contracting parties. . . . In the past slaves could not marry without the consent of their masters, and today, in many civilized states, children cannot marry without the consent of their parents or guardians if they are minors. . . . The birth of children is the goal and end of marriage] (*Encyclopédie, ou dictionnaire raisonné des sciences et des arts*, vol. 10 [Stuttgart: Friedrich Fromman Verlag, 1966], 103).

25 Flandrin, *Familles: Parenté, maison, sexualité dans l'ancienne société* (Paris: Seuil, 1984), 117. From the 1500s to the 1700s, reinforcement of paternal and marital power was accompanied by that of private property; the exchange remained obedience in return for protection. On the juridical front, women had lost ground after the 1200s according to Flandrin, with the affirmation of patrilinearity and by their inability to fulfill vassal obligations. In the 1300s there came the use of the patronym, the exclusion of women from the French throne, their inability to transmit the right of the throne, and especially the juridical restrictions variously imposed on them from this century on (117–24).

pens when a new diffused authority supplants the father. The *drame bourgeois* and its successors replace the father's weakened sense of authority with a family based on the reciprocal relations of its members, whose support and actions make possible a new family structure. A sequence of stories in Beaumarchais's trilogy renders the new order. *Le Barbier de Séville, Le Mariage de Figaro,* and *La Mère coupable* constitute what I have loosely called a case; a text, event, or trial becomes the point of reference for a sequence extending over time. The trilogy functions as a roundhouse, with several intersecting sequences. The first involves the three plays themselves, in which the characters remain the same and the preface of each play comments upon and announces the plays to come.[26] The second concerns the tradition of "exogamous imitations" (Michel Delon's term), based upon Beaumarchais's trilogy and written following *Le Barbier* and *Le Mariage.* Some were prolongations of *Le Mariage,* which added little to the model; others attempted to follow *Le Mariage* as it followed *Le Barbier,* with modifications, progressions, mutations, and after-the-fact follow-ups; then there was a sequence of operatic writings, most notably by Mozart and Rossini; and Beaumarchais's rereading of the Miss Polly Baker affair in Marceline's speech.[27] All of them focus on bastardy and the family constellation. Many eighteenth-century authors, including Olympe de Gouges, attempted to create a sequel for the charming child-adolescent Chérubin, but no one engages the character Marceline, for several reasons.

In Beaumarchais's Aeschylean trilogy the Almaviva family undergoes considerable change. He describes the relationship among the three plays in his 1797 preface to *La Mère coupable*: "[Dans] le roman de la famille Almaviva . . . les deux premières époques ne semblent pas, dans leur gaieté légère, offrir de rapport bien sensible avec la profonde et touchante moralité de la dernière; mais elles ont, dans le plan de l'auteur, une connexion intime, propre à verser le plus vif intérêt sur les

26 For analyses of Beaumarchais's works, see M. Descotes, *Les Grands rôles du théâtre de Beaumarchais* (Paris: Presses Universitaires de France, 1974); René Pomeau, *Beaumarchais ou la bizarre destinée* (Paris: Presses Universitaires de France, 1987); and Jacques Scherer, *La Dramaturgie de Beaumarchais,* 2nd ed. (Paris: Nizet, 1980). See also *Europe* (April 1973) and *Revue d'histoire littéraire de la France* (September–October, 1984) for special issues on Beaumarchais and *Le Mariage de Figaro.*

27 See Michel Delon, "Figaro et son double," *Revue de l'histoire littéraire de la France* 5 (1984): 774–84.

184 *Christie McDonald*

représentations de *La Mère coupable*" [In the novel of the Almaviva family . . . the light gaiety of the first two periods do not seem to have much in common with the profound and touching morality of the last period; but in the author's plan they do have an intimate connection, guaranteed to shed light on and create interest in the performances of the *La Mère coupable*] (599). Both *Le Barbier* and *Le Mariage* are called comedies and take place in Spain, while *La Mère coupable* is listed as a *drame* and is set in France in 1790.

In the spirit of continuity, the original actors, with Beaumarchais's approval, had intended to present the play in three consecutive performances: the first day, one would laugh during *Le Barbier*; the second day, one would view the foibles of man's virility; the third day, one would see that most men end up good by the inexorable wear and tear of age, particularly if they are fathers. Beaumarchais planned to reveal certain other issues as well, some of which seem today the most innovative and revolutionary of all: the ability of servants, mothers, and women in general, for example, to recast the events of their lives through a redistribution of roles within the family constellation. In more contemporary, less good-humored terms, one could describe these three days somewhat differently: during the first day an illegitimate child finds work and a family, and love gives the illusion of equality in social relations; during the second, the male sex-right is foiled and a family discovered; during the third, equality of rights is not borne out by the portrayal of the "facts" of the characters' lives when feeling reconfigures a family.

Finding a master in the person of Count Almaviva, Figaro helps him to marry, thus creating a family into which he himself will be integrated. The concept of the family in the ancien régime included the servants, and the family in which a valet worked was considered his real one, for his raison d'être and legitimacy derived from his master. At a time when, as Philippe Ariès has shown, a new feeling and sense of the family were developing, Figaro discovers himself to have a biological as well as a social family.[28]

28 Ariès, *L'Enfant et la vie familiale sous l'Ancien Régime* (Paris: Seuil, 1973), 251. In 1948, with his groundbreaking study *Histoire des populations françaises et de leurs attitudes devant la vie depuis le dix-huitième siècle,* Ariès began to reveal what had until then remained family secrets.

In the prefatory letter to *Le Barbier*, Beaumarchais fills in Figaro's background: Before abandoning him and his mother, Marceline, Bartholo the doctor branded Figaro's right arm with a hieroglyph. A Bohemian chief kidnapped Figaro, and a celebrated astrologer whom his mother had consulted prophesied:

> Après avoir versé le sang dont il est né,
> Ton fils assommera son père infortuné:
> Puis, tournant sur lui-même et le fer et le crime,
> Il se frappe, et devient heureux et légitime. (275)

> [After shedding the blood that bore him, your son will fell his unfortunate father: then, turning the criminal blade upon himself, he wounds himself and becomes happy and legitimate.]

Destiny weighs lightly in this alternative to the story of Oedipus, who was "destined by fate to kill his father and take his mother to wife."[29] The plays carry out the prophecy: Marceline, Figaro's birth mother, now an old governess in the house of Doctor Bartholo, fulfills the first part when her foot is bled offstage;[30] Figaro innocently thrashes the Doctor, fulfilling the second; later, Figaro cuts himself on his chin or throat; and ultimately, the Doctor marries Marceline in *Le Mariage*, making Figaro legitimate and, presumably, happy.

In *Le Barbier*, the Count has fallen in love with and desires to marry Rosine, an orphan of noble extraction imprisoned in the care of her tutor/guardian, Bartholo. As such, Bartholo has a seigneurial and legal hold over her, as well as a familial function.[31] With his philosophy of "le droit du plus fort" [the law of the jungle], he plans to marry Rosine despite abusing her.[32] Rejecting the power of rank and position ("le rang doit être ici sans force" [348]), the Count claims Rosine through love, focusing on their equality and her freedom to choose a partner.

---

29 Sigmund Freud, "Some Thoughts on Development and Regression—Aetiology," in *New Introductory Lectures*, trans. James Strachey (New York: Penguin, 1976), 373.

30 In Sophocles' *Oedipus* it was Oedipus's foot that bled.

31 Marcel Garaud, *La Révolution française et la famille*, ed. Romuald Szramkiewicz (Paris: Presses Universitaires de France, 1978), 145.

32 Since Bartholo is a bourgeois professional, not a noble, his power over Rosine could be disputed. "Conjugal power is not paternal, but part of masculine sex-right, the power that men exercise as men, not as fathers" (Pateman, 22).

He challenges Bartholo by proclaiming Rosine's emancipation, protection under the law, and recourse to just magistrates.[33]

The preface to *Le Barbier* begins a network of familial images and a sequence continued in the other plays. Not only is the action based on disguised identity, deception, and recognition, as well as changing roles and sexual identity, but language constantly crosses sexual boundaries and kinship lines. When the Count asks Figaro if he knows Bartholo, who is actually his biological father, Figaro replies, "comme ma mère" [As if he were my mother] (298). Elsewhere accusing Bartholo of being a bad father, Figaro calls him a "père marâtre" [a father like a stepmother].[34] Beyond biological ties, Rosine refers to Figaro affectionately as "un bon parent" [a good relative], and even as her son, as does Suzanne in *Le Mariage*.

In *Le Barbier* the Count abolishes what is referred to throughout the trilogy as the *droit du seigneur*. The many rights of seigneury included a quasi-feudal law that had become common practice: the right of the lord to deflower his vassal's wife on her wedding night.[35] In the *Dictionnaire philosophique*, this right appears under the heading *droit de cuissage ou culage*. None of the general dictionaries or treatises on the rights of seigneury from the period specifically reference it; Voltaire, pointing out that this tyrannic excess had never really been passed into law, applauds the evolution from *culage* to *cuissage*. Beaumarchais, however, prefers the generic euphemism, *droit du seigneur*, as a touchstone for

33 "Les vrais magistrats sont les soutiens de tous ceux qu'on opprime" [True magistrates are ever the defenders of the oppressed] (*Le Barbier*, 349); Beaumarchais, "*The Barber of Seville*" and "*The Marriage of Figaro*," trans. John Wood (New York: Penguin, 1964), 102.

34 As a category beyond sexual definition, Rétif de la Bretonne calls the bad mother "marâtre" in *La Mauvaise Mère*, in *Les Contemporaines, ou aventures des plus jolies femmes de l'âge présent* (Geneva: Slatkine, 1988).

35 It has been argued that the lord could claim this as a penalty only if his vassal had failed to pay some fee. See Vivienne G. Mylne, "*Le Droit du seigneur* in *Le Mariage de Figaro*," *French Studies Bulletin* 11 (1984): 4–5; Robert Niklaus, *Le Mariage de Figaro* (London: Grant and Cutler, 1983), 32–3. For discussion of the *droit du seigneur* see Alain Boureau, *Le Droit de cuissage: La Fabrication d'un mythe* (XIIIe–XXe siècle) (Paris, 1995); and Suzanne Pucci, "The Currency of Exchange in Beaumarchais' *Mariage de Figaro*: From the 'Master Trope' Synedoche to Fetish," *Eighteenth-Century Studies* 25 (fall 1991), pp. 57–84. See also Antoine Laplace, *Introduction aux droits seigneuriaux* (Paris, 1749); M. Renauldon, *Dictionnaire des fiefs et des droits seigneuriaux* (Paris, 1765).

criticizing privilege in general and the power of men over women in particular.[36]

Having staked a claim for equality and liberty through love in *Le Barbier*, the Count does an about-face in *Le Mariage* once he and Rosine are married: in the second play, he intends to take advantage of the outmoded right to seduce Suzanne on her wedding night. The Count thereby repeats claims to the male sex-right that he himself had formerly denounced. As the Countess, Figaro, and Suzanne try to prevent the Count from exercising his privilege, it becomes clear that the Count, vacillating in his attitude toward power and privilege, will not challenge traditional authority.

The turning point comes in the third act of *Le Mariage*: family relations are realigned through the revelations of Marceline and Figaro's trial. In the transformation of the family house to a courtroom, the Count becomes the judge, as was his seigneurial right by the law of the land. At issue are a contract and a marriage, an absurd revamping of the *droit du seigneur* with the sexual roles reversed. Figaro had borrowed money from Marceline, promising to marry her if he defaulted. Now he wants to break the contract, but Marceline wants to keep the contract because of her love for Figaro, which she has misconstrued as passionate rather than maternal. The Count's conflict of interest disposes him to want Figaro to marry Marceline in order to clear his way to Suzanne. Everyone has a particular interest in breaking or holding to the contract, even those who should be the most impartial.

At the trial, the play on family names and genealogy indicates the force of tradition and the need to resist it to bring about change. Marceline answers to names that characterize her as a surrogate and a passionate adult female: Barbe-Agar-Raab-Madeleine-Nicole-Marceline de Verte-Allure. Figaro leaves his Christian name blank and marks his family background as "anonymous," apparently positioning himself as a self-created hero.[37] He evokes the belief that he is from a lost noble family,

36 Voltaire, *Dictionnaire philosophique*, in *Œuvres complètes*, vol. 18 (Paris: Garnier, 1878), 299–302. One of Voltaire's characters in *Le Droit du seigneur* calls it an "impudent custom" (*Œuvres complètes*, 5:10), p. 10. Desfontaines wrote a play of the same title in 1783.

37 See Beaumarchais, *Œuvres*, 441. For an analysis of the fundamental theme of the bastard and the foundling, see Marthe Robert, *Roman des origines et origines du roman* (Paris: Grasset, 1972).

is a gentleman or even a prince—the belief that Freud later analyzed in *Moses and Monotheism* as a revolutionary fantasy. In this case, however, the Oedipal trio is involved in a trial over a breach of contract.

The first issue is to reach a consensus on the correct reading of the contract; is it "Laquelle somme je lui rendrai, ET je l'épouserai," or "laquelle somme je lui rendrai OU je l'épouserai,' ce qui est bien différent" [Which sum I will repay her *and* I will marry her; which sum I will repay her *or* I will marry her] (*Le Mariage*, 442). As both judge and interested party, the Count interprets the contract as an either/or clause, condemning Figaro to marry Marceline. Wriggling to avoid the sentence, Figaro recalls the parental authorization necessary for marriage, recounts how he was stolen as a child, and reveals the proof of his identity: the hieroglyph on his arm. Marceline and Bartholo recognize him as their son, Emmanuel. But when Bartholo points to Marceline, saying, "Voilà ta mère" [Behold your mother], Figaro balks in disbelief, asking if she isn't rather his mother substitute, or wet nurse (*Le Mariage*, 445). His dream of noble parents ends with the recognition of a resistant bourgeois father and a mother who has pursued him in marriage.

The reinstatement of a genetic line dissolves the judgment and the contract and fulfills the prophecy of legitimacy.[38] The recognition of filiation suggests that Figaro has based his sense of personal merit on the false assumption of nobility, but it averts the threat of Oedipus's tragic crime to the natural and social order. In the end, it is the wrong contract, based on wrong assumptions at the wrong time, and biology is there to dispel it. Moreover, Figaro's identifying hieroglyph proves paternity where it is usually surmise, since only the mother is known for certain in the tradition. Yet Marceline's transformation is perhaps most crucial. Initially portrayed as a ridiculous, unlikeable hag, she gains, by acknowledging her status as mother, a grace and a sensitivity that her demeanor, actions, and the rest of the play bear out.[39] As farce

38 For an elegant historical analysis of literary recognition, see Terence Cave, *Recognitions: A Study in Poetics* (Oxford: Clarendon, 1990) and Marshall Brown's perceptive discussion of this trial as a moment in the breakdown of classical unity in *Le Mariage* (*Preromanticism* [Stanford: University of California Press, 1991] 252–60).

39 See Agnes G. Raymond, "Figaro, fils naturel de Polly Baker? ou la réhabilitation de Marceline," *Comparative Literature Studies* 12 (1975): 36, concerning negative criticism about this passage for its cynicism and *bouffonnerie*.

turns into serious drama, Figaro too shows sensitivity. Unlike Diderot's notion of an ideal model, Figaro is unique not only because of his brilliance and agility, but because as a child who is lost, found, and reintegrated with both his biological and social family, he occupies a doubly legitimate place. In giving up the dream of noble parents, Figaro moves out from his personal family romance to that of society at large, demonstrating how one might live with equality among individuals in a cohesive bond where differences also prevail.

During the trial itself Marceline is defended by, and has as her judicial counsel, the very man who had abandoned her, Bartholo. She uses her own voice only after being recognized as a single mother. With the legal case dissolved, change now occurs. Marceline condemns in general the way men abandon women, although Beaumarchais carefully cut out an entire passage in which she characterizes herself as a victim of a derelict past. In it Marceline argues that although she was born to be wise and make use of her reason, inexperience could not withstand the pressure of vile seducers.

> Hommes plus qu'ingrats, qui flétrissez par le mépris les jouets de vos passions, vos victimes! c'est vous qu'il faut punir des erreurs de notre jeunesse; vous et vos magistrats, si vains du droit de nous juger, et qui nous laissent enlever, par leur coupable négligence, tout honnête moyen de subsister.

> [You men, lost to all sense of obligation, who stigmatize with your contempt the playthings of your passions—your victims! It's you who ought to be punished for the errors of our youth—you and your magistrates so vain of their right to judge us, who by their culpable negligence deprive us of all honest means of existence.][40]

Marceline's plea that justice in equality prevail recalls another famous speech: that of Miss Polly Baker, whose legal case was first pub-

---

40 *Le Mariage*, 446; *The Marriage*, 175–6. In a longer earlier version, intended for act 4, scene 11, Marceline first pleads that women without money and manners are slaves. Then she painfully recounts the events of her past: While working as a domestic, she fell ill and was treated by a doctor, who bled her; he took advantage of her weakness, and she was thrown out when Figaro was born. What had been her loss became her gain, her son, until he was stolen. She went to a judge who threw her in prison, but once his father became rich, the judge took her in as his servant.

lished in 1747. She denounced the inequality of a judicial system that punished only the mother for the birth of bastard offspring, and her story—like that of the contemporary television character Murphy Brown—had an extraordinary life in the media.[41] Widely publicized for over forty years, it became the subject of debate, from Diderot and Voltaire in France to the common readers of the press in Europe and the New England colonies. It was followed passionately for many years as a factual case and accepted as authentic by Abbé Raynal in *l'Histoire des deux Indes* (1770), until Benjamin Franklin confessed to having invented and written it, as Thomas Jefferson attested in 1818.[42] The latest reprint of Franklin's piece appeared on the op-ed page of the *New York Times* on 15 June 1992 as an ironic comment on the Dan Quayle–Murphy Brown controversy about single parenthood and family values. In Franklin, the passage is humorous; in Raynal, acerbic; in Diderot, light; and in Beaumarchais, serious again.

In pleading her case, Marceline not only goes beyond Miss Polly's stance but also shows a solidarity among women not found among the male characters of Beaumarchais's trilogy:

> Dans les rangs mêmes plus élevés, les femmes n'obtiennent de vous qu'une considération dérisoire; leurrées de respects apparents, dans une servitude réelle; traitées en mineures pour nos biens, punies en majeures pour nos fautes! ah, sous tous les aspects, votre conduite avec nous fait horreur ou pitié!

> [Even in the more exalted walks of life you accord us women no more than a derisory consideration. In a state of servitude behind the alluring pretenses of respect, treated as children where our possessions are concerned we are punished as responsible adults where our faults are in question! Ah! Whatever way one looks at it your conduct towards us must provoke horror or compassion!] (*Le Mariage*, 446–7; *The Marriage*, 176)

The problem of social and sexual inequality runs throughout the three plays—a girl must obey her tutor, a wife and servant must obey the

41 I would like thank Walter E. Rex for pointing out this convergence to me while I was working on the versions of the Baker story by Franklin, Diderot, and Raynal.

42 For a detailed account of this case, see Max Hall, *Benjamin Franklin and Polly Baker: The History of a Literary Deception* (Pittsburgh, Pa.: University of Pittsburgh Press, 1990).

master of the house, and only a woman may be punished for an illegitimate child. Marceline's speech addresses the public, though the story is not hers alone. If she is an ordinary woman, her ability to speak—like Miss Polly's—is not at all an ordinary occurrence. Women had no legal status or right to public speech, according to scholars of jurisprudence; the system of authority did not center on the individual, and dignity derived from being nothing in oneself.[43] Beaumarchais proposes, in Marceline's name, a new set of values about the individual, although they remained largely unexplored because Marceline's words were suppressed in performance until the 1950s.

The model for her exceptional discourse comes from criticism leveled at the feudal system, since her inability to speak, her status as juridical minor, could only be considered scandalous in a world where the individuality of a woman—like that of a man—was valued (Guilbert-Sledziewski, 38). Marceline's message is clear: "sois belle, si tu peux, sage si tu veux; mais sois considérée, il le faut" [Be fair if you can, wise if you will, but be circumspect you must] (*Le Mariage*, 388; *The Marriage*, 113–4). Perhaps what rendered Marceline's speeches unacceptable for so long was the force of this outraged female cry, this maternal call for dignity. Indeed, there was a considerable reaction against the character: her speeches were not performed; actresses did not want to play the part; and even today few analyses of the character exist. Does her speech possess a force far surpassing the condition of the character? Beaumarchais had suggested as much in his *Mémoires contre Goëzman*, when he denounced the defense of a woman—Mme Goëzman—who justified her having accepted money from him by saying that she was weak and inexperienced. On the contrary, he contended, her discourse was strong, provocative, insulting, and seductive—full of "mâles injures." With Marceline, however, Beaumarchais spins the same argument positively to show that moral discourse always centers on the woman's role.[44]

43 Elisabeth Guilbert-Sledziewski, "Naissance de la femme civile: la Révolution, la femme, le droit," *Pensée* 238 (1984): 37. A woman's judicial incapacity was clearly stated in the *Etablissement de 1270* by Louis IX: "De response de fame—Nule fame n'a response en cour laie, puisque ele a seigneur" (Guilbert-Sledziowski, 38).

44 "Mais que nous font, mon fils, les refus d'un homme injuste? ne regarde pas d'où tu viens, vois où tu vas: cela seul importe à chacun" [But what if an unjust man

With newfound maternal force, Marceline advises looking ahead, not back; Bartholo, in contrast, brushes off the past, avoiding responsibility by pleading youthful insanity in both his promises and actions. Thus rehabilitated through the maternity that formerly condemned her, Marceline reconstitutes her family: Figaro as her son, Suzanne as her future daughter-in-law, and Bartholo, who finally gives in to become her husband. Marceline's fate stands as a warning to the Count about the injustice of misplaced power and conduct toward women. What Figaro expresses to him about the inequity between merit and birthright, women could transpose to men: "Qu'avez-vous fait pour tant de biens? vous vous êtes donné la peine de naître, et rien de plus" [What have *you* done to deserve such advantages? Put yourself to the trouble of being born—nothing more] (*Le Mariage*, 469; *The Marriage*, 199).

In two important speeches, Marceline and Figaro address the audience and society, moving to a larger court of social jurisprudence, which, as Anne Ubersfeld suggests, is the goal of all theater. For each, the issue is the condition of their identity. Marceline's speech is as revolutionary as Figaro's, yet while both concern the accidents of birth, Figaro focuses on general inequities of rank and fortune in society, whereas Marceline criticizes the inequality between the sexes in reproduction and in family matters. Clearly, the plea for equality and justice still can be posed in two separate and paradoxical arguments, the first through a definition in which all parties are equal, the second through a conception of equality based on the complementarity of difference. The problem with the first argument is that universal equality may be firmly rooted in a specific set of parameters, whereas the problem with the second is that no addition of single identities or interests adds up to a universal principle. The ideal falls short because it cannot reconcile universality and difference.

Figaro's speech gained celebrity; Marceline's was silenced until recently, as seen in the history of the play's performances. Starting in 1785, Marceline's speech from act 3, scene 16, has been bracketed in

---

denies us justice, my son? Think no more about whence you came but whither you are bound. That is all that matters to any of us] (*Le Mariage*, 447, *The Marriage*, 176). "Nos jugements sur les mœurs se rapportent toujours aux femmes" (Beaumarchais, "Préface," *Le Mariage*, 362).

almost all editions; Beaumarchais indicates in a note that it was eliminated from the first performance in Paris by the actors themselves.[45]
Editions used by directors at the Comédie-Française show that throughout the eighteenth century, and during the twentieth century until
1956, Marceline's speech was never performed. In 1953, Jean Meyer
invoked the same tradition.[46] Jean Vilar's inclusion of the speech in
1956 at the Théâtre National Populaire marked a turning point,
because it has been performed ever since. Why this suppression? The
inappropriateness of dramatic tone (it was said to spoil the comic
momentum)? The story of a woman with doubtful mores (the argument of the censors)? Or the "ridiculousness of the character"? All of
these arguments have been used, but none satisfactorily explains the
continued suppression of a passage that Beaumarchais cared about
deeply; he not only insisted on restoring it to the written text of the
play but quoted from it extensively in his preface.

In addressing questions of inequality through birth, fortune, and
rank, does Figaro ask a broader, more inclusive question about injustice and inequality than Marceline, justifying in some sense the suppression of her speech within the play? Or is the concept of equality
different for men and for women, in which case a tradition of performance repeated this difference until the 1950s? To answer this question, we must first see how *La Mère coupable* completes the trilogy.

La Mère coupable takes place in 1790, twenty years after *Le Mariage de
Figaro*. The Count and Countess have lost a first biological son, and both
have illegitimate children, though neither is aware of the other's child;
nor do the children, who are in love with each other, know their situation. At the beginning of the play, the family consists of the Count and
Countess, Léon, Florestine, and the servants, Suzanne and Figaro. Léon
is the "natural child" of Chérubin and the Countess. The Count has
named himself godfather and guardian of Florestine, who is really his
love child. The action concerns the recognition of kinship lines and the
moral consequences of reconfiguring family relations in this context.

L'Autre Tartuffe, ou La Mère coupable, takes the first half of its name
from the character Bégearss, a traitorous Tartuffe figure. Hovering

45 See Beaumarchais, "Préface," 367–8.
46 Beaumarchais, *Le Mariage de Figaro*, ed. Jean Meyer (Paris: Seuil, 1953).

between drama and incipient melodrama, its major themes are the status of illegitimate children and a sympathetic if damning analysis of women's place in society. Bégearss's power comes from knowledge, not religion, a weapon he wields first to scare Léon and Florestine into believing they have the same father, and then to trick the Count into allowing him, rather than Léon, to marry Florestine and inherit the Count's fortune. Although the title suggests that Bégearss and Rosine figure symmetrically in their immorality, it is the Count and the Countess—Beaumarchais belabors the point—whose lives are parallel, as the libertine parents of illegitimate children.

Beaumarchais presses the asymmetrical judgment of their symmetrical roles, calling on the spectator to mix tears with the pain and pious repentance of the unfortunate Countess. "Les larmes qu'on verse au théâtre, sur des maux simulés qui ne font pas le mal de la réalité cruelle, sont bien douces" [The tears shed at the theater because of simulated evils, which hurt no one in reality, are quite sweet]. Through identification in feeling Beaumarchais seeks a moral end: "On se trouve si bon après la compassion" [It feels so good to have been compassionate] ("Un Mot sur *La Mère coupable*," 600). Compassion defines being as fundamentally sentient rather than rational, and Beaumarchais links himself with Rousseau in adapting this essential, presocial faculty to the notion of mixed gender: "j'[ai] composé [*La Mère coupable*] dans une intention droite et pure: avec la tête froide d'un homme et le cœur brûlant d'une femme, comme on l'a pensé de Rousseau" [My intention in *La Mère coupable* was straight and true: to write with the cool head of a man and the burning heart of a woman, just as Rousseau is thought to have done].

Beaumarchais thus uses the metaphor of the hermaphrodite to show that an aesthetic and moral alliance must be constructed between feeling and thought.[47] Sensibility may be primarily a female attribute, but its appropriation by men becomes a humanizing force.[48] Beyond the

47 "J'ai remarqué que cet ensemble, cet "hermaphrodisme" morale, est moins rare qu'on ne le croit" [I have noticed that this whole, this moral hermaphroditism, is not as rare as one might think] ("Un Mot sur *La Mère coupable*," 600–601).

48 In the *Encyclopédie*, sensibility is called "mother of humanity"; in *L'Orphelin de la Chine* (1755), Voltaire's character Idamé changes the warrior despot Genghis into a just leader, proving that her apparent weakness, maternal compassion, was in fact a

immediate moral lesson of *La Mère coupable*, Beaumarchais promotes the centrality of the woman's story for all moral discourse. By putting the errors of adultery in the past, he writes that he can concentrate on a woman's grave betrayal of her duties as a wife; otherwise, he would have had to call his play the *L'Epouse infidèle* or, more equally, *Les Epoux coupables*. Although libertine man and woman have been returned to the family economy, adultery is still a more serious offense for women than for men. The Count laments:

> Nos désordres, à nous, ne leur enlèvent presque rien; ne peuvent du moins leur ravir la certitude d'être mères, ce bien inestimable de la maternité! tandis que leur moindre caprice, un goût, une étourderie légère, détruit dans l'homme le bonheur . . . le bonheur de toute sa vie, la sécurité d'être père. Ah! ce n'est point légère- ment qu'on a donné tant d'importance à la fidélité des femmes! Le bien, le mal de la société, sont attachés à leur conduite; le paradis ou l'enfer des familles dépend à tout jamais de l'opinion qu'elle ont donnée d'elles.

> [Our own disorders take almost nothing away from them; at least they cannot rob them of the certainty of being mothers, the invaluable property of maternity; whereas the least whim or care- less fancy destroys happiness in men—the happiness of their own lives—the security of being fathers. It is not without good reason that the fidelity of women has been accorded so much impor- tance. Social good and evil are related to their behavior; familial paradise or hell is forever dependent on the opinion that they pro- ject of themselves.] (*La Mère coupable*, 620–1)

Here the Count announces that women carry the burden because of the certitude of maternity and the anxiety of uncertainty surrounding pater- nity. They are at the center of the family, the ones on whom the cohe- siveness of the whole depends. Even Marceline does not dispute that the

---

virtue (*Œuvres complètes* [Paris, 1877], 4:303–54). For the architect Le Doux the effects of feminization were so positive that he erected columns upon which the vir- tuous stories of mothers were inscribed, so that fathers and sons might praise them (*L'Architecture considérée sous le rapport de l'art, des mœurs et de la législation* [Paris, 1804], 160).

nature of woman differs from that of man with respect to children. In a variant she rejects the very possibility of abandoning her child: "L'abandonner! Oui, l'homme en est capable. Mais une mère! Un fils! . . . la femme inexperte ou sensible peut quelquefois manquer aux lois de la décence ou de la société, jamais à celles de la nature" [Abandon him! Yes, man is capable of such an act. But a mother! A son! . . . Being unskilled or sensitive, a woman sometimes fails before the laws of decency or society, but never before those of nature] (*Le Mariage*, 1385).

In the search for a more democratic family contract than the ancien régime had allowed, the clinging to a definition based in nature creates a dislocation in the concept of equality. Natural law was not considered to have been transgressed when men and women could follow a so-called natural vocation: power and public life for men, motherhood and the family for women.[49] The division between men as the principal authorities and women as the subordinate agents of natural regeneration of the family and society is borne out by the very different reactions of the Count and Countess to the discovery of the illegitimacy and true identity of Léon and Florestine. Whereas the Count had pleaded for equality in love in *Le Barbier*, in *Le Mariage* he contradicts himself concerning the Countess's infidelity and even threatens divorce. The Countess, who had pardoned the Count in *Le Mariage* in a way she says he never would have done, pleads in *La Mère coupable* for equal indulgence and caring for all. Acknowledging their respective transgressions of an outdated marriage arrangement, she proposes a renewal of marriage in reciprocity: "Faisons, sans nous parler, l'échange de notre indulgence!" [Silently, let us exchange forgiveness!] (*La Mère coupable*, 639).[50]

Attempting to make the characters accountable for their destiny, Beaumarchais, throughout these plays, heightens the role of mothers and diminishes the authority of fathers. Bartholo is the only father in the first two plays; as a "père marâtre," he is no role model at all. The Countess, however, chooses to "serve . . . as mother" to Florestine, whom she

49 See Elke Harten and Hans-Christian Harten, *Femmes, culture et révolution*, trans. Bella Chabot, Jeanne Etoré, and Olivier Mannoni (Paris: Des Femmes, 1988), 22.

50 See also *La Nourrice républicaine ou les plaisirs de l'adoption: Répertoire du théâtre républicain ou recueil de pièces imprimées avant, pendant, et après la République Française*, vol. 7 (Geneva: Slatkine, 1986).

likens to her own flesh. Occupying the double position of biological and substitute mother, she brings the illegitimate child into a new structure that fuses both a "natural" and a social family. Despite her own liberal view, the Countess still acquiesces to an unequal vision of the moral drama, crying out abjectly that the guilt is hers:

> Mère coupable! épouse indigne! Un instant nous a tous perdus. J'ai mis l'horreur dans ma famille! J'allumai la guerre intestine entre le père et les enfants! Ciel juste! il fallait bien que ce crime fût découvert! Puisse ma mort expier mon forfait!

> [Guilty mother! Unworthy wife! An instant has caused us to lose everything. I put horror into my family! I ignited an internecine war between father and children. Just heaven, this crime had to be discovered! May my death expiate (atone for) this infamous crime!] (659–60)

By the contrast between the Count and the Countess, and her assumption of guilt (evident in the title of the play), Beaumarchais tacitly asks whether the Countess is any guiltier than the Count. The answer may be no in twentieth-century terms, and even according to Rousseau's social contract, but the myth of natural regeneration through the mother was doubly threatening with the progressive loosening of the father's role, and may have made the answer, in the eighteenth century, yes, she is guiltier. If it then seems clear that there is some "natural vocation" attached to a notion of "nature" that none of the characters quite relinquishes, it is unclear how anxiety and guilt play themselves out in the context of these changing roles and political determinations.

Freud suggested that the fraternity of the primal horde had created the collective guilt that life in politics and the family seemed constantly to revive. To alleviate anxiety, he argued that women had to remain pure; neither the Countess nor Marceline had, yet their mistakes were no worse than those of the men. But Freud made the "sense of guilt of the son" fundamental, corresponding to one of the two repressed wishes of the Oedipus complex: parricide and the taboo of incest as the inauguration of social organization.[51] Two points are of interest in

51 The other was sparing the totem animal as the undoing of parricide (*Totem and Taboo*, trans. A. A. Brill [New York: Vintage, 1918], 185).

this regard. *La Mère coupable* premiered in 1792, the year of the arrest and condemnation of the king.[52] By showing the Count in the role of benevolent father and making him repent, Beaumarchais suggested that it was unnecessary to condemn the father/authority/aristocrat; it was only necessary to condemn and exclude Bégearss. We can then say of this drama what Hunt says of the French Revolution, that it is "about conflict between father and son and about the threat of violence to the community."[53] After all, the last line of *La Mère coupable* is Figaro's: "Ne plaignons point quelques moments de trouble; on gagne assez dans les familles, quand on en expulse un méchant" [Let us not regret a few moments of turmoil; the family gains considerably when a villain has been expelled] (672). Second, when Figaro ultimately figures out the strategy deployed by Bégearss to evoke fear of recognition and the horror of incest within the family, he states the biological facts: Léon and Florestine are in fact not kin to each other; they endanger no one, and nothing at all. So the two "children" are free to marry.

Whereas the trial between Marceline and Figaro in *Le Mariage* removes incest by recognizing mother, father and son, and leads paradoxically to the legitimation of the biological family through a marital contract, in *La Mère coupable* incest is never really a problem. In a curiously regressive move, nature prevails over convention; it is the contract between Marceline and Figaro that seemed to threaten the order of nature and society by institutionalizing incest. When the three plays end, Marceline, the Count, and the Countess have all experienced a similar problem—the illegitimacy of a child. This symmetry permits the passage from the old, hierarchical family to a new, perhaps even harmonious, family; the Count assumes his legal role as father of Léon, and the Countess chooses the function of substitute mother for Florestine. The new family contract redomesticates conflict by basing order on a feeling that extends the concept of mother and father beyond biological to social bonds.

52 Written in 1790, finished in January 1791, *La Mère coupable* was first presented at the Théâtre du Marais in 1792, for fourteen performances. In 1797, there were only five performances; the critics were harsh, and the audience was bored (see Beaumarchais, 1476).

53 Hunt threads her way between a Freudian and a Girardian analysis of the foundation of society (12).

Marceline's demand for equality in *Le Mariage* is reinforced by the Countess's plea for mercy in *La Mère coupable*. Not only tone but position differentiates them: Marceline rises in status from an old maid to a single, unwed mother (one of whose names is that of the biblical surrogate Hagar) to wife and legitimate mother; the Countess, on the other hand, harbors her illegitimate son in the privacy of her "legitimate" family. Prior to the scenes of recognition, these two women play out two opposed forms of action. Marceline can speak out in the name of equality and rights because she has nothing to lose; viewed as neither wife nor legitimate mother, she is not subject to the former laws of the family. Speaking out ran deeply counter to a wife's function in the ancien régime; although a woman agreed to marriage as a free contractant, she lost that status the moment she entered into the contract and became defined once again as a minor.[54] The Countess, however, tries to cope within an outdated feudal structure; her "natural" vocation as woman is obscured by the tradition of punishing adultery in women alone by up to three years' confinement in a convent at the husband's behest.

La Mère coupable was staged just as discussions of the marriage contract began in 1792. The Constituent Assembly fundamentally upset the theoretical and actual status of women in an article from 3 September 1791, decreeing that marriage was no longer a sacrament but a contract based purely on civil right. The contractual partner was made equal in capacity, consistent with the principles of freedom and equality pronounced in 1789. Women ceased to be Eve or Mary, at least before the law; they were no longer viewed as creatures determined according to their species, designed to marry and conceive children (Guilbert-Sledziewski, 34). Thus, the ability to marry as equal partner contained in theoretical germ the ability to divorce.

The equalizing of positions was a step toward the democratization of the family hierarchy; now a combination of reason and sensibility held the structure together. In the discussions surrounding the causes for divorce, M. Aubert-Dubayet proclaimed the equality of partners in their right to separate:

54 Nadine Bérenguier points out this transformation in her unpublished manuscript "L'Infortune des alliances: Contrat, mariage, et roman au dix-huitième siècle," (1993), 79. Not until 1792 was the concept of equality between married partners put forth.

Il est temps de le reconnaître, le contrat qui lie les époux est commun; ils doivent incontestablement jouir des mêmes droits, et la
femme ne doit point être l'esclave de l'homme. L'hymen n'admet
point l'asservissement d'une seule des parties.

[It is time to recognize that the contract that binds spouses is common; they must unquestionably enjoy the same rights, and a woman
must not be the slave of a man. Marriage does not admit the sub-
servience of either party.] (*Moniteur universel,* 30 August 1792)

In another speech, Léonard Robin traced this right to a universal law
of freedom:

La Déclaration des droits et l'article de la constitution, qui veut que
le mariage ne soit regardé, par la loi, que comme un contrat civil,
vous ont paru avoir consacré le principe, et votre décret n'en est que
la déclaration. . . . Le comité a cru devoir conserver ou accorder la
plus grande latitude à la faculté du divorce, à cause de la nature du
contrat de mariage, qui a pour base principale le consentement des
époux, et parce que la liberté individuelle ne peut jamais être alié-
née d'une manière indissoluble par aucune convention.

[The declaration of rights and the article of the constitution which
says that marriage must only be regarded as a civil contract in the
eyes of the law has appeared to you to have sanctioned the principle, and your decree is the declaration of that. . . . The committee
felt that it had to maintain or award the greatest latitude to the
right of divorce because of the nature of the marriage contract,
which has as its basic principle the consent of spouses, and
because individual liberty can never be alienated indissolubly by
any convention.] (*Moniteur universel,* 7 September 1792)

The advocates of divorce abandoned the sacred view of marriage in
a return to natural law, which would then ground conventional rule.
But M. Sédillez warned about the discrepancy between rights and facts:
"Il est à craindre que dans les mains du mari ce ne soit un moyen de
plus d'abuser de sa puissance; car, oserai-je le dire? la liberté et l'égal-
ité n'existent pas encore en France pour les femmes. Le divorce ne
sera jamais pour elles qu'un triste remède" [It is to be feared that in

the hands of the husband (divorce) may become yet another means of abusing his power; for—dare I say it?—liberty and equality do not yet exist for women in France. For women, divorce will never be more than a meager remedy] (*Moniteur universal,* 15 September 1792). The clarity of purpose in the speeches cited from *Le Moniteur* was not always followed by the stories of individuals, as *La Mère coupable* demonstrates poignantly. Beaumarchais situates the play in 1790, prior to the decrees on divorce and marriage, but the Count invokes divorce on several occasions. Neither he nor the Countess seems to understand that they have become more equal, for not only is there reticence about the new law, but the Count misconstrues its consequences, seeking in his jealousy to blackmail and wreak vengeance upon the Countess. Neither grasps that the decree on divorce effects a juridical and political change from a state of *incapacity* to one *capable of action* (Guilbert-Sledziewski, 45).

Women and men were thus empowered to exert their will, and women were no longer minors but adults. Neither the model for moral conduct in the *drame bourgeois* nor the happy endings of Beaumarchais's plays could quell the emerging question of the individual in relation to all others: Who am I? And who are you (the spectator)? The characters can no more answer these questions than restore order to an increasingly disordered world. If these plays grew out of the *drame bourgeois,* they unraveled the model for a moralizing stance. What followed was the cultural explosion of the Revolution, as Anne Ubersfeld has shown.[55] The absurdity of the action nullifies any pretense to political positioning. It is not clear, for example, which is more threatening: the *droit du seigneur* as a specter of power from the past or the uncalculated risk and unknown damage that the civil contract may bring.

The dissolution of what had been up until then an indissoluble contract awarded legal symmetry to both men and women in nonfoundational principles of civil law (Guilbert-Sledziewski, 42). The fear remained, however, that the family would explode, so that individuals, encouraged to make their differences explicit, would be atomized under civil rule. Women gained a new status as the sacred institution of

55 The above commentary rephrases Ubersfeld's argument in "Un Balcon sur la Terreur: *Le Mariage de Figaro,*" *Europe* (April 1973), 105–15.

marriage yielded to the will and rights of the individual. As family cohesion under the authority of the father weakened, both the individual and the state gained strength.[56] This fragmentation continued with the decree on succession (August 1791) and was radicalized during the Legislative Assembly with the suppression of *patria potestas* (the power of life and death over sons) in August 1792.

A great deal of conflict still surrounds these questions and similar topics as the end of the twentieth century approaches. Today's reader of Beaumarchais must glean the movement toward civil and human rights from stories fraught with contradiction and human flaw. As Flax has suggested, "[A]mbivalence is an appropriate response to an inherently conflictual situation. The problem lies not in the ambivalence, but in the premature attempts to resolve or deny conflicts. The lack of coherence or closure in a situation and the existence of contradictory wishes or ideas too often generate anxiety so intense that aspects of the ambivalence and its source are repressed"(11). Is that what happened to Marceline's speech? Both *Le Barbier de Séville* and *Le Mariage de Figaro* have survived in the repertory of the Comédie-Française and live on in the works of Rossini and Mozart, among others. But it was not until 1964, when Darius Milhaud set Madeleine Milhaud's libretto to music, that *La Mère coupable* found its operatic voice. The 1990 performance of the play by the Comédie-Française was the first since 1850. *La Mère coupable* had been criticized in much the same terms as Marceline's speech: it was not comic or light enough, and its tone was "wrong." But the director articulated its modernity through its melodrama and its ability to bring the great themes of the *Oresteia* to everyday life.[57] By questioning "the temptation to construct a 'successor project' to fill the void left by the failures of the Enlightenment"(11), Flax recognizes the need to resist shutting out a troubling scenario or grasping at new metanarratives; it is important to stay with the anxiety that individual stories may create.

Péguy was right to align the movement of Beaumarchais's trilogy

56 Legislation on bastards is a good example, as I have argued in "Legitimating Change: The Decrees on Bastardy during the French Revolution," *University of Toronto Quarterly* 61 (1992): 449–59.

57 "Cette légère irréalité si familière: Un Entretien avec Jean-Pierre Vincent," *Comédie-Française* 183 (1990): 21.

with the changing temper and concerns of the years from 1775 to 1792. The connection with our own times has now been fancifully mapped out in the opera commissioned by the Metropolitan Opera Company for its hundredth anniversary: composer John Corigliano and librettist William M. Hoffman's *Ghosts of Versailles, Suggested by "La Mère coupable" of Pierre-Augustin Caron de Beaumarchais*, performed in 1992. Because a single voice, theory, or solution, like one politics or politician, may dominate at a given time, one can hope that the political correlative of change might be tolerance for other voices as well as the creation of new solutions and forms—be they philosophic, literary, or social. A new social form rooted in an identity willed from a rereading of the past renews and recombines received patterns in a dialogue with that past. Literature's function in effecting change and literature's changing affect allow anxiety to reconstruct imaginative scenarios that create, sustain, and accompany us, however discontinuously, on our journey.

The

Eighteenth-Century

Beauty Contest | Michael B. Prince

Take a good look at this woman," the cover of a recent special edition of *Time* proclaims. "She was created by a computer from a mix of several races. What you see is a remarkable preview of . . . The New Face of America." Her name is reassurance: mixture obeying an inner rule, disproving all the feared consequences of miscegenation. Her truth is beauty: a placid sensuality whose immediate appeal suspends all doubts about her questionable origin. She is the future reproducing the past, assuring us that despite the very real changes in the demographic complexion of America, Greek Beauty, Helen with a tan, will always be our point of return, as she was the point of departure for so many ill-fated ships.

Not content with the image alone, as if, by itself, the picture could not be counted on to provide *that* much assurance, the managing editor finds it necessary to add an account of her genesis. "When the editors were looking for a way to dramatize the impact of interethnic mar-

I thank the following individuals who read the manuscript and gave me sound advice: Julia Brown, Abigail Gillman, Jon Klancher, Raimonda Modiano, and Charles Rzepka. I also thank Marshall Brown for the opportunity to present this essay orally at the Modern Language Association convention in Toronto, 1993. The American Council of Learned Societies and the Boston University Humanities Foundation supported the research for this essay.

Cover, *Time*, fall 1993 special issue. © 1993 Time Inc. Reprinted by permission.

riage, which has increased dramatically in the U.S. during the latest wave of immigration, they turned to [a computer process called] morphing to create the kind of offspring that might result from seven men and seven women of various ethnic and racial backgrounds" (2). Morphing, short for "metamorphosis," allows the computer "to produce the various combinations of offspring" likely to result when an African female model and a Chinese male model, or a Vietnamese female model and an Italian male model, mate. The editor fails to mention, however, that the cybergenetic cover girl has not been derived from any specific interracial coupling: she is the fantasy work of male cybergeneticists, who have constructed an ideal face from the best sight bytes of all the beautiful female models. She is 15 percent Anglo-Saxon, 17.5 percent Middle Eastern, 17.5 percent African, 7.5 percent Asian, 35 percent Southern European, and 7.5 percent Hispanic. Although racially mixed, her perfection resides in the effacement of any telltale sign of a particular race or ethnicity. She does not exist, the editor reminds us, "except metaphysically."

Despite the claim that the image is new, the editor's explanation constantly alludes to the Western metaphysical and literary tradition. "As the onlookers watched the image of our new Eve begin to appear on our computer screen, several staff members promptly fell in love. Said one, 'It really breaks my heart that she doesn't exist.' We sympathize with our lovelorn colleagues, but even technology has its limits. This is a love that must forever remain unrequited" (2). Postmodern Pygmalions, cybernetic Petrarchans, they need the cold image of absolute beauty to stop the flow of change, and then they wish she would change into something a little warmer. *Odi et amo. quare id faciam, fortasse requiris?* (Catullus: "I hate and I love. Why do I do this? You may well ask").[1] Fortunate man! thought Petrarch of Dante, whose breathing love died so that she might through his verses live on, "a privilege of lovers released from all human qualities."[2]

What is the origin of this modern, technologically assisted beauty contest, in which multiple, anonymous female contestants sit before

1 Catullus, *The Poems*, ed. Kenneth Quinn, 2d ed. (New York: St. Martin's, 1973), no. 85, p. 78.

2 *Petrarch's Lyric Poems: The Rime Sparse and Other Lyrics*, trans. and ed. Robert M. Durling (Cambridge, Mass.: Harvard University Press, 1976), Rime Sparse no. 15, p. 50.

male judges? Is the obsession with fixing beauty as old as human desire and the inevitable encounter with death, as Elizabeth Bronfen has argued?[3] Or does the calculus of beauty have a more recent origin, dating, as Naomi Wolf has claimed, from the early nineteenth century, when the threat of female emancipation brought about new forms of physical and psychic control?[4] While the postmodern beauty contest has its roots in antiquity and in the tradition of Christian Neoplatonism descending through Renaissance humanists such as Agnolo Firenzuola, the beauty contest takes its modern form in the mid–eighteenth century, when the vestiges of Christian Neoplatonism encounter the secularizing and calculating tendencies of Lockean empiricism. Beauty and science fuse, so as to assign inevitability (predictability) to realms of being not open to precise calculation. With the emergence of philosophical aesthetics, the beauty contest divests itself of older, theologically driven inquiries to rule new disciplines such as anthropology, sociology, genetics, and the sciences of domesticity.

The Eighteenth-Century Beauty Contest

The phrase "beauty contest" is not being used metaphorically, in the sense that the entire search for a standard of taste or judgment characteristic of the first half of the eighteenth century could be described as an extended beauty contest. Twentieth-century morphing has its eighteenth-century equivalent in an equally rigorous rating system. Joseph Spence claims that "a Scale might be settled, by which one

3 See Bronfen, *Over Her Dead Body: Death, Femininity, and the Aesthetic* (New York: Routledge, 1992), esp. pt. 1. "We invest in images of wholeness, purity, and the immaculate owing to our fear of dissolution and decay. . . . Pleasure at the Beauty of Woman resides in the uncanny simultaneity of recognizing and misrecognizing it as a veil for death. . . . Beauty always includes death's inscription" (62–3).

4 See Wolf, *The Beauty Myth: How Images of Beauty Are Used against Women* (New York: Doubleday, 1991). "The beauty myth in its modern form is a fairly recent invention. The myth flourishes when material constraints on women are dangerously loosened. . . . The beauty myth in its modern form gained ground after the upheavals of industrialization. . . . Most of our assumptions about the way women have always thought about 'beauty' date from no earlier than the 1830s, when the cult of domesticity was first consolidated and the beauty index invented" (14–5).

might judge tolerably well of the proportional excellence in any of our most celebrated beauties."[5]

> I should assign to Lady B, * * *, Eight for Color, Four for Shape, Twenty-five for Expression, and Ten for Grace; in all, Forty-seven; not quite half-way in the complete Sum of Excellence:—To Mrs. A * * *, Eight for Color, Seventeen for Shape, Fifteen for Expression, and Twenty for Grace; in all, Sixty Degrees of Excellence:—And to Mrs. B * * *, Eight for Color, Ten for Shape, Twenty-five for Expression, and Thirty for Grace; in all Seventy-three. And that is the highest Sum, that I could in Conscience allow to any Woman that I have ever yet seen. (44)

One might dismiss Spence's scale as the machination of a minor figure plying an outmoded genre (dialogue-imitation), hardly representative of the religious and philosophical tradition (Christian Neoplatonism) Spence hopes to defend.[6] Yet, as Walter Benjamin observes, the minor work, the hopelessly flawed instance of a genre, often manifests the most characteristic features of a philosophy or an ideology.[7] So it is with Spence: the dialogue on beauty ending in a beauty contest literalizes the dominant claim of philosophical aesthetics from Shaftesbury through Kant—that a mixed, increasingly heterogeneous audience could in theory be united through its shared responsiveness to select aesthetic phenomena. The numerical evaluation of known beauties renders theory concrete: it proves that men of discernment (but, by extension, all correctly trained individuals) can make judg-

---

5 Sir Harry Beaumont [Joseph Spence], *Crito; or, A Dialogue on Beauty* (1752; rpt. New York: Garland, 1970), 44.

6 The purpose of his analysis of female beauty, as Spence writes, is to reveal "the real Beauty of the other Works of Nature . . . one great universal Beauty of all created Matter taken in one View . . . the Goodness of God, as displayed in the Works of the Creation" (p. 57).

7 "We will be guided by the assumption that what seems diffuse and disparate will be found to be linked in the adequate concepts as elements in a synthesis. And so the production of lesser writers, whose works frequently contain the most eccentric features, will be valued no less than those of the great writer. It is one thing to incarnate a form; it is quite a different thing to give it its characteristic expression. Whereas the former is the business of the poet elect, the latter is often done incomparably more distinctly in the laborious efforts of minor writers" (Benjamin, *The Origin of German Tragic Drama*, trans. John Osborne [London: Verso, 1977], 57–8).

ments of value according to a shared norm, the perfect one hundred. Thus, the task of evaluating beautiful women serves a higher ideal, bridging sensible and supersensible realms, providing a calculus for comportment.

Calculating female beauty begins much earlier than the eighteenth century. In Firenzuola's *Dialogue on the Beauty of Women* (1548) the philosophical gallant, Celso, teaches four ladies of the Prato how to conceive of the ideal (intellectual) beauty, what rules of mathematical proportion inform the perfection of each body part, and how the best parts of each woman might be borrowed and combined in an ideal portrait.[8] Firenzuola makes it clear that his sources are both classical (Plato's *Symposium*, Aristotle's *Nichomachean Ethics*, and Cicero's *Tusculan Disputations*) and Christian (Petrarch's *Canzoniere*, Ficino's *Commentary on Plato's Symposium on Love*, and Alberti's *On Painting and on Sculpture*). Like many Renaissance Neoplatonists, Firenzuola's mouthpiece likens his derivation of the ideal beauty to the story of Zeuxis of Heraclea, who, when asked to paint a portrait of Helen, requested that five beautiful women be brought before him to donate their best parts to his composite. They sat still, while they were first dismembered, and then remembered in light of the ideal.[9]

To some extent, Spence's *Dialogue on Beauty*, along with numerous Platonic imitations appearing during the mid-1700s, represents a continuation of this Christian, Neoplatonic tradition.[10] But in one impor-

8 See the edition of *On the Beauty of Women*, ed. Konrad Eisenbichler and Jacqueline Murray (Philadelphia: University of Pennsylvania Press, 1992).

9 "Thus, I will take from each one of the four of you," Celso tells the women, "and will do like Zeuxis" (Firenzuola, 13). The dialogue is in many ways more interesting than its eighteenth-century successors because the women are permitted to venture questions and objections. Why, asks one, is Zeuxis's composite derivation of the ideal beauty limited to an extrapolation from women? "When you speak of beauty in general," Mona Lampianda asks, "are you referring to men or to women, or are you speaking of one and the other interchangeably?" (15). Elsewhere, Selvaggia playfully literalizes Celso's fantasy of taking the best parts of different women: "Leny, bring the scissors here so we can cut it [Verdespina's hair]. But how would you like her to cut it? Close-cropped?" (48).

10 Testimony to the proliferation of translations and imitations of Plato comes from Richard Hurd. He complains, "Not that I presume to think it [Platonic dialogue] unworthy of imitation. But the public taste, as appears, is running full fast that

tant respect, the example of Zeuxis and the Renaissance appropriation
of Plato's *Symposium* are quite different. Zeuxis has ascended the Platonic ladder of material beauties, as Socrates (paraphrasing Diotima)
describes it in the *Symposium*, and has returned to earth, his knowledge
of the ideal intact, to sit in judgment over inferior forms. He, like
Celso, knows the ideal before borrowing spare parts from living
women. The power to judge, to discriminate good from bad, right
from wrong, healthy from deformed, resides in this prior acquaintance
with unadulterated Beauty. But by the mid–eighteenth century direct
access to the divine archetype has been lost, and the beauty contest, a
soon-to-be pop-cultural ritual embedded in serious philosophical discourse, seeks to recover it.

How the template was lost is part of the complex history of secularization, which I shall not attempt to detail here. But one aspect is
important to stress. If Zeuxis's painting and the image on the cover of
Time prove the efficacy of an inductive logic moving transcendentally
from lower (physical) beauties to the highest (metaphysical) Beauty,
skeptics such as David Hume were dismantling the theoretical basis for
this operation. They denied the very logic of abstraction, which had
always sustained the teleological ascent from nature to revelation. "If
they tell me," writes Hume, "that they have mounted on the steps, or by
the gradual ascent of reason, and by drawing inferences from effects to
causes, I still insist that they have aided the ascent of reason by the
wings of imagination."[11] He mocks transcendental induction as a by-
product of pseudo-empirical procedures, a projection of desire and
imagination rather than the result of inductive method. Elsewhere, he
even more explicitly negates the analogical move from lower effects to
higher causes and then back:

In general, it may, I think, be established as a maxim that where
any cause is known only by its particular effects, it must be impos-

way, insomuch, that some may even doubt, if the state of literary composition be more
endangered by the neglect, or vicious imitation, of the Platonic manner" (in Q. Hor-
atii Flacci, *Epistolae ad Pisones, et Augustum: With an English Commentary and Notes*, trans.
Richard Hurd, 3 vols., 5th ed. [London: T. Cadell, 1776], 1:250).

11 Hume, "Of a Particular Providence and of a Future State," in *An Inquiry concerning Human Understanding*, ed. Charles W. Hendel (Indianapolis, Ind.: Bobbs Mer-
rill, 1955), 147–8.

sible to infer any new effects from that cause, since the qualities which are requisite to produce these new effects along with the former must either be different, or superior, or of more extensive operation than those which simply produced the effect, whence alone the cause is supposed to be known to us. (Hume, 154 n. 7)

The maxim deprives transcendental induction of its vertical axis, knocking the ladder out from under Zeuxis. His progress from known beauties to the ideal form, and then back, begins with an ordinary preference for one beauty over another (which Hume would allow) but moves then to the metaphysical claim that by abstracting from personal preferences one could arrive at an ideal Beauty, somehow causing or participating in all lesser effects.

Hume's source for this extreme skepticism may well have been the ancient Greek skeptic Pyrrho, given new currency in Thomas Stanley's *History of Philosophy* (3d ed., 1701) and in Pierre Bayle's favorable essay on Pyrrho in *Dictionnaire historique et critique* (1697).[12] Summarizing Sextus Empiricus's account of Pyrrhonism, Stanley transmits the following critique of transcendental induction:

> Induction . . . may easily be overthrown; for . . . by it they [dogma-tists] would prove an Universal from Particulars. [But] either they must do it, as having examined all Particulars, or only some. If only some, the Induction will not be valid, it being possible, that some of the omitted Particulars may be found contrary to the Universal Proposition. If they would examine all, they attempt Impos-sibles, for Particulars are infinite and undeterminate. Thus it happens, that Induction cannot *subsist* either way.[13]

12 Stanley's *History* appeared between 1655 and 1662 and reached a fourth edi-tion in 1743. On the transmission of Pyrrhonism to the eighteenth century see Richard H. Popkin, "Sources of Knowledge of Sextus Empiricus in Hume's Time," *Journal of the History of Ideas* 54 (1993): 137–41.

13 Stanley, *The History of Philosophy: Containing the Lives, Opinions, Actions, and Dis-courses of the Philosophers of Every Sect*, 3d ed. (London: W. Battersby, 1701), 505. Induc-tion is precisely the operation claimed to be taking place in what the postmodern cybergeneticists describe as "morphing." From known instances of beauty, they have induced, through a computer-generated program, a series of abstractions, producing the divine image. They have thus rescued from a time of cultural and intellectual indeterminacy the ultimate Platonic abstraction.

The philosophical Christianity common to Sprat, Locke, and all pro-
ponents of physico-theology depended upon the intellectual operation denied in this Pyrrhonian commonplace. Early apologists for the
Royal Society held that the empirical sciences posed no threat to Christianity because an impartial investigation of natural effects (Particulars) would disclose a beautiful contrivance (the Universal Proposition), thus securing both design here, and by analogy, a benevolent
Designer there. A more fully secularized empiricism, with its emphasis
upon particulars freed from any a priori interpretative scheme, threatens this analogical structure. And Pyrrhonian skepticism, as adopted by
Hume, subverts the very logic of analogy.

Philosophical aesthetics attempts to rescue design from the Pyrrhonian abyss. If Hume and the skeptics denied the logic of analogy linking known effects (for example, order in natural phenomena) to an
unknown cause (God as providential Orderer), then perhaps it would
still be possible to identify certain exemplary objects (natural or artistic) whose inner organization exhibited such a wondrous sense of
contrivance, that one had to grant the hypothesis of design. Without
recourse to the endangered analogy referring every sign in the book of
nature to a coordinate in the book of revelation, one would still have
to acknowledge a marvelous relation of part to whole within the exemplary object. The search was on for an earthly sign (an empirical fact)
so invested with the aura of divinity (with inner creative purposiveness)
that it became in itself part and whole, physical mark and metaphysical
emblem.[14]

Philosophical aesthetics begins in Shaftesbury's late essays on the

14 As M. H. Abrams has shown, philosophical aesthetics is radically continuous
with the older project of rational Christianity (physico-theology). It merely transfers
design from a quality attributed to all of nature to one exemplified by certain aesthetic objects. "The antecedents of heterocosmic theory emerged in critics of literature who, beginning in the late fifteenth century, reversed the traditional comparison
of God the creator to a human artisan by making the portentous comparison of the
literary artisan to God the creator. . . . [But] not until the eighteenth century was the
divine analogy converted from a topic of laudation into a principle of critical theory,
for only then was the concept that a poem is its own world exploited so as to qualify,
then to displace, the concept that a poem is a credible imitation of the existing
world" (Abrams, "From Addison to Kant: Modern Aesthetics and the Exemplary Art,"
in *Studies in Eighteenth-Century British Art and Aesthetics,* ed. Ralph Cohen [Berkeley:
University of California Press, 1985], 28–9).

fine arts (1712–13) and in Hutcheson's *An Inquiry into the Original of Our Ideas of Beauty and Virtue* (1726) as an attempt to locate an exemplary object of beauty whose inner contrivance, the dialectical reduction of parts to whole, would convince all (correctly ordered) viewers of a transcendental cause for order. Shaftesbury's definition of the "heroic tablature" suggests how the vocabulary of design passes out of a more comprehensive Christian Neoplatonism and into the special study of plastic art: the tablature is "a single piece, comprehended in one view, and formed according to one single intelligence, meaning, or design; which constitutes a real whole, by a mutual and necessary relation of parts, the same as of the members of a natural body."[15] Studying design in the fine arts, which Shaftesbury calls "second characters," becomes a precondition for knowing the principle of order in ethics, politics, and divinity, which he calls "first characters." With the aesthetic reversal, the attributes of beauty provide an inner rule for all of creation, as Shaftesbury outlines in *Plastics; or, The Original Progress and Power of Designatory Art* (1712). The Divine Creator becomes a "creatrix, or sovereign plastic nature," ensuring that "within the inward, several species (within the genus) as in dogs and fowls, which breed with one another, a natural propensity [exists] for like joining with like; so that the breed when mixed or blended, in time and after several consequent generations displays and opens itself, and the orders return to their first natural secretions, purity and simplicity of form" (Rand, 121–2).

Shaftesbury's great disciple, Francis Hutcheson, would develop this argument, asserting that a uniform responsiveness to beautiful objects proves the existence of a shared moral sense and thus a concrete basis for a universalist ethics. "It plainly appears 'that some Objects are *immediately* the Occasions of this Pleasure of Beauty, and that we have Senses fitted for perceiving it. . . . The Ideas of Beauty and Harmony, like other sensible Ideas, are *necessarily* pleasant to us, as well as immediately so.'"[16] If such were the case, then the logic of transcendental dialectic would be restored under the single representative sign of

15 Cited in *Second Characters; or, The Language of Forms*, ed. Benjamin Rand (Cambridge: Cambridge University Press, 1914), 32.

16 Hutcheson, *An Inquiry into the Original of Our Ideas of Beauty and Virtue*, 2d ed. (1726; rpt. New York: Garland, 1971), 11–2.

Beauty. Our immediate, virtually intuitive response to the exemplary material sign acquaints us with higher principles of virtue founded upon the equation of natural and divine order. "Nor could *Example* any more engage us to pursue Objects as *Beautiful* or *Harmonious* had we no *natural Sense* of *Beauty* or *Harmony*" (Hutcheson, 94).

Why did this compression of the design argument into a search for the single exemplary sign occur during the first half of the eighteenth century? To the extent moral philosophers continued to operate within a metaphysical (Neoplatonic) tradition, the recovery of the larger sense of design required only that one locate somewhere in the natural order a single example of a natural correspondence of parts within the whole. Pope may have feared, "From Nature's chain whatever link you strike, / Tenth, or ten thousandth, breaks the chain alike," but to the metaphysical mind, the chain was equally upheld by locating a single link whose spontaneous obedience to an inner hierarchical necessity verified the causal logic animating hierarchy all the way up the scale of being.[17]

In addition, the collapse of design into a quest for the exemplary image was a defensive strategy against skeptics who were ready to extend the Pyrrhonian attack against induction into a critique of signification itself. Because, according to Sextus Empiricus, a sign operates like a demonstration, and because that demonstration also depends on abstracting from particulars (e.g., different instances of trees) to generalities (e.g., the idea derived from the sign, "tree"), the Pyrrhonian critique of dialectical induction is no less applicable to signification itself. Here again is Stanley, summarizing Sextus Empiricus summarizing Pyrrho and sounding much like Derrida:

> An Endictick sign . . . is that, which is not observed together with an evident significate, but of its own nature and constitution signifieth that whereof it is a sign. . . . Now if it be a sign detective of the Consequent, either the Consequent is manifest or unmanifest; if manifest, it needs no detective, for it will be comprehended together with the other [sign], neither is it a significate, and there-

---

17 Pope, "An Essay on Man," in *The Poems of Alexander Pope*, ed. John Butt (New Haven, Conn.: Yale University Press, 1963), ll. 245–6.

fore this is not its sign; if unmanifest . . . it will be unmanifest whether the Connex speaks true. (499)

For signs to function in a determinate way, passage must take place from the body of the letter to the spirit of its meaning. Yet once Pyrrho stresses the gap between manifest and unmanifest signs, he challenges the very notion of a "sign detective of the Consequent." Because he defines the sign as "a demonstrative axiome, antecedent in a sound connex, detective of that which followeth" (498), the implication is that nothing followeth of necessity from any sign. Words are as helpless as syllogisms: "The Genus of demonstration being a sign, when we question whether there is a sign, we question whether there is a demonstration" (499).

Yet if Hutcheson is right that "some Objects are *immediately* the Occasions of this Pleasure of Beauty, and that we have Senses fitted for perceiving it"; if a mixed (though implicitly male) audience responds in the same way to a beautiful or sublime object; if, in short, signs exist that are self-interpreting, then the Pyrrhonian critique must be false. For in such a sign (beauty, sublimity), manifest (concrete, physical) existence means the same thing as its unmanifest significate (truth, virtue), an identity proven by the uniform response of all interpreters. Not only does the exemplary object of beauty rescue the design argument, then, but it also revives the very possibility of reading signs as they used to be interpreted in allegory, as indications of a transcendental dimension.[18]

In this context beauty offers an instance of what Paul J. Korshin calls an abstracted (or detached) type. Signs become "abstracted" when they are "drawn away from the theological field of action," which had

18 Following Angus Fletcher, I am using the term "allegory" to refer both to a specific genre and to a mode of reading: "Allegory is properly considered a mode: it is a fundamental process of encoding our speech" (Fletcher, *Allegory: The Theory of a Symbolic Mode* [Ithaca, N.Y.: Cornell University Press, 1964], 2–3). What counts in allegory "is a structure that lends itself to a secondary reading, or rather, one that becomes stronger when given a secondary meaning as well as a primary reading" (7). In Christian allegory one assumes a stable pattern of correspondence or translation between the first and second readings. In the eighteenth century "the cosmic matrix for imagery such as Spenser, Shakespeare, or even Milton could draw on no longer carried conviction with the poet who must equally reckon with the rising wave of scientific skepticism and with the progressive widening of middle-class materialist values" (237–8).

previously assigned meaning, and begin to function as autonomous reminders of an entire system of value. "Types are always *signs* whose meanings would be known to those fortunate enough to 'read' the code they embody and of which they are a part. . . . [Yet the abstracted type] can be shifted about from one text to another, always keeping the same approximate significance."[19] What good is a typological sign unmoored from its "code," floating about from text to text? Philosophers, artists, and editors of popular magazines focus on the isolated sign of beauty when it becomes evident that a culture has lost, or is in the process of losing, an older mythic dimension within which an entire network of symbols formerly conveyed meaning and upheld values. They hope that the sign for beauty, by itself, will revive a way of reading all phenomena, of assigning transcendental meaning to apparently mundane, inchoate particles, of replenishing allegory even in the moment of its dissolution. The lost code enters the material sign of beauty itself, providing both dimensions—pleasure and virtue, body and spirit, nature and revelation—in the selfsame image. Like Auerbach's *figura*, beauty restores the parallel between micro- and macrocosm: "An occurrence on earth signifies not only itself but at the same time another, which it predicts or confirms, without prejudice to the power of its concrete reality here and now. The connection between occurrences is not regarded as primarily a chronological or causal development but as a oneness with the divine plan."[20]

The aesthetic sign overcomes the Humean critique of transcendental induction by embodying transcendence while remaining grounded in the phenomenal realm. In its immediate and uniform effect the object reaffirmed divine teleology. The difficult negotiation between earthly and transcendental realms paradoxically required the physical sign both to attach our desire and to point elsewhere "without prejudice to the power of its concrete reality here and now." Even within medieval Christian Neoplatonism the balance was precarious. In a remarkable discussion of the "symbolist mentality" of twelfth-century allegory, de Chenu writes that "the symbol, in order to effect the transference for which it is a vehicle,

19 Korshin, *Typologies in England, 1650–1820* (Princeton, N.J.: Princeton University Press, 1982), esp. 104–6.

20 Erich Auerbach, *Mimesis: The Representation of Reality in Western Literature*, trans. Willard R. Trask (Princeton, N.J.: Princeton University Press, 1953), 555.

calls for matter which does not disappear in the process of signifying . . .
[yet] in turning reality into nothing but a figure, tropology weakens itself.
. . . Moralization, even in the masterly commentary of St. Gregory on Job,
ended up in attenuated abstraction, for it dissolved the natural or historical materials upon which it operated."[21] Genres such as allegory provided the interpretative framework within which "historical materials"
functioned as "signs detective of the consequent," the consequent
being a realm beyond history and the body.[22] Deprive beauty of its
generic emplacement, transform it into a detached type still expected
to signify in the same way, and the pressure to control beauty by other
means will become inescapable.[23]

It was not enough for moral philosophers of the early eighteenth
century to perpetuate Neoplatonism through the condensation of
design into the exemplary image of beauty. The image alone might
easily be misunderstood. "Imagine then, good Philocles," says Theo-
cles in Shaftesbury's dialogue, *The Moralists*, "if being taken with the
Beauty of the Ocean which you see yonder at a distance, it shou'd
come into your head, to seek how to command it; and like some
mighty Admiral, ride Master of the Sea: wou'd not the Fancy be a

21 Marie-Dominique de Chenu, *Nature, Man, and Society in the Twelfth Century*,
trans. Jerome Taylor and Lester K. Little (Chicago: University of Chicago Press,
1968), 132−3.

22 In a similar context, Michel Foucault observes that "the sixteenth century
superimposed hermeneutics and semiology in the form of similitude" (*The Order of
Things* [New York: Vintage, 1973], 29). Within the "semantic web of resemblance"
characterizing belief in a divine analogy between micro- and macrocosm, a framework of interpretation—what Foucault calls hermeneutics and I am calling genre—
establishes the code within which signs become meaningful. When powerful images
such as sublimity and beauty come unmoored from these hermeneutic contexts, writers will need to supply new guidelines for interpretation, whether through the self-
conscious revival of older forms (Platonic dialogue, Spenserian allegory), or through
the development of new professionalized disciplines (such as modern literary criticism), or through the development of new technologies such as morphogenesis, or
through special rituals, such as the beauty contest, which transform anxiety about the
loss of interpretative standards into a spectacle affirming their restitution.

23 John Barrell makes a similar point. During the eighteenth century "public
images of Venus must be enclosed within narratives which leave us in no doubt of her
bad character. . . . As soon as Venus finds her way into a history painting, she must be
shifted from formal to moral, from the body as symmetry to the body as moral tale"
(*The Birth of Pandora, and the Division of Knowledge* [Philadelphia: University of Pennsylvania Press, 1992], 75−6).

little absurd?"[24] Beauty always invites the wrong response, either, as in the above, by provoking desire for physical possession, or, as one frequently finds in early discourses on aesthetics, through an error only seemingly opposite—beauty's attenuation into pure abstraction, a mere sign function whose purpose is to rescue the concept of necessary connection from Humean critique.[25] In addition to generating the special sign of beauty, then, early philosophical aesthetics had to establish the conditions governing its proper interpretation.

Uniform Response to the Beautiful

The need to stipulate norms of response to aesthetic display is implicit in Hutcheson's confident assertion that "some Objects are *immediately* the Occasions of this Pleasure of Beauty, and that we have Senses fitted for perceiving it." While this axiom of early philosophical aesthetics has generated extensive commentary about the special sense (that is, the "moral sense") fitted to perceive beauty, less attention has been paid to the fact that the claim envisions a performative scene in which a group of individuals ("we") responds immediately and identically to a given aesthetic object. In the theoretical formulation, "we" is universal humanity; in practice, however, "we" is most often a coterie of privileged gentlemen who define their shared preferences as normative for all healthy individuals. To avoid contradiction the coterie must · represent its preferences in a way that assigns universal validity to them. In this respect, early philosophical aesthetics cannot remain a

24 Shaftesbury, *Characteristics of Men, Manners, Opinions, Times*, 3 vols., 6th ed., corrected (1737), 2:396.

25 At one point in the *Inquiry*, Hutcheson admits that all he really needs beauty for is to disprove chance: "Let it be observ'd, 'That the preceding Reasoning from the frequency of regular Bodys of one Form in the Universe, and from the Combination of Bodys, is intirely independent on any Perception of Beauty; and would equally prove Design in the Cause, altho there were no Being which perceiv'd Beauty in any Form whatsoever: for it is in short this, That the recurring of any Effect oftener than the Laws of Hazard determine, gives Presumption of Design'" (56). Beauty preserves predictability; yet beauty excites unpredictable desires. In this passage, Hutcheson seems willing to jettison beauty altogether, assuming other evidence for "the recurring of any Effect" can be found. Lacking such evidence, beauty will need to be simultaneously summoned and controlled—especially when beauty is a woman. See also Ian Hacking, *The Taming of Chance* (Cambridge: Cambridge University Press, 1990).

theoretical inquiry into the status of beauty as a special kind of sign; its central arguments immediately entail a search for new (or renewed) modes of representation within which judgments of taste may be represented as exemplary for the widest possible audience.

Hutcheson confronts this very problem at the end of the *Inquiry*. He questions whether philosophical treatises such as his will ever be able to represent beauty and the uniform response it evokes:

> Where we are studying to raise any Desire, or Admiration of an Object really beautiful, we are not content with a bare Narration, but endeavour, if we can, to present the Object it self, or the most lively Image of it. And hence the Epic Poem, or Tragedy, gives a vastly greater Pleasure than the Writings of Philosophers, tho both aim at recommending Virtue. The representing the Actions themselves, if the Representations be judicious, natural, and lively, will make us admire the Good, and detest the Vitious, the Inhuman, the Treacherous and Cruel, by means of our moral Sense, without any Reflections of the Poet to guide our Sentiments. (262)

Ironically, Hutcheson has just finished a long work in which he felt compelled to add secondary "reflections" to establish the equation between beauty and virtue. Although he admires the true artist who without apparent effort raises our desires through direct representations of beauty, the moral philosopher understands the danger these powerful images present. In praising the epic poem and tragedy at the expense of "philosophical narration," Hutcheson is not so much lamenting his inability to compose real literature, as he is designating an ideal performative genre that both represents the object of beauty and stipulates the appropriate response to it. His interest in tragedy, like that of his moral sense successor Adam Smith, is not with the action on the stage, but with the uniform secondary response triggered in a large, heterogeneous audience. The passion raised by tragedy interests us, writes Smith, "not as a passion, but as a situation that gives occasion to other passions that interest us; to hope, to fear . . . it is with these secondary passions only that we can properly be said to sympathize."[26]

---

26 Smith, *The Theory of Moral Sentiments*, ed. D. D. Raphael and A. L. Macfie (1976; rpt. Indianapolis, Ind.: Liberty Classics, 1982), 32.

Philosophical aesthetics thus always requires a supplemental assurance that the image operates immediately and uniformly on all correctly formed individuals. "As the onlookers watched the image of our new Eve begin to appear on our computer screen, several staff members promptly fell in love." We need to be told this because by itself the image cannot be counted upon to resurrect the lost code. In the same way, when eighteenth-century moral philosophers celebrate the pleasure of beauty or the power of sublimity or the catharsis we feel viewing tragedy, what delights them most is not the *frisson* of the passions, but the *Einstimmung* of a mixed audience all feeling the same thing at the same moment. In their many translations and imitations of Platonic dialogues on art and beauty such as the *Symposium, Ion,* and *Greater Hippias,* mid-eighteenth-century moral philosophers were able both to represent the object of beauty (usually in the person of a beautiful woman) and to dramatize the correct way of reading her as a sign prescribing political, racial, and sexual norms. "You would be widely mistaken," says Socrates in another of George Stubbes's imitations of Plato, "in confining this Rule [for judging beauty] to a fond Indulgence to my peculiar Fancy. On the contrary, it is my Ambition to render it [the rule] suitable to the various Tastes of all my Friends."[27]

These works are then at once marginal and representative; their failure results less from a lack of genius on their authors' part than from a tendency to depict aspects of philosophical aesthetics that the dominant figures usually have the good sense to avoid. In the preface to the *Critique of Judgment* Kant says that he will not stoop to discuss mere examples: "The examination of the faculty of taste, as the aesthetical judgment, is not here planned in reference to the formation or culture of taste (for this will take its course in the future as in the past without any such investigations)."[28] Nor will he describe how a mixed audience arrives at a uniform response to the beautiful: "The necessity of the universal agreement that is thought in a judgment of taste is a sub-

27 Stubbes, *A Dialogue on the Superiority of the Pleasures of the Understanding to the Pleasures of the Senses* (London: W. Wilkins, 1734), 9.

28 Immanuel Kant, *Critique of Judgment,* trans. J. H. Bernard (New York: Hafner, 1951), 6. On Kant's relation to the example, see Jacques Derrida, *The Truth in Painting,* trans. Geoff Bennington and Ian McLeod (Chicago: University of Chicago Press, 1987), esp. 37–82.

jective necessity, which is represented as objective under the presupposition of a common sense" (76).[29] By excluding both of these empirical questions from truly philosophical concern, Kant makes systematic idealist aesthetics possible. Spence's beauty contest and the spate of Platonic imitations confirm Kant's good judgment in ruling out a too-explicit representation of either the object of beauty or the process by which a select "we" produces a standard of judgment for the larger "we." Crito arrives at the crass numerical evaluation of known beauties while proving that "the necessity of the universal agreement that is thought in a judgment of taste is a subjective necessity, which is represented as objective under the presupposition of a common sense." He thinks he is giving the presupposition of a common sense a more rigorous philosophical basis by placing several approximations to beauty before a panel of judges whose (necessarily) shared preferences prove the existence of a sense (aesthetic) they share in common.

The mid-eighteenth-century imitators and translators of Plato seek to perpetuate the tradition of Renaissance Neoplatonism represented by Firenzuola's *Dialogue on the Beauty of Women* under conditions that have become inimical to it. Hume's critique of transcendental induction is thoroughly anti-Platonic. Yet the midcentury Platonists, summoning the intellectual and discursive authority of their great precursor, were able to reestablish a basis for the endangered dialectic. Floyer Sydenham, the most prolific of the midcentury translators, introduces his version of *The Greater Hippias* with the claim that "the design of this Dialogue is little by little to unfold the Nature of true Beauty; and gradually to conduct our Minds to the View of that Being, who is Beauty itself; and from whose Original Ideas, all of them essential to his Nature, is copied every Particular Beauty."[30] Here again is the assertion Hume had mocked—the notion that all particular beauties are

29 The sentence heads sec. 22.

30 Sydenham, *A Synopsis; or, General View of the Works of Plato* (London: S. Richardson, 1759), 5–6. Describing the plot of another dialogue in 1767, Sydenham repeats the point, through an allusion he shares with his Renaissance precursors: "The Philosophy of Socrates is like the Ladder in the Patriarch Jacob's Dream: his Metaphysics ascend gradually up to the First Cause of Things; from which depend, and from whence come down to Earth, the Sciences of Ethics and Politicks, to bless Mankind" ("The Rivals, a Dialogue concerning Philosophy," in *The Dialogues of Plato*, 2 vols. [London: W. Sandby, 1767], 2:32).

more or less faithful copies of a transcendental template arrived at inductively through abstraction.

Knowing the original from which all lesser effects have been copied, the eighteenth-century moral philosopher and the twentieth-century cybergeneticist also know the distance every lesser effect must travel to reach perfection. Beauty supplies the rule, not only for itself (a fruitless reflexivity) but also for determinations of value in ethical and political domains. "All Virtue is Order and Proportion, whether in the Soul of Man, or in a Civil State," writes Sydenham. He then maps out the concentric circles defining the relevance of beauty to the exercise of power:

> The Rule, according to which the Mind by [Virtue's] Will then governs, is Beauty itself; and the Science, through which She governs, is the Science of that Beauty. For Truth and Beauty concur in One; and where-ever They are, there is also Good. The Love of Beauty then is nothing different from that First and Leading Motive in all Minds to the Pursuit of every Thing . . . the DESIRE of GOOD. Thus the Perfection of Man consists in his Similitude to this SUPREME BEAUTY; and in his Union with it is found his SUPREME GOOD."[31]

Beauty provides the rule for politics and ethics. What supplies the rule for beauty? The science of beauty, which provides rules for itself. In effect, the correspondences argue that science will now supply the rule for politics and ethics. Such an assertion, so directly stated, might occasion disagreement, as would the claim that human genetics has identified the qualities of a master race. Therefore it is necessary to position the "universal" category of beauty between science and ethics: just as beauty need not turn to anything outside itself to postulate rules for its own interpretation, so a science modeled on beauty need not justify its applicability to any and all areas of human experience. Beauty has

31 Sydenham, 17–8. When so programmatically stated, the Platonic doctrine bears perhaps a greater resemblance to the terms of Plotinus's *Enneads*, 1:6: "Soul, then, when it is raised to the level of intellect increases in beauty. Intellect and the things of the intellect are its beauties. . . . For this reason it is right to say that the soul's becoming something good and beautiful is its being made like to God, because from Him come beauty and all else which falls to the lot of real beings" (*Plotinus*, trans. A. H. Armstrong, 6 vols. [Cambridge, Mass.: Harvard University Press, 1966], 1:251).

the remarkable advantage of being both autonomous and legislative of values outside the aesthetic realm.

The divine and benevolent simplicity of the equation between beauty and truth belies the tendentious consequences that follow from any actual attempt to put beauty's rule into sociopolitical effect. Kant, sharing in the effort to situate aesthetic judgment between natural philosophy (science, nature) and moral philosophy (ethics, desire), wisely rules out any specific "reference to the formation or culture of taste." But in the minor works of concern here, no attempt is made to conceal beauty's immediate utility in prescribing norms of conduct and value.

Beauty is truth, truth beauty. But in George Stubbes's *Dialogue on Beauty in the Manner of Plato* (1731), truth requires a beautiful young woman named Aspasia, who sits posing for a portrait, to renounce her immediate temporal interests and to join Socrates in the quest for the ideal beauty. This "new kind of Chase, unknown to Diana and her Nymphs" (11), while it potentially equates male and female intellects, eventually leads Aspasia to declare herself no "less desirous to lay hold on the friendly Aid [of Socrates], than the creeping Vine is ambitious to clasp with her Tendrils the supporting Elm, and rear to the Sun her feeble Branches" (50).

In Spence's *Crito; or, A Dialogue on Beauty*, the equation between beauty and truth proves that women are beautiful only for a brief moment, while the male judges are beautiful for a lifetime. The dialogue begins when Crito admits to having observed a Mrs. B through a crack in her door, as she sits weeping. "The Distress in her Countenance, and the little Confusion that appeared about her Eyes," says Crito, "added so much to the other Beauties of her Face, that I think I never saw her look so charming in my Life" (4). Asked to account for this phenomenon, Crito begins to set down rules for judging female beauty, applicable to any and every woman. He makes it clear that his preference for a woman in tears derives not from his own kinky taste but from timeless aesthetic ideals.[32] Because beauty is, finally, an intellectual ideal, those who possess the

32 The ideal color, we learn, is a mixture of red and white. This tint conveys a "natural liveliness" and the idea "of good Health." The basis for this ideal remains what it had been for Hutcheson, a measure of diversity (the darker tints—redness) blended into the harmony of an ordered whole (whiteness). The pleasure afforded by such diversity in unity helps explain why the sight of a beautiful woman in pain causes

standard (the male judges) are *always beautiful*, regardless of age or physical appearance. Those, on the other hand, who provide the objective examples of physical beauty are beautiful only so long as their bodies, like their faces, express the ideal balance between change (diversity) and permanence (unity). It follows, for Spence, that a woman is most beautiful when her body first suggests a readiness for procreation, but before pubescence can degenerate into womanhood. The peak of female beauty must be short-lived, the ripeness all:

> It might sound odd to you, if I should say, that a Woman is like a Pine-apple; yet the Similitude would hold much farther, and in more Particulars, than anyone would at first imagine. She has her Season of growing to her greatest State of Beauty, of Continuance in it, and of a Decay from it, as well as that; and the highest Season of their Beauty is just as properly timed in the one Case, as in the other. (43)

The similitude becomes more apt than Spence could possibly wish, assuming that, like most contributors to the philosophical exposition of early modern aesthetics, he wants to keep the metaphor of "taste" from becoming re-entangled with the cluster of terms evoking salivation, mastication, and swallowing. We draw a habitual connection between the appearance of a pineapple of a certain hue and the deliciousness of its ripe fruit. Salivation provides the bridge between stimulus and response, cause and effect, the same for all. Similarly, the appearance of a woman of a certain age, showing traces of childhood but a readiness (as the man imagines it) for intercourse (of course for the purpose of procreation) evokes the equivalent of salivation in the male. Sensual arousal becomes the bridge between stimulus and response. Within this aestheticized short-circuit, transcendence is being nudged out of the picture: sublimation of desire has been replaced by its gratification. It becomes increasingly difficult to hear the connoisseur's definition of grace—"a certain Deliciousness that almost always lives about the Mouth" (29) in quite the sense he intends it.

---

delight: the uniformity of a beautiful face (threatening to become only a white lifeless abstraction) is humanized (diversified) by the traces of red suffering, and although *she* is not aware of her greater appeal at that moment, the man of taste is. He has a preference for "that Magdalen-look in some fine faces, after weeping." Grief gives the complexion a "Softness or Silkiness" (11–2).

Here again, the embarrassments of the minor work are indicative of larger movements in literary and intellectual history. As moral philosophers turned their attention from metaphysics to aesthetics in the hope of discovering an empirical basis for uniform response, they faced the philosophically unwelcome conclusion that the best evidence for such uniformity was to be found in a purely sensual arousal. They were committed, in other words, to locating more and more powerful triggers stimulating less and less rational responses. That is why the focus of aesthetics shifts during the eighteenth century from the beautiful to the sublime to an eroticized gothicism to (in Sade) "experiments" in involuntary arousal.[33]

Despite—or perhaps because of—the ephemeral nature of female beauty, it becomes possible and necessary to establish a hundred-point rating system to test women's beauty. Most of the dialogue concerns Crito's explication of this system. Women will be assessed according to their color (ten points), form (twenty points), expression (thirty points), and grace (forty points).[34] The calculus of beauty makes it clear that although a small coterie of gentlemen fix a standard of taste, their determinations attain mathematical certitude and are valid for humanity in the widest sense.[35] The eighteenth-century rating system,

33 An instructive work in this regard is "A Dialogue concerning Decency," attributed to Benjamin Buckler (London: James Fletcher, 1751). The main character in this dialogue holds that universal response is verified by the shame people feel defecating in public.

34 Spence derives his rating system from Roger de Piles's *Cours de peinture* (Paris: Jacques Estienne, 1708), which ends with a chart ranking Renaissance painters numerically on the basis of composition, design, color, and expression. For a discussion of this work see Andrew McClellan, *Inventing the Louvre: Art, Politics, and the Origins of the Modern Museum in Eighteenth-Century Paris* (Cambridge: Cambridge University Press, 1994), 33–4. On the quantification of an affect, especially as regards women, see also Terry Castle, *The Female Thermometer: Eighteenth-Century Culture and the Invention of the Uncanny* (New York: Oxford University Press, 1995).

35 Through their rating system, the gentlemen in the *Dialogue on Beauty*, like Zeuxis and the editors of *Time*, produce what Joel Black has called a "holotype," "a type-specimen abstracted from a variety of individual specimens in nature" ("The Aesthetics of Gender: Zeuxis' Maidens and the Hermaphroditic Ideal," *New York Literary Forum* 8–9 [1981]: 190). Black argues that Zeuxis's method of composition transforms aesthetic representation into political representation, since what is at issue is the way "a select group of individuals organizes itself into a compact whole or 'fair sample' which in turn 'acts for' a larger constituency or 'body politic'" (192). Black goes on to show that if aesthetics were genuinely rigorous in forming its composite

like twentieth-century morphing, assures us that the gentlemen concern themselves with "such [beauty] as is natural or real, and not such
as is only national or customary; for I would not have you imagine, that
I would have any thing to do with the beautiful thick Lips of the good
people of Bantam, or the excessive small Feet of the Ladies of Quality
in China" (7).

In Joseph Spence's hands, philosophical dialogue becomes that
ideal performative genre called for but not provided at the end of
Hutcheson's *Inquiry*: hovering between philosophical narration and
dramatic enactment, dialogue both represents objective instances of
beauty and provides directions for the proper interpretation of the
sign. Testimony to our ability to know the absolute through beauty now
comes not from the single love-struck poet or the philosophical gallant of Renaissance Neoplatonism but from the male panel of judges,
Petrarchans in the age of Locke, whose shared determinations of taste
prove the efficacy of a measuring science equally applicable to material
form and spiritual substance. Similarly, the paragon of beauty, the
Greek Helen or Christian Laura, has become multiple anonymous
contestants who approximate the ideal.

While the late Platonists of the eighteenth-century struggle to retain
the equation between aesthetics and ethics, the situation changes by
the early nineteenth century. Writers who identify themselves with new
professional disciplines separate concepts of sympathy, the moral
sense, and innate benevolence from the emerging science of beauty in
order to supply themselves with a methodological grounding. Anthropology and medicine, for instance, adopt the science of beauty as the
foundation for a remarkable set of findings in the work of T. Bell,
M.D.[36] "Whilst man acts on external objects by the power of his organs,
or by the ascendancy of his genius, woman acts on man by the reduction of her manners and by the continual observation of all that can
engage his heart, or captivate his imagination. . . . Her highest duty is

ideal, its data would have to include members of both sexes, thus producing, as its
average, a hermaphroditic ideal (as is found in Winckelmann). Observe the morph-
ers of *Time*, "One of our tentative unions produced a distinctly feminine face—
sitting atop a muscular neck and hairy chest" (66).

36 *Kalogynomia; or, The Laws of Female Beauty: Being the Elementary Principles of That
Science* (London: J. J. Stockdale, 1821).

to please him to whom she has united her days, and to attach him to home by rendering it agreeable to him" (64). Here we find science legislating norms for conduct, norms that might appear controversial were they not founded upon a principle of subordination in nature:

> Female beauty differs among the various races of mankind. There is, however, a standard of beauty independent of all idea of that partiality which is wounded by pride, and which self-love with such obstinacy maintains. The negro, who wisely in a hot clime prefers for his mate a woman of color, always awards the superiority in beauty to the white. . . . Everywhere throughout the universe a young and beautiful woman of the European race commands the admiration and receives the homage of men. (67–8)

The woman's reduction to the man, the black's subordination to the white, only replicate the hierarchical relation of lesser beauties to a single standard in nature. And if the oppressed have a mind to complain, let them remember that their own intuitive preference for the white over the black and the beautiful over the ugly confirms the eternal justice of their prostration. In this way, the science of beauty creates necessary monsters.[37]

Beauty is truth, truth beauty. But what the equation goes on to provide in Alexander Walker's *Beauty: Illustrated Chiefly by an Analysis and Classification of Women* (1836) is an "anthropological science in modern times."[38] This work begins with a veritable synopsis of the dominant arguments of early philosophical aesthetics, "a Critical View of the General Hypotheses Respecting Beauty, by Hume, Hogarth, Burke, Knight, Alison, etc." Once again, beauty functions as a principle of invariability that grounds ethical and political valuations in an absolute sanction: "If I can here show that, in the material qualities of the objects of nature and art, there exists elements of beauty equally invari-

37 For an argument that the "root theory" of many forms of modern racism are to be found in the "universalist, benign, and neutral" accounts of the nature of man promulgated during the Enlightenment, see Richard H. Popkin, "The Philosophical Basis of Eighteenth-Century Racism," *Studies in Eighteenth-Century Culture*, ed. Harold E. Pagliaro, vol. 3 (Cleveland, Ohio: Case Western Reserve University Press, 1973), 245–62.

38 Walker, *Beauty: Illustrated Chiefly by an Analysis and Classification of Women* (London: Effingham Wilson, Royal Exchange, 1836).

able in themselves; and in the kind of effect they produce upon the mind, it is evident there can be no further dispute about the standard of beauty" (Walker, 70).[39]

Invariability in art underwrites an anthropological science whose consequences extend immediately beyond the aesthetic into human genetics. Walker's main concern, like that of the editors of *Time*, is with the control of breeding practices: "The forms and proportions of animals—as of the horse and the dog; have been examined in a hundred volumes. Not one has been devoted to woman, on whose physical and moral qualities the happiness of individuals and the perpetual improvement of the human race are dependent" (vii). Unless men of privileged station learn to "read" the indications of beauty correctly, mating only with good breeders, their runtish offspring will bear diminishing resemblance to the invariable norm. Beauty needs to be classified in 1836 (as in 1993) to assure the "perpetual improvement of the human race," that is, to control demography. When the love of beauty combines with nationalist and imperial ambitions, the transition from genetics to eugenics is imminent.[40]

Walker fixes the standard of beauty as a prelude to even more remarkable discoveries. Before the mind can admit ideas of absolute beauty, special conditions must exist, such as the right climate producing brains capable of "vigorous thought, sound judgment and exquisite taste" (187–8). Absence of these conditions produces "deformities" in the organism, false preferences for dark skin, fat lips, short figures, and the like. "In the case of the African, he is born whitish, like the European, but he speedily loses such beauty for that of adaptation, by his

39 This methodology leads to the odd but entirely expected claim that the more human beings imitate "those simpler elements of beauty, which characterize inanimate bodies . . . the more beautiful these [beings] become" (199).

40 On the transition from genetics to eugenics see Mikuláš Teich, "The Unmastered Past of Human Genetics," in *Fin de Siècle and Its Legacy*, ed. Mikuláš Teich and Roy Porter (Cambridge: Cambridge University Press, 1990). Teich draws attention to the ease with which the metaphor of breeding, which we already saw in Shaftesbury's discussion of beauty, could become the basis for both a positive eugenics (whose aim was to produce human beings endowed with desirable genetic traits) and a negative eugenics (whose aim was "to reduce if not eliminate hereditary physical and mental defects . . . by preventing the propagation of undesirable genetic constitutions" [303]). The eugenic dream of human hybridization bears an uncanny resemblance to the morphogenetic production of *Time*'s new face of America.

color, to the hot climate in which he exists. . . . The climate of Africa, the cerebral structure of its inhabitants, and the degree of their civilization are as unfavourable to the existence of beauty, as to the power of judging respecting it" (199). Dr. Bell's *Kalogynomia* settles the point: "England, perhaps exclusively, presents the combination of those circumstances which are essentially favorable to beauty" (77).

Conclusion: The Beauty Contest Contested

Pierre Bourdieu and Terry Eagleton have recently linked the origin and ideology of philosophical aesthetics to a hegemonic discourse serving the interests of an emerging middle class.[41] Their discussions, however, neglect the active opposition that arose during the eighteenth century to the premise of uniform response to the beautiful. Not surprisingly, works like Spence's *Crito* and Walker's *Beauty* that literalized the claims of high philosophical aesthetics provoked a reaction. Critics of the aesthetic attacked what they took to be the root cause of misguided practices, namely, a late Platonic metaphysics serving retrograde forms of social control. Such early analyses are prescient in explaining why *Time* would produce an avowedly metaphysical image of beauty to deny actual processes of social change.

Because the "native" critique of the aesthetic during the eighteenth century would in itself be the subject of a much longer essay, a single example must suffice here. Joseph Spence's equation of women and pineapples was itself ripe for ridicule, and parodied it was three years later in the first sustained critique of the aesthetic in English, a *Dialogue on Taste* (1755) by Allan Ramsay (the younger). At one point the main character, George Freeman, relates his encounter with Sir Harry Beaumont (the pseudonym for Joseph Spence):

> Col. Freeman: I happened to be walking in the Mall with Sir Harry Beaumont, about a week after Crito was published, when Sir Roger came up to us, and, after congratulating his brother Baronet upon the success of his performance, and the figure it was like to give

41 See Pierre Bourdieu, "The Historical Genesis of the Pure Aesthetic," *Journal of Aesthetics and Art Criticism* 46 (1987): 201–9; and Terry Eagleton, *The Ideology of the Aesthetic* (Oxford: Blackwell, 1990).

him in the eyes of the Misses, as an arbiter of beauty, Sir Harry, says
he, I observe that in your distribution of grace you give twenty
degrees to Mrs. A * * *, and thirty to Mrs. B * * *. Now I do not find
fault with your tables, but I should be glad to know by what scale,
weight, or measure you compute their several shares with so much
precision. You certainly, answered Sir Harry, did not read my paper
with much attention, or else you would have seen that I did not
pretend to have made my calculations exactly; but rather to point
out what might be done by more exact judges of beauty. Ay, but, Sir
Harry, says the old Knight, let who will calculate those tables of
beauty, it will have but a very unscholarlike appearance, if, when
the exactness of their calculations happens to be called into question, they should have nothing better to appeal to, than the infalli-
bility of their own judgments. I am afraid that method would
hardly pass muster at the Royal Society.[42]

Now the attempt to combine epistemology, ethics, and aesthetics, to
provide a calculus of beauty, becomes self-parodying. By what precise
calculation has the extent of grace in a face been determined? To what
criterion did the judge of beauty appeal beyond his own whim? Freeman offers to help Beaumont with his figures:

I have . . . been thinking that the rule of three or rule of proportion, might be applied so as to become a golden rule in comparing
beauties as much as any thing else. It is performed, you know, by
multiplying the first by the second, and dividing by the third; and
being curious this morning to know with exactness how much Mrs.
D * * * excelled in beauty Mrs. C * * *, I thus stated the question,
as a cat is to a wheelbarrow, so is Mrs. C * * * to Mrs. D * * *; but
though I tried till my brain was ready to crack, I could never con-
trive how to multiply a cat by a wheelbarrow. . . . Now if you, or any
other virtuoso, could fall upon the method of multiplying and
dividing such matters; I am persuaded you . . . would prevent it
[the judgment of beauty] from being any longer left, as you justly
complain, to the particular whim of ignorant people. (31)

42 Allan Ramsay (the younger), *A Dialogue on Taste* (London: 1762), 30–1. The
first edition appeared in the *Investigator*, no. 322 (London: A. Millar, 1755). Subsequent citations refer to the 1762 edition.

Borrowing a page from Swift, Ramsay's persona eagerly takes over the project of quantifying beauty, suggesting his own improvements. The rule of three is not an arbitrary contribution. Although he muddles the formula (if $a:b$ as c:an unknown value, then the unknown is c times b divided by a, not a times b divided by c), Freeman manages to parody the operation that is really intended by the conflation of beauty and math. For the rule of three derives an unknown value from known values. Like transcendental induction, Ramsay's weird math moves from a comparison of supposedly similar effects (the beauty of Mrs. A and Mrs. B) to the overriding constant that makes the comparison possible (a specular Mrs. Z whose perfect beauty provides the standard). The point is not to begin with the ideal, but to arrive at it through a mundane process of comparison, a beauty contest. Ramsay's Knight argues that differences in beauty pertain to quality and cannot sensibly be compared in quantitative terms. The effort to do so says more about the judges than the judged. Ramsay, who was a friend and admirer of David Hume, views the effort to quantify beauty as an elaborate and doomed response to Hume's critique of induction. His parody of the beauty contest therefore travesties the attempt to extend the rule of three to questions of moral and aesthetic value.[43]

Ramsay undermines the transcendental "plot" of the mid-eighteenth-century Platonic dialogues and with it the conceptual structure of the beauty contest. Instead of asking his female auditors to sublimate the temporal dimension in the name of an ideal Beauty, Freeman hopes to teach them the techniques of comparative historical analysis: "History, Lady Harriet, and the investigation of facts will always enable us to set the true stamp upon such sublime pretensions. . . . All sham claims to divinity are easily exposed, whenever the proper means are employed" (16). In an early version of Bourdieu's critique of distinction, Freeman identifies all preferences with contingent and politicized processes of value formation. Indeed, philosophical aesthetics—the science of taste—itself has a history:

43 For Ramsay's relationship to Hume and a discussion of the *Dialogue on Taste*, see Alastair Smart, *Allan Ramsay: Painter, Essayist, and Man of the Enlightenment* (New Haven, Conn.: Yale University Press, 1992), 139–49.

For many ages had bishops and barons, monks and knights errant, kept the people of Europe in slavery and dissention, sloth, ignorance and misery. All the arts which tended to render life more humane and agreeable, were utterly discountenanced and forbid. . . . Canon law to defend the worldly pretensions of church-men, and metaphysics to promote and defend their spiritual absurdities, for the same gainful purpose, were what passed currently by the name of learning. When these failed, in determining the truth or falsehood of a proposition, recourse was had, legally and cooly, to single combat. . . . Painting and sculpture were not yet found necessary to be called in aid of these holy cheats. (43–4)

Freeman, like some of his contemporaries, describes aesthetics as a substitute theology.[44] It arose when a metaphysically sanctioned religion was losing its hold over Europeans. Debates about art then replaced the duel in the panoply of persuasive devices. This genealogy explains why those who set themselves up as arbiters of taste are often ready to second their preferences with a more direct exercise of power: "It has sometimes, too often, happened that in default of reasons, force, and terror have been applied, in order to produce an uniformity of thinking, and to render the taste and opinion of the strongest, the catholic, or universal. And then, woe! to the wretched sons of Adam!" (76). Seventy years before Bell and Alexander, Ramsay describes how the supposedly benevolent love of beauty will be used as an instrument of domination.

44 In 1744 Philip Skelton mocked what he called the new "Religion of Taste": "Our great Folks, not liking the vulgar Religions, with which these Countries abound, as being both expensive and inconvenient, were on the point of renouncing all Religion, when his Lordship [Shaftesbury], who knew what they wanted, revealed to them the Religion of Taste. This Religion sits easy, and breaks no Squares. It neither shocks nor offends. It neither hampers, nor restrains. It can never occasion either Disputes, or Wars. It distinguishes the polite Part of the World from the Vulgar, who cannot participate in it. But it may be, thou wilt ask me what it is? I tell thee again, It is Taste and good Breeding" (*The Candid Reader; or, A Modest, yet Unanswerable Apology for All Books That Ever Were, or Possibly Can Be Wrote* [Dublin, 1744; rpt. London: M. Cooper, 1744], 29). Skelton writes from the viewpoint of a High Church country parson who twice sold his library to relieve the poor of his parish during times of famine. He suspects that Shaftesbury's "religion of taste" has no other purpose than to absolve wealthy Whigs of traditional Christian obligations to feed and clothe the poor.

And two hundred and thirty years before Bourdieu, Ramsay asserts that pressures of the marketplace shape the production of aesthetic ideals. When one of the women asks whether the repetition of symmetrical and proportionate images in Greek statuary indicates a universal standard for beauty, Freeman replies,

> No sooner were the arts of painting and sculpture brought to some degree of excellence, but the artists, in representing a Venus, an Helen, or any other personage, from whom beauty was expected, must have found all their endeavours to please rendered ineffectual by the variety of sentiments which different men, by the various structures of their nerves and organs, have of beauty. . . . Here necessity, the mother of invention, would come to his assistance, and set him upon a method that, although it might charm few, would disgust no body; that is, to form a face that should affect a medium in all its features and proportions, carefully avoiding anything extraordinary. (23–4)

The ideal of Greek beauty is here redescribed as a sales gimmick, a necessary response to the irreducible variety of tastes among the buyers of sculptures and paintings. Unwilling to offend any, the artist tries to please all by seeking out the most mediocre expression: "All the antique statues now remaining . . . by their great similarity, plainly appear to be all copies, more or less exact, of one original, framed upon this cautious principle" (25). That principle, formerly the artist's ability to copy the Platonic ideal, now becomes the pure calculation of profit, which instigates not a quest for beauty but a search for the average. Our historical detour has brought us back to "the new face of America."

In this essay I have argued that the origin of the postmodern, technologically assisted beauty contest can be traced to the eighteenth century, when philosophical aesthetics, the science of beauty, emerges to rescue the method of transcendental induction (abstraction) from Pyrrhonian critique. Then as now, the beauty contest transforms a culture's anxiety about the contingency of its defining values into a spectacular reenactment and overcoming of that very anxiety. A story about method, the beauty contest makes a virtue of necessity: it stages the process by which the sign for beauty is cured of contingency (other contestants) and rendered fit for use as a sociopolitical norm. While men of taste give way to scientists who give way to computer programmers, the panel of judges continues to function as an apparatus generating infinite desire for an unattainable abstraction. It pieces together an ideal from unspared parts, then calls it the necessary dream of the whole. It replaces God with an image that promises everything and delivers something less, which is to say, nothing. And so we also hate her, want to ruin that beautiful face so it cannot remind us of our self-deception. The woman you see on the cover does not exist, except metaphysically.

Descartes's Cogito, Kant's

Sublime, and Rem-

brandt's Philosophers:

Cultural Transmission as

Sanford Budick | Occasion for Freedom

For Stanley Cavell

I seek to demonstrate that Descartes, Kant, and Rembrandt can be understood as bound together by their connection with a particular place, namely, Amsterdam. Even work so unworldly as that of the philosophers may share worldly imagery with a certain painting, or series of paintings, by Rembrandt. A hitherto unnoticed intimacy of consciousness links the three figures.

It may alleviate the initial strangeness of what I am asking the reader to consider if I explain that I have assembled the following sequence of thoughts, arrived at from other directions, in response to a challenge issued in Bernard Williams's *Descartes: The Project of Pure Enquiry.* For me Williams raises the deepest questions about what a shared intimacy of consciousness would have to entail. The challenge emerges from the claim that in Descartes's cogito ("I think, therefore I am") the move from a consciousness of thinking to the existence of a thinker ("A is thinking") logically requires an impersonal formulation, but Descartes does not, and cannot, supply it. Achieving the "separateness" of an impersonal formulation, Williams argues, would imply "relativizing the content of the impersonally occurring thoughts."[1] In other words, if a

1 Williams, *Descartes: The Project of Pure Enquiry* (Atlantic Highlands, N.J.: Humanities, 1978), 98.

place could be found for the subject to stand outside first-person thoughts (such as the thought of the cogito), the relativized subject could prove that *it* thinks and hence that it exists substantively, beyond consciousness, where others might have access to it. But any such "literal place" or "concrete relativization . . . even if it could fall short of requiring a subject who has the thoughts . . . has to exist in the form of something outside pure thought. . . . The Cartesian reflection merely presents, or rather invites us into, the perspective of consciousness" (98–100).

Williams repeatedly suggests that "it is not at all clear that we really can grasp . . . in the abstract" the difference between thought in Descartes's first-person form and thought in Williams's impersonal form (96). Thus a concrete relativization might offer some unexpected clarity. In fact, the cue for my line of questioning is Williams's imagining for Descartes—to be sure, as a "problem"—a possible "relation between the 'I think' in the content of the thought" and "what is objectively involved in the state of affairs which constitutes its being thought" (100). As I interpret this suggestion, Williams wants to reconceive the relation of thought to its contents, such that the state of affairs being thought is not merely assumed but recognized as necessary. Following this interpretation, my informal proposal is that without the existence of Amsterdam and Rembrandt, Descartes's thoughts (of himself) would not be what they are. The cultural achievements of the Amsterdam of that period and of Rembrandt in his images are the conditions needed for Descartes's supposing of presence. These achievements liberate his thought from an illusory (and perhaps fetishized) immediacy and dispose it to a subjunctive mood that may indeed be the hallmark of what we think of as works, or the work, of culture. This disposition of thought amounts to a significant kind of freedom.

Informally, then, I propose that a semantic requirement of Williams's has a cultural realization.[2] At the end of this essay I will specify as nearly as I can the implications of this proposal for the materials I have presented.

---

2 I stress that this possible picture of Descartes's thought as what is objectively involved in the state of affairs that constitutes its being thought is an informal proposal rather than a formal crossing of a logical demarcation. I do not require prior acceptance of this proposal to get on, now, to the presentation of materials that will unhurriedly lead the reader to his or her own judgments.

Descartes lays special emphasis on freedom of choice as one kind of thinking. Even in the Second Meditation he includes *affirming* and *denying, willing* and *rejecting,* on his short list of what a thinking being thinks.[3] In the Fourth Meditation "volition" is said to be "the liberty of the free will" (PE, 85); moreover, it is the highest (the divine) mark of human thinking, because it is the freedom to decide between "two contraries" while no "external force" constrains the mind.[4] In the *Discourse on Method,* in Descartes's description of the moment when he came to his cogito, the central term for representing the thinking of freedom is *resolving* or *choosing.* After years of delay Descartes finally set down his system because he was "honest enough not to desire to be esteemed as different from what I am" (*Works,* 1:100). In the same paragraph he commences to lay the groundwork of the sameness or repetition of his "I am" and does so by "resolving." I refer to Descartes's first "resolve" [*résoudre* (31)], which is to remove himself from all acquaintances, to Holland. In the following paragraph he again "resolves" [*résolus* (32)], this time to choose the hyperbolic doubt of "everything that ever entered into my mind." This resolve is what makes possible the experience of the cogito itself.

It is striking that the first resolve already sketches many, perhaps all, of the second resolve's principal elements, most especially something very like hyperbolic doubt:

> [1] It is just eight years ago that this desire made me resolve to remove myself [*me fit résoudre à m'éloigner*] from all places where any acquaintances were possible, and to retire to a country such as this, where the long-continued war has caused such order to be established that the armies which are maintained seem only to be of use in allowing the inhabitants to enjoy the fruits of peace with

3 Descartes, *Philosophical Essays,* trans. Laurence J. Lafleur (New York: Bobbs-Merrill, 1964), 85. Citations from Descartes in English are either from this collection (hereafter *PE*) or from *The Philosophical Works of Descartes,* trans. Elizabeth S. Haldane and G. R. T. Ross, 2 vols. (New York: Dover, 1955) (hereafter *Works*). Citations from the *Discourse on Method* in French are from *Discours de la méthode: Texte et commentaire,* ed. Etienne Gilson (Paris: Vrin, 1925).

4 "Our free will consists," says Descartes, in behaving "in such a way that we do not feel that any external force has constrained us in our choice . . . of one or the other of . . . two contraries" (*PE,* 113).

so much the more security; and where, in the crowded throng of a great and very active nation, which is more concerned with its own affairs than curious about those of others, without missing any of the conveniences of the most populous towns, I can live as solitary and retired as in deserts the most remote [*j'ai pu vivre aussi solitaire et retiré que dans les déserts les plus écartés*]. (*Works*, 1:100)

[2] I resolved [*résolus*] to assume that everything that ever entered into my mind was no more true than the illusions of my dreams. But immediately afterwards I noticed that while I thus wished to think all things false, it was absolutely essential that the "I" who thought this should be something. . . . remarking that this truth "*I think, therefore I am*" was so certain and so assured that all the most extravagant suppositions brought forward by the sceptics were incapable of shaking it. (*Works*, 1:101)[5]

How are we to understand the verb *to resolve*, either in the first resolve, which apparently describes no more than Descartes's account of his removal to Amsterdam, a place of estrangement, he says, where no acquaintances were possible; or, in the next paragraph, in his resolve to assume that everything that had ever entered into his mind was no more true than the illusions of his dreams?

I propose that in his representation of the origins of his philosophy Descartes's resolve to experience hyperbolic doubt is occasioned by a line of representations—each of which lets us see its inadequacy as a representation—that together form a particular culture. By "culture" I mean no more or less than the patterns of cultural transmission specified by the works of given cultures. Focusing the term *culture* in the subterm *cultural transmission* is, I believe, commensurate with widely accepted usage. Clifford Geertz, for example, writes:

The culture concept to which I adhere has neither multiple referents nor, so far as I can see, any unusual ambiguity: it denotes an historically transmitted pattern of meanings embodied in symbols, a system of inherited conceptions expressed in symbolic forms by means of which men communicate, perpetuate, and develop their

5 I amend Haldane and Ross's "'I' who thought this should be somewhat" to "'I' who thought this should be something."

knowledge about and attitudes toward life. Of course, terms such as "meaning," "symbol," and "conception" cry out for explication. But that is precisely where the widening, the broadening, and the expanding come in.[6]

Among other things, the present essay explores the possibility that in a given history of culture the means of cultural transmission (or communication, perpetuation, bequeathing/inheriting, or development from one generation to another) already determine the meanings, symbols, and conceptions of that culture. If so, then the means of cultural transmission are central to what culture is.

I am therefore particularly concerned with the fact that Descartes resolves to remove himself not just to anywhere but to a culture transmitted by partially dispossessed representations. Already in his opening words he shows (although he camouflages it) that the line of transmission that he experiences in, or *as,* this culture holds open the opportunity of hyperbolic doubt, which enables his freedom of choice.

I wish to note certain symmetries among the representations that make up Descartes's first resolve. Each representation is dual. Each is constituted by delineating first a totality suggestive of great activity, or even material turbulence, and then a withdrawal from part of the totality, leaving a place of emptiness within the maelstrom. In ways that are not immediately clear, Descartes locates his "I am" in a line of points within vortices.

Descartes's first representation is of the peculiar activity of the Dutch,

> a great and very active nation . . . more concerned with its own affairs than curious about those of others.

The great, divided activity of Dutch life—that is, its active concern with worldly affairs side by side with its indifference to neighbors or acquaintances—is conserved by an equally paradoxical representation of armies that

> seem only to be of use in allowing the inhabitants to enjoy the fruits of peace with so much the more security.

Thus Descartes's resolve

6 Geertz, *The Interpretation of Cultures: Selected Essays* (New York: Basic, 1973), 89.

to remove myself from all places where any acquaintances were possible, and to retire to a country such as this

—which is to say, to remove or withdraw or retire to "peace"—is formally symmetrical with the prior representations constituted by the paradox of self-immersion in the activity of the world and then, somehow as a result, withdrawal from it to the place where the condition of "I can live" is attained:

In the crowded throng of a great and very active nation . . . I can live as solitary and retired as in deserts the most remote.

The continuing line of representations of subtraction in Descartes's first resolve already heralds his cogito with a veiled announcement from the depths of his withdrawal into a condition highly congenial, and perhaps indispensable, to his hyperbolic doubt. Into *les déserts les plus écartés*, that is, Descartes withdraws from everything but the pronouncement, by way of an anagram, of his own name: here "I . . . live," or, here I am, in *les* déserts *écart és*.[7]

From this serially emptied place Descartes immediately sets out to represent his resolve to hyperbolic doubt. When in the first sentence of part 4 he speaks of "the first meditations there [*y* (31)] made by me," he means the meditations experienced in *les* déserts *écartés*, which is his thinking of freedom and his "I am," in other words, his cogito.

---

7 *René* can be read here, too, in *et re tiré que dans les*, which is perhaps plausible only immediately before *les* déserts *les plus* écartés. If such an interest in anagrams seems out of character for Descartes, think of the anagrammatic side of Saussure. Two other points about *les déserts les plus écartés* are worth making. First, when two paragraphs later Descartes says that for the "existence" of his cogito "there is no need of any place, nor does it depend on any material thing," he knows that he has already represented such an immaterial place by expressing his solitary cogito as no more than "I . . . live" in *les* déserts *écartés*, amid "the crowded throng," which is to say, amid the whirl of unlimited material things in "the most populous towns." Second, the lineage of Descartes's utterance of his "I . . . live" or "I am" is immeasurably long. Given the isolation in this clause of his "I . . . live" or "I am" together with his self-naming *les* déserts *les plus* écartés, Descartes is almost certainly thinking not only of God's most explicit Old Testament naming of himself, *Ego sum qui sum*, "I am that I am" (whose connection with Descartes's "I am" has been frequently noted), but also of its placement *ad interiora deserti*, "behind/after the desert" (Vulg. Exod. 3.1, 14). In this sense Descartes's double resolve and double pronouncement of his "I am" echoes God's doubled naming of himself in the deepest desert.

There is thus an indispensable continuity between the first and second resolves. The first is a series of representations of subtraction or removal, each of which reveals its own incompleteness of representation; thus each succeeding representation is chosen from the freedom of a nothingness (a space of withdrawal or occlusion) opened by a previous representation. Continually removed from all external objects or forces that might constrain his freedom of thinking and choosing, Descartes remains solitary, unconstrained, in the remotest desert, "there," and in this void his second, apparently more significant resolve is freely enacted.

Despite the very continuity of the representations that culminate in the freedom prerequisite to his cogito, Descartes will soon claim that an infinite series of representations must be denied or halted. He is well aware, however, of at least his initial experience of that continuity. In the Third Meditation he lays down the following propositions:

[1] One idea gives birth to another idea.
[2] Ideas in me are like paintings or pictures. (*PE*, 98)

But Descartes is silent about the kind of nothingness opened, in the *Discourse* at least, within each chosen representation (or painting or idea). Instead he ascribes the freedom of volition in his "present" moment of being to God's *concursus* [concurrence], which alone allows him to return from nothingness. Moreover, the *concursus* of God's being and his own nothingness is the very image in which the continuous "regress" of representations comes to a halt:

> Step by step we finally arrive at an ultimate cause which will turn out to be God. And it is very obvious that in this case there cannot be an infinite regress, since it is not so much a question of the cause which produced me in the past as of that which conserves me in the present. (*PE*, 106)

"To be conserved at every moment that it endures," Descartes explains, "a substance . . . needs the same power and the same action which would be necessary to produce it and create it anew if it did not exist" (*PE*, 105). The scene of the *concursus* is therefore the most fateful moment imaginable for human being per se. God alone gives Descartes the present experience of both nothingness and being. To be created "at every moment . . . anew" means to be created at every moment ex nihilo; hence at every moment every created thing must have just been nothing.

In the Fourth Meditation Descartes says precisely the same about his own thinking and being in his cogito:

> There is present in my thought not only a real and positive idea of God, or rather of a supremely perfect being, but also, so to speak, a certain negative idea of nothingness. . . . I see that I am, as it were, a mean between God and nothingness. . . . Placed between the supreme Being and not-being . . . I consider myself as some-how participating in nothingness or not-being. (*PE*, 110)

In Descartes's experience, every created thing not only tends con-stantly to slip out of existence but in fact has already slipped, at every moment, into the nothingness from which God at every moment newly creates it.[8]

Yet Descartes's claims about his experience of nothingness diverge significantly from his representations of it. No doubt Descartes believed that his slipping into nothingness was a quasi-religious expe-rience. But his representation of his oscillation between being and nothingness, as well as of his freedom to choose from nothingness, is accounted for within the structure of his representations, especially those in which he is engaged in his first and second resolves.[9] I pro-

8 Descartes's "doctrine" that "every created thing tends constantly to slip out of existence, being kept in being only by the continuous activity of God" is, Williams remarks, "one of the most genuinely religious elements in Descartes' outlook" (149). I suggest that Williams's statement can be amended as proposed here.

9 There may be another consequence for Descartes's religious outlook in his com-ments on nothingness. Descartes names being "God" and not-being "nothingness." Insofar as God has created him as "a mean between God and nothingness . . . placed between the supreme Being and not-being," Descartes's freedom of choice requires the freedom to deny one of the two contraries in the midst of which he is placed, namely, the existence of God, for even an instant; otherwise he could never *affirm* the existence of God. The tacit implication of Descartes's freedom of choice may account for the veiled force of the word *somehow* in Descartes's statement that God has created him with the possibility of "somehow participating in nothingness." In effect, Descartes describes a divinely sanctioned oscillation between nothingness and being, and between affirming and denying God, that is perhaps as bold as the same element of Nietzsche's "death of God" theology.

pose that his sketch of the *concursus* of being and nothingness itself points to the freedom that he encounters in his continuous line of culture.[10] Far from identifying a halt to representation in this image, Descartes advances it as his most powerful symbol of necessitated transmission in his line of representations, each of which lets us see its own inadequacy as representation.

Nicholas Malebranche, Descartes's disciple, intended to reveal God's direct action in Descartes's picture of the *concursus* of being and nothingness. Instead he demonstrated how Descartes's picture of the *concursus* is spectacularly occasioned by the continuity of cultural transmission. Malebranche observed that Descartes's conception of God in the *concursus* drew on a formulation commonplace in the New Testament, especially in the Pauline epistles. Malebranche, who styled it "that we see all things in God," meant that we see only in the light provided by God; for example, "Not that we are sufficient of ourselves to think any thing as of ourselves; but our sufficiency is of God" (2 Cor. 3.5); or "That which may be known of God is manifest in them [the Gentiles]; for God hath shewed it unto them" (Rom. 1.19).[11]

The provenience that Malebranche gives for the *concursus* shows that for Descartes the *concursus* of being and nothingness must be, among other things, the representation of a line of representations of Paul's representation of it. Because of the nothingness described by each representation within the series, each prior representation (whether we can specifically identify it or not) functions as the enabling ground of freedom for thinking and choosing. Descartes's regress of "ideas" or "paintings" is a spiraling line—more precisely, a vortex—of representations of being and nothingness, each of which is a concursus. Part of what is encountered in the *concursus*—as in all derivations and transmissions of culture in the mode of partial withdrawal of representation—is its endless, unrepresentable repetition from the past. Descartes traces his line of cultural transmission forward in his own rep-

10 See also Descartes's *Principles of Philosophy*, part 1, principle 51: "We perceive that all other things [besides God] can exist only by the help of the concourse of God" (*Works*, 1:239).

11 Malebranche, *Recherche de la vérité*, ed. Geneviève Rodis-Lewis, 3 vols. (Paris: CNRS, 1962–64), 1:439–40.

resentations of his first and second resolves. His experience entails his free choosing from the contraries of being and nothingness endlessly encountered in representations of the *concursus*.

The Pauline provenience of Descartes's *concursus* also helps us, I believe, locate the "great and very active" achievements of Dutch culture that so deeply impressed Descartes, even though he declined to specify them. To begin with, I offer a very brief exemplification of the part of the vast map of contemporary Dutch culture that most directly concerns us.

Among such achievements in the culture of partially withdrawn representations, Rembrandt's *Saint Paul in Prison*, painted in 1627, two years before Descartes reached Holland, is virtually a schematic representation of Paul's meditation on the *concursus* (fig. 1). The light entering the window of the otherwise dark cell is mediated for Paul by the crucifix handle of his "sword of the Spirit" (Eph. 6.17), supported on both sides by such texts as a saint keeps by him, reminding him that he can think nothing by himself. Rather, his sufficiency to think is of God. The pen in his hand indicates that he is writing the very texts that inscribe this scene.[12] Rembrandt strongly suggests that the texts are themselves reworkings, or representations, of sacred commonplaces of the *concursus* in the piles of scriptures that Paul keeps at his side and on his lap. (Who would not, under the same circumstances, think back, for example, to Psalms 36.9: "With thee is the fountain of life: in thy light shall we see light"?) Within the Rembrandtian iconographic economy it may even be plausible that Paul opens his eyes wide and brings his hand to his mouth because he suddenly realizes that he has just been created anew, from nothing, by the text that he is meditating on or is about to write down. At the very least, the scene is a stark representation of the Pauline *concursus* of being and nothingness that Malebranche paraphrases.

Aside: If such a philosophical reception of Rembrandt's painting seems unimaginable for 1627–29, I may instance here the intellectual

---

12 Rembrandt seems to join himself to the effects of God's light (and *fiat lux*) and concurrence by writing in large letters, at the top of Paul's page, "Rembrand [*sic*] fecit" [Rembrandt made this], although J. Bruyn et al. express doubt that Rembrandt himself inscribed these words (*1625–1631*, vol. 1 of *A Corpus of Rembrandt Paintings*, trans. D. Cook-Radmore [The Hague: Martinus Nijhoff, 1982], 146).

Figure 1   *Saint Paul in Prison* (Bredius 601). Courtesy Staatsgalerie Stuttgart.

range of Constantijn Huygens, patron to Descartes and Rembrandt and one of the "great and very active" Dutch whom Descartes came to know best after his arrival in Amsterdam in 1629–30. In 1629 Huygens wrote in his diary that Rembrandt, then only twenty-three years old, was already the equal of the most famous painters of Europe and predicted that he would soon surpass them. In 1632 Huygens began the relationship with Descartes that lasted until the end of Descartes's life. Descartes indicates that he composed the first draft of the *Meditations* about this time.[13] Rembrandt moved from Leiden to Amsterdam permanently in 1631–32. It seems clear that Rembrandt knew Descartes directly; apparently, he even painted Descartes in a place of honor in *The Hundred Guilder Print*.[14]

To resume: The art historian Jakob Rosenberg observes that the "motif" of the meditating philosopher "seems particularly close to Rembrandt and can be called one of his most personal choices." Whereas in other, contemporary Dutch painters "the outward attributes" of the philosopher's inquiry are most prominent, in Rembrandt the emphasis is on "the old philosopher enjoying the privilege of meditating in complete seclusion in his search for truth. Light and shade, a penumbral atmosphere, . . . gain a particular importance in connexion with this subject."[15] By the end of the eighteenth century, at the latest, Rembrandt's work was associated in the public mind with a single representation of the philosopher thinking, *Old Man in an Interior with a Winding Staircase* (1633). I believe that this painting already held a special significance for Descartes when he composed the *Discourse*. In France the painting had come by the following century to be called *Le Philosophe en contemplation* (fig. 2).[16] A recurrent

13 See Elizabeth S. Haldane, *Descartes: His Life and Times* (London: John Murray, 1905), 121. Haldane largely relies on Descartes's remarks in what I call his first resolve.

14 Howard White precedes me in noting resemblances between Rembrandt's and Descartes's handling of light ("Rembrandt and the Human Condition," *Interpretation* 4 [1974]: 17–37). White also draws special attention to Rembrandt's picturing of philosophers in cavernous rooms with windows and to the possibility that Huygens provided a link between Descartes and Rembrandt. Yet White's interpretations of Rembrandt and Descartes seem to me almost wholly mistaken. They are given as general impressions rather than derived from the structures of thought and object that Rembrandt and Descartes show. Curiously, White does not note Descartes's philosopher-in-the-cellar-with-windows passage, quoted below.

15 Rosenberg, *Rembrandt: Life and Work*, 2d ed. (London: Phaidon, 1964), 266–7.

16 Ironically, although the painting "helped to determine the image of Rembrandt's work to an unwarranted extent" (Bruyn et al., 642), it is currently ascribed (at least by Bruyn et al.) only to his workshop, not to Rembrandt himself. The distinction would, I suspect, have been lost on Descartes and most of his contemporaries. The same point applies to Bredius 427, mentioned below. (Bredius numbers

Figure 2   *Le Philosophe en contemplation* (Bredius 431). Courtesy Musée du Louvre, Paris. © Photo RMN.

feature in Rembrandt's paintings of the philosopher is that he meditates near a window or windows, usually in a darkened room. From roughly the same period as *Le Philosophe en contemplation* we have other well-known paintings of the scholar or philosopher thinking near a window (cf. figs. 3–4).[17]

In the late 1620s and early 1630s Rembrandt made his mark spectacularly as the master of chiaroscuro. Can it be purely by accident that in the *Discourse* Descartes evokes something very like Rembrandtian

are given according to A. Bredius, ed., *Rembrandt: The Complete Edition of the Paintings*, rev. H. Gerson, 3d ed. [London: Phaidon, 1969].)

17 From Rembrandt's later years we may instance the famous *Scholar in His Study* (1652), usually called the *Faust Etching*. The status of this setting for European philosophical culture at the end of the eighteenth and the beginning of the nineteenth centuries can hardly have been attested in a more remarkable way than by its free adaptation to illustrate the first edition of Goethe's *Faust* (1808).

Figure 3   *A Scholar in a Lofty Room* (Bredius 427). Courtesy of the National Gallery, London.

Figure 4 *A Scholar in a Lofty Room* ("St. Anastasius"), (Bredius 430).
Courtesy of the Statens Konstmuseer, Stockholm.

technique when setting down his own philosophical ways of representing thought and knowledge of "material things"?

> I intended to include . . . all that I thought I knew . . . concerning the nature of material things. But I found myself in the same state as painters, who cannot equally well represent in a two-dimensional

painting all the various faces of a solid body, and so choose one to bring to the light, and leave the others in shadow. (*PE*, 31–2)

For Descartes one face of every material thing, or of every cogito, in every *concursus*, is turned toward nothingness. For us the significance of the relation of Descartes's ideas to Rembrandt's highly contrastive chiaroscuro does not lie merely in the models that may have influenced Descartes.[18] Rather, the transposition of a painter's language of chiaroscuro into Descartes's language allows us to glimpse something like the cultural enabling of Descartes's freedom of choice between light and shadow, being and nothingness. That Descartes neglects to name specific cultural objects, or occasions, of this kind creates a false impression of his intellectual independence, which is contradicted by the way in which freedom becomes available, or is derived, in his own representations and resolves. Specific occasions of partially withdrawn representations, rendered by a painter like Rembrandt—or by extraordinarily close equivalents of Rembrandt—are, I suggest, the missing terms (the experienced openings of freedom) in Descartes's account.

Thus it may be especially significant for our understanding of how Descartes's cogito was enabled that one begetting representation of his freedom is eerily reproduced in the *Discourse*. In one of Descartes's most striking images of the courage of his philosophical resolve, opponents to his way of thinking

> appear . . . similar to a blind man who wishes to fight on even terms with one who can see, and so brings him to the back of some very dark cellar. These people, I may say, are interested in my abstaining from the publication of my principles of philosophy; for since these are very simple and evident, I would be doing much the same to them as though I opened some windows and let the

18 Moshe Barasch has pointed out to me that the chiaroscuro of the late sixteenth century, say, that of Caravaggio or even that of Dutch Caravaggesque painters, uses shadow to bring into relief the material reality of the bodies on which shadow and light are seen together. In Caravaggio we see the outlines of the body through the shadow. In Rembrandt, however, the outlines of the body tend to be lost in darkness. Descartes's reference to painters' use of shadow therefore corresponds quite closely, even distinctively, to the chiaroscuro that Rembrandt was innovating at the time of Descartes's arrival in Holland.

light of day enter into that cellar where they had descended [*descendus* (71)] to fight. (*PE*, 51)[19]

I turn again to *Le Philosophe en contemplation*, which by 1738 was also called *Tobias, and a Winding Stair*. The subject is clearly identified from its relation to the Book of Tobit (in the Jewish Apocrypha) and to the many representations of it that Rembrandt executed. The episode superimposed on the meditating philosopher here is that of the victory of Tobias, blind Tobit's son, over a demon who has attempted to murder him in a dark room below the stairs. Tobias, pictured at the window, overcomes the demon without striking a blow and also restores his father's sight. The advanced age of the man at the window suggests that, in addition to being an exemplum of Rembrandt's philosopher, he is also a composite of son and father, the dual heroes of the Book of Tobit.[20]

This painting and Descartes's pictured scene share the specific combination of familiar primary theme and exotic secondary theme. The former is that of the philosopher and his windows; the latter, that of the battle fought (without blows) between the hero and the demon (one of whom is blind) in an intensely dark room to which they have

19 I amend Lafleur's translation "cave," for the French *cave*, to "cellar."

20 Rembrandt painted blind Tobit many times, and more than once at a window where Tobias restores his sight to him. In *Tobias, and a Winding Stair* the female figure at the lower right burns incense, presumably at Tobias's direction, to drive away the demon, as the Book of Tobit requires. Unaccountably, Bruyn et al. claim that the identification of the painting with the story of Tobias "is certainly incorrect since there are two women in the picture and there is no specific motif from the story of Tobias" (642). In fact, even the second woman, about to leave at the head of the stairs, is clearly indicated in this episode: "Then they [Tobias's in-laws] went forth and shut the door of the chamber" (Tob. 8.2; cited from *The Book of Tobit*, ed. Frank Zimmermann [New York: Harper, 1958]). The woman who helps Tobias by taking "the liver of the fish and the heart out of the bag"—perhaps like the bag that Rembrandt places at the bottom of the stairs—and puts them "on the ashes of the incense" (Tob. 8.2) is identifiable with Tobias's bride, Sarah. The result is that "the smell of the fish repelled the demon, and he fled into the upper parts of Egypt" (Tob. 8.3). This is the place to recall that in Descartes's third dream of 10 November 1619, which he regarded as an oracle of his philosophical future and of what must happen to him for the rest of his life ("Ce dernier songe . . . marquoit l'avenir selon lui; & il n'étoit que pour ce qui devoit luy arriver dans le reste de sa vie"), he saw copper-plate etchings ("les petits Portraits de taille-douce") that were at the time inexplicable to him: see *Oeuvres de Descartes*, ed. Charles Adam and Paul Tannery (Paris: Vrin, 1966), 10:185.

descended, as from a staircase. The correspondences, though vivid, possess only archival interest in themselves. What may have decisive significance for Descartes's "principles of philosophy," however, is the location of the opening to his freedom in the repetitions from this regress (or progression) of partially withdrawn images, in paintings or in texts, each a *concursus* unto itself. Most important, both painting and text are chiaroscuro arrangements of being and nothingness in which the painter and the philosopher, each a mean between being and nothingness, resolve to participate. Each finds a freedom enabled by his inherited images of *concursus*. Each chooses between the contraries of being and nothingness within his effectively endless line of culture, and each is created anew in his representation within his line of culture.

Hanging on a wall of Descartes's Dutch world, the painting (or its twin) opens a window for Descartes's windows and for his free, peaceful battle on behalf of philosophy. Something very like this unnamed transmission of a *concursus* enabled the freedom of Descartes's "principles of philosophy." Specifically, Descartes obtained the freedom of his *déserts écartés* and of his cogito in a concrete *there* of this culture.

I turn now to Kant's sublime. In the "Analytic of the Sublime," and even in the *Critique of Judgment* as a whole, the mind's a priori ground of the sublime is announced as the "point of capital importance."[21] Kant claims that the freedom experienced in it is entirely independent of any object or any definite concept (90, 104). He attaches central significance to the independence of sublime experience because, in his view, it is identified with the freedom of aesthetic judgment and its consequence, "moral feeling" (116–7).

Yet the immediacy of the provocation required by the sublime casts doubt, from the start, on Kant's claim.[22] Thus I will propose a counter-

21 Kant, "Analytic of the Sublime," in *The Critique of Judgement*, trans. James Creed Meredith (Oxford: Clarendon, 1973), 102, 117. I do not reproduce Meredith's capitalizations of certain nouns (e.g., *Object*). Citations from the "Analytic of the Sublime" in German are from *Kants Werke: Akademie-Textausgabe*, vol. 5 (Berlin: Walter de Gruyter, 1968).

22 In a future discussion I hope to elaborate on the causes of Kant's blindness to what seems like an obvious contradiction on an elementary point. Kant's contradictions regarding the occasion of the sublime have been noticed before. See, for example, Paul Crowther, *The Kantian Sublime: From Morality to Art* (Oxford: Clarendon,

claim: in the "Analytic of the Sublime" Kant's representation of the mind's "*a priori* . . . transcendental" freedom (116–7) is indispensably occasioned by a particular cultural transmission, signaled by a specific work of art; that is, in his experience of the sublime Kant resists, in freedom, a particular representation of resistance in freedom.[23] This prior representation enables Kant's freedom; furthermore, it is experienced by him in an infinite progression—or infinite regress—of representations, each of which lets us see its own inadequacy as representation. These representations form the immediate (always culturally transmitted) objects of Kant's experience of the sublime. Kant's own language indicates that he takes in this prior representation, in its line of representations, "at one glance" [*in einem Augenblick*], but he chooses to "resist" [*widerstehen*] what he has seen and in effect "no longer sees" [*nicht* . . . *ansieht*] what he has seen.[24]

It will help clarify the nature of my counterclaim to note that it corresponds to Kant's way of setting off his representation of sublime experience. Kant's framing predicate, near the beginning of section 28, is the phrase *wenn* . . . *wir uns bloss* . . . *denken* (103) [our simply imagining in thought (110)]. These words clearly indicate a supposition or subjunctive condition, or, as we now say, a counterfactual: the very supposition *wenn* . . . *wir uns bloss* . . . *denken* denies that the representation (the pictured case or situation) is the reality that it represents.[25] F. H. Bradley long ago supplied (without specific reference to Kant) the basic logic of the supposition. With regard to its givens, Bradley made it clear that although a supposition is "known to be ideal . . . it is not the

<hr />

1989), 108–35. Although my interpretation of Kant's representation of sublime experience is very different from Crowther's, I take heart from his attempt to find in Kant an "artefactual sublime" (162), that is, "a sense of the scope of human artifice" (153) that has gone into the production of a given work of art and that therefore can give us "species solidarity" (173).

23 I do not find that Kant maintains a significant distinction between presentation and representation, *Darstellung* and *Vorstellung*, in the "Analytic of the Sublime."

24 To be viewed within Kant's own picture of the sublime, these terms require an appropriate framing, which I try to give below. The terms occur on pages 107, 110, and 114 of *The Critique of Judgement*; on pages 99, 103, and 108 of *Kritik der Urteilskraft*.

25 I am grateful to Dieter Henrich for pointing out to me the counterfactual form of Kant's phrase and for proposing the translation "our simply imagining in thought" in place of Meredith's "simply picturing to ourselves." Meredith's phrase apparently anticipates the emergence of a picture in Kant's text; Henrich's is more neutral.

mere *idea* of existence that is used. What we use is the real that is always in immediate contact with our minds." With regard to what a supposition produces, he observed that "the real is not qualified by the attribute we apply to it. But, so soon as we judge, we have truth or falsehood, and the real is at once concerned in the matter." Bradley added that what a supposition affirms "is the mere ground of the connection; not the actual existing behavior of the real, but a latent quality of its disposition, a quality which has appeared in the experiment."[26] These comments bear on the apparently loose relations among the representations that I describe in Kant's supposition. Furthermore, the status of the supposition obtains equally in the relations among the representations that I have proposed for Descartes. For the meaning of literary history there are important lessons to be learned from the ways in which Kant's and Descartes's representations leave virtually no traces of influence (anxious or unanxious) even as they are powerfully implicated in the relations of a highly specific cultural transmission. One might indeed object that such relations as I propose amount to no more than strings of possible associations that might just as well have led the viewer in many other directions. Yet the experience of cultural transmission—that is, of cultural transmission that continues to find recipients—is characteristically of this kind.

Just in this way, I suggest, Kant's invoking of the suppositional frame for his representation of sublime experience captures a feature of representations that may be all too easily lost on art critics and historians. That is, the status of supposition that conditions Kant's representation reproduces the status of supposition that necessarily inheres in the representations that he takes in. In addition, in the specific representations that Descartes and Kant encounter, as in their own representations, the status of supposition is highlighted by a form of representation that lets us see its own inadequacy as representation.

In Kant's supposition of sublime experience and moral feeling, no less than in Descartes's resolve to the hyperbolic doubt from which his cogito issues, the thought recorded (including its subtractive elements) could not have come into existence without the real that was

26 Bradley, *The Principles of Logic*, 2d ed., 2 vols. (London: Oxford University Press, 1922), 1:85–7.

in immediate contact with their minds. My supposition, accordingly, is that a significant part of the real, for both Descartes and Kant, was provided by an existing line of representations. The disposition for connection that Descartes and Kant came to share is a recurring quality of the line of representations that they chose to join or, as Descartes would say, to remove themselves to. It follows that my own supposition regarding these matters must be formulated in a subjunctive mood, immediately real though I believe the force of the supposition to be.

Here I briefly summarize what Kant says about the half dozen chief elements of his supposition, or picture, of sublime experience, that is, the experience that he claims is of the mind "of itself alone":

1 "As is allowable," says Kant, his presentation of the sublime is drawn exclusively according to experience of the sublime occasioned by "objects of nature," not from experience occasioned by objects of art or culture (91). Thus, for example, Kant asks us to imagine some vast peak whose top we cannot see, "shapeless mountain masses towering one above the other in wild disorder" (104).

2 The experience of the sublime occurs in the mind as the result of a contradiction between two mental capacities. While our imagination attempts to follow a progression that has no end in sight— for example, "masses towering one above the other"—our reason tries to grasp a whole idea of that progression. Oddly, the incapacity created by this contradiction sets in operation the innate capacity to feel the presence of something unknown to the senses, or "supersensible." The supersensible is not necessarily supernatural or divinely mysterious. For Kant the sublime is the mind's capacity or "faculty" to continue to think about a given representation of an object even though the mind has exhausted its resources for sensory perception (measurement) of that object:

Because there is a striving in our imagination towards progress *ad infinitum*, while reason demands absolute totality, as a real idea, that same inability . . . is the awakening of a feeling of a supersensible faculty within us. . . . Consequently it is the state of mind evoked by a particular representation engaging the attention of the reflective judgment, and not the object, that is to be called sublime. (97–8)[27]

For the logical unfolding of the experience of the sublime Kant offers a shorthand that renders the instantaneous character of the experience. The mind's experience of the sublime is "owing to the impossibility of the absolute totality of an endless progression" (104).

3 The experience of the sublime occurs only when the individual mind initiates it by freely inducing its own incapacity, which is the mind's subjection to "the impossibility of the absolute totality of an endless progression." Thus the mind's act of freedom is a willed self-deprivation of freedom, which paradoxically creates greater freedom:

> The sublime . . . is a feeling of imagination by its own act depriving itself of its freedom. . . . In this way it gains an extension and a might greater than that which it sacrifices. But the ground of this is concealed from it, and in its place it *feels* the sacrifice or deprivation . . . a deprivation of something—though in the interests of inner freedom. (120–3)

4 Only in "a negative presentation" can the mind present to itself the idea of freedom, because "the inscrutability of the idea of freedom precludes all positive presentation" (128), that is, all presentation in any bounded or defined body.

5 "Melancholy," one of Kant's principal names for the mind's representation to itself of its sublime thought and emotion, is the effect on the mind of combining its "serenity" with the abrupt "movement" of the mind aroused by the object (121). This movement, an "alternating repulsion and attraction" (107), follows from "resistance" or "opposition" to the sensory object (91, 110, 118–9), which "the mind [which] is all life (the life-principle itself)" experiences in the sublime as a moment of dying. We are reassured that this "momen-

---

27 I have given "state of mind" for Kant's *Geistesstimmung* (85), where Meredith has "disposition of soul," although Meredith usually translates Kant's words for the location of the supersensible faculty as "mind." J. H. Bernard's translation of the *Critique of Judgment* (New York: Haffner, 1931) gives "state of mind" for *Geistesstimmung*.

tary check to the vital forces" (91) [*augenblicklichen Hemmung der Lebenskräfte* (75)] is "followed at once by a discharge all the more powerful." Yet it is not obvious in Kant's account of the sublime, any more than in Descartes's sudden awareness of his "I am" after hyperbolic doubt—or, incidentally, than it becomes in Hegel's Kant-derived account of the birth of self-consciousness after "dying-away" in "sublimation"—how the "vital forces," which have been checked or radically suspended or have died-away, are able to recover.[28]

6   Surprisingly, Kant withholds discussion of the feeling that a viewer may have on seeing the Pyramids of Egypt or Saint Peter's in Rome, that is, the feeling when it "comes home to him of the inadequacy of his imagination for presenting the idea of a whole within which that imagination attains its maximum, and, in its fruitless efforts to extend this limit, recoils upon itself [*in sich selbst zurück sinkt* (88)], but in so doing succumbs to an emotional delight" (100). Kant's withholding, a key element in his representation of the sublime, expresses itself as a refusal

at present . . . to deal with the ground of this delight, connected as it is, with a representation in which we would least of all look for it—*a representation, namely, that lets us see its own inadequacy,* and consequently its subjective want of finality for our judgment in the estimation of magnitude. (100; emphasis added)

Such a representation—a work of art or a representation of culture, in other words—has been crafted to let the viewer see its (the art object's) own inadequacy to full or complete representation. Kant appears to distinguish this withdrawn representation from "works of art, e.g. buildings, statues and the like, where a human end determines the form as well as the magnitude" and also from "things of nature, that in their very concept import a definite end" (100). Inexplicably, Kant is "disposed" (100) to deal only with objects of nature that occasion the sublime by not "import[ing] a definite end," and not with works of art that might do the same negative thing.

28   I comment on Hegel's account of "dying-away" in "The Experience of Literary History," *New Literary History* 25 (1994): 749–77.

Yet Kant's own representation of sublime experience, considered in the
array of visualized predicates that constitute that representation, allows
us to suppose that another picture, prior to Kant's picture of his "a priori . . . transcendental," may enable the freedom that leads to moral
feeling, that is, for Kant himself. For the following list of those predicates I use only the details of Kant's own terms and phrases, most of
them from sections 28 and 29 of the "Analytic of the Sublime." Using a
typical Kantian formulation, I ask, what must a representation be to
include the predicates that Kant supposes?

1 The individual experiencing the sublime simply imagines in
   thought the experience of the sublime.
2 He views a desolate place, isolated from all society.
3 He is withdrawn from the world and its affairs.
4 The place to which he has withdrawn is not altogether inhospitable.
5 His mood is that of melancholy—or *apatheia* or *phlegma in significatu bono* [phlegmatic in a good sense]—or "an interesting sadness."
6 He is helpless.
7 He sees that he is safe.
8 He experiences deprivation as if by his own will.
9 He resists (or has resisted) God's commandments.
10 He is now resigned to God's will or wrath.
11 He is conscious of his own uprightness before God and man.
12 God's wrath is shown in the violence of nature.
13 Nature's violence is shown to be God's outburst of wrath or the
   pouring forth of the vials of his wrath.
14 The individual who experiences all of this at this moment no
   longer sees the violence wrought by nature in fulfillment of God's
   wrath.

   In principle it must be possible to identify the specific representation that Kant chose to resist (i.e., not to acknowledge specifically)
even while he supposed all of its predicates. Of course, I do not insist
that the work of art that I will propose, and suppose, must be the one
that "immediately . . . provokes" Kant's sublime experience (90). But,

following Kant's own terms, I do insist that his sublime experience was immediately provoked by some work of art virtually identical with the one that I will propose. (It is my hope that other readers will propose other possibilities that include all of Kant's predicates.) In Kant's own terms for experience of the sublime and of freedom, only one work at a time could occasion "at once" (103), "at one glance" (107), the instant of "a momentary check to the vital forces." This immediately experienced, particular work signaled for Kant the experience of a particular endless transmission of culture. In the "Analytic of the Sublime" Kant resists this derivation of sublime experience yet actively, specifically, represents it.

That is, Kant's representation of sublime experience must in itself be an experience (as well as a representation) of an effectively endless line of prior representations of that experience. It must be occasioned by a particular object that "immediately . . . provokes" this sublime experience, which thus expresses a definite concept of the line of culture (the line of withdrawn representations) subjunctively directed, with a certain disposition, toward an end.[29] All elements of Kant's representation of the experience of the sublime are necessarily represented as commonplaces (topoi). In the experience of the sublime Kant experiences the utter (sublime) commonplaceness of his own thinking of the sublime, because commonplaces are figures or representational predicates (always expressed in the subjunctive mood) derived from an endless progression or line of prior representations. In the representation of sublime experience the lineage of commonplaceness is itself part of the representation.

This perspective on the function of the commonplace within sublime representation at least partly meets, and embraces in advance, the objection that Kant surely recalled numerous other representations (including discursive descriptions) of the sublime that were very similar to the one I will suppose. In addition, this perspective suggests that in Kant's experience of the sublime per se only those elements—including selection and arrangement—that are part of an effectively endless progression of prior representation are admissible to Kant's picture of the sub-

29 Stanley Cavell suggested to me the emphasis, at this juncture of my argument, on the expressibility of the concept and on the directedness (of sublime experience) toward an end.

lime. Here *prior* can only mean "identical to," or at least "identified with," the latest representations in the progression. Of course, there will always be the individual's fingerprints on the sublime transmission of culture, and there will always be new contextualizations or historical landscapes in which the call and the silence of a transmission of the sublime are heard. These fingerprints and contextualizations may be of great interest in themselves, but they do not occasion the sublime experience per se as Kant describes it. Thus Kant's selection and arrangement of commonplaces must be experienced by Kant as the recurrence of a prior, particular selection and arrangement of commonplaces. In this way Kant's representation represents the experience of a particular line or effectively endless progression of sublime representations, which is to say, the sublime suppositions of a given line of culture.

Within Kant's line of culture, an endless progression of representations frees him to resist or choose the object of culture. Yet since freedom is to resist or choose *something*, Kant is free to resist or choose that something only if it has been part of his experience; if, in this case, he stands within his line of cultural transmission. Otherwise his resistance or choice is only the effect of prejudice, that is, of someone else's resistance or choice imposed (however subtly) on him. Kant's act of freedom in resisting or choosing this line of cultural transmission can have occurred only in his experience of this line of his culture. His act of freedom in resisting is achieved by "simply imagining in thought" (i.e., by simply supposing, counterfactually) a "righteous man" wishing to "resist God and His commandments" (110). Although Kant denies that experience of the sublime intrinsically depends on an experience of culture, he must both resist and repeat this particular, prior representation within his line of culture.

The particular representation that I have in mind and that Kant may very well have had in mind—a widely circulated etching of a painting by Rembrandt—was known in Germany, in Kant's time, both as *Le Philosophe dans sa grotte* [The philosopher in his cave] and as *Loth in der Höhle* [Lot in the cave].[30] (At the end of the nineteenth century, a hun-

---

30 Bruyn et al. point out that the painting was called *Lot in der Höhle* as early as 1767 (282). They mistakenly suggest, however, that the title *Le Philosophe dans sa grotte*

dred years after Kant wrote the "Analytic of the Sublime," the painting received a new title, *Jeremiah Lamenting the Destruction of Jerusalem* [fig. 5], which in effect made the connection with Kant impossible to see.[31] A number of Kant's predicates have no place in Jeremiah's situation but correspond in detail to Lot's.)

Already in the eighteenth century Rembrandt's works were very popular in Germany, especially in northern (Protestant) Germany. The etching of Rembrandt's painting to which I draw attention became commonly available in Kant's part of the world precisely when he was writing the "Analytic of the Sublime." The copper-plate etching was made in Berlin in 1768 by Georg Friedrich Schmidt, engraver to the king of Prussia and one of the most famous engravers of the day. Schmidt's Rembrandt etchings (eight in all) were widely admired as the pinnacle of engraving in that century, surpassing (it was said) the engravings of Rembrandt himself.[32] In the Keyserling palace, where

dates from C. Vosmaer, *Rembrandt Harmens van Rijn: Sa vie et ses oeuvres* (The Hague, 1868), 2–3. Already in A. Crayen's *Catalogue raisonné de l'oeuvre de feu George Frédéric Schmidt, graveur du roi de Prusse*, published in London in 1789 (i.e., a year before the publication of Kant's "Analytic of the Sublime"), Schmidt's etching of Rembrandt's painting is itemized as "No. 166 *Le Philosophe dans sa grotte . . . le nom qu'on donne ordinairement à cette estampe*" (104).

31 I comment on the iconography of this painting (although without reference to Kant) in "Rembrandt's *Jeremiah*," *Journal of the Warburg and Courtauld Institutes* 51 (1988): 260–4 and plate 41; and in "Rembrandt's and Freud's 'Gerusalemme Liberata,'" *Social Research* 58 (1991): 189–207. Schmidt's etching is extremely faithful to Rembrandt's painting, except for a slight change in the shape of the bag (here a kind of hat) beside the old man, the absence of the inscription "BiBeL" (perhaps a late addition to the painting) on the book, and the omission of a tiny, insectlike figure over the fire. In addition, of course, Schmidt's etching (dedicated, left to right, to his friend Hoffrath Johann George Lesser, physician to the king) reproduces Rembrandt's painting in reverse. If the accepted date of the painting (1630) is correct, then it was painted shortly *before* Rembrandt moved permanently to Amsterdam, although most of his paintings in the philosophical genre were painted in Amsterdam.

32 The contemporary art connoisseur Matthias Oesterreich, for example, explicitly made this claim in *Beschreibung der Königlichen Bildergalerie und des Kabinets in Sans-Souci*, 2d ed. (Potsdam, 1770), 29. In a similar vein, and with regard to the failure of Schmidt's black-and-white etching to reproduce the richness of Rembrandt's painting, it is interesting to recall Kant's comment that, in our experience of painting, "the *charm* of colors" may distract the aesthetic judgment from "what is essential," namely, "the *design*" (67–8).

Figure 5　*Jeremiah Lamenting the Destruction of Jerusalem* (Bredius 604).
Courtesy Rijksmuseum, Amsterdam.

Kant was a frequent guest beginning in 1772, Königsberg (one of the
king's official residences) boasted one of the finest collections of copper-
plate etchings in Europe. Considering the prominence of etchings in
everyday artistic education of the times and Kant's particular opportunities for special attentiveness to Schmidt's rendering of Rembrandt's
picture of the philosopher (rendered, in turn, from the Bible), it

requires an effort to imagine that Kant never at least glanced at it. How he may have been affected by it is, of course, another matter. The representations that I have in mind, then, side by side, are Schmidt's etching of Rembrandt's *Philosopher in His Cave/Lot in the Cave* and the collection of visual predicates from Kant's "Analytic of the Sublime."[33] In the predicates Kant simply imagines in thought the individual in the moment of experiencing the freedom of the sublime, necessarily in resistance (fig. 6). If we put together the title *Lot in the Cave* and the story told in Genesis, the buildings burning to Lot's right may be supposed to be those of Sodom and Gomorrah. Here God expresses his wrath through violent nature: earthquakes, brimstone, and fire. Formerly fearful of this violence, Lot has for a time even resisted divine

---

33 Aside from the passages quoted earlier, the principal passages I have in mind are the following: (1) "The irresistibility of the might of nature forces upon us the recognition of our physical helplessness as beings of nature, but at the same time reveals a faculty of estimating ourselves as independent of nature, and discovers a pre-eminence above nature that is the foundation of a self-preservation of quite another kind from that which may be assailed and brought into danger by external nature. This saves humanity in our own person from humiliation, even though as mortal men we have to submit to external violence. . . . We must see ourselves safe in order to feel this soul-stirring delight" (111–2). (2) "Only when [a man] becomes conscious of having a disposition that is upright and acceptable to God, do those operations of might serve to stir within him the idea of the sublimity of this Being, so far as he recognizes the existence in himself of a sublimity of disposition consonant with His will, and is thus raised above the dread of such operations of nature [i.e., 'God in the tempest, the storm, the earthquake, and the like, . . . presenting Himself in His wrath'], in which he no longer sees God pouring forth the vials of his wrath [*und dadurch über die Furcht vor solchen Wirkungen der Natur, die er nicht als Ausbrüche seines Zornes ansieht, erhoben wird* (108)]" (113–4). (3) "(As seems strange) even *freedom from affection* (*apatheia, phlegma in significatu bono*) in a mind that strenuously follows its unswerving principles is sublime. . . . Such a stamp of mind is alone called noble" (124–5). (4) "*Isolation from all society* is looked upon as something sublime, provided it rests upon ideas which disregard all sensible interest. To be self-sufficing, and so not to stand in need of society, yet without being unsociable, i.e. without shunning it, is something approaching the sublime" (129). (5) "There is an *interesting* sadness [*eine interessante Traurigkeit* (127)], such as is inspired by the sight of some desolate place into which men might fain withdraw themselves so as to hear no more of the world without, and be no longer versed in its affairs, a place, however, which must yet not be so altogether inhospitable as only to afford a most miserable retreat for a human being.—I only make this observation as a reminder that even melancholy, (but not dispirited sadness,) may take its place among the *vigorous* affections, provided it has its root in moral ideas" (130).

Figure 6   Schmidt's etching of *Le Philosophe dans sa grotte/Loth in der Höhle* (*Jeremiah Lamenting the Destruction of Jerusalem*). Courtesy Staatliche Museen zu Berlin. Photo: Jörg P. Anders.

counsel to flee the city (Gen. 19.16, 18, 20), but now he sits alone in a desolate cave, apathetic or melancholy. (He reclines in the pose that iconographically stands for melancholy [see Bruyn et al., 281].) Aware that he is safe from the conflagration, out of sight of God's wrath, Lot might be taken (as his daughters take him) for the last man alive. He has accepted God's decree, having earlier risked his life (and that of his daughters) to observe the customs of hospitality and to protect the stranger.

"We may look upon an object as *fearful*, and yet not be afraid *of* it," says Kant,

> if . . . our estimate takes the form of our simply imagining in thought the case of our wishing to offer some resistance to it, and recognizing that all such resistance would be quite futile. So the righteous man fears God without being afraid of Him, because he regards the case of his wishing to resist God and His command-ments as one which need cause *him* no anxiety. But in every such case, regarded by him as not intrinsically impossible, he cognizes Him as One to be feared. (110)

To take the estimate of Kant's true picture of sublime cultural experi-ence, we need to paraphrase his words in something like the following way, that is, in order to suppose (to imagine in thought) Kant's resis-tance to the prior representation (especially of the inadequacy of rep-resentation) that he fears:[34]

> We may look upon an object of culture—"a representation, namely, that lets us see its own inadequacy, and consequently its subjective want of finality for our judgment in the estimation of magnitude" (100)—as fearful and yet not be afraid of it. . . . Our estimate takes the form of our simply imagining in thought the case of our wishing to offer some resistance to this "it" and recognizing that all such resistance would be quite futile.
>
> So the philosopher, or man who experiences the sublime, fears the endless progression of artistic, or cultural, presentations of sub-

34 Kant further specifies the importance of resistance in his experience of the sub-lime: "The *sublime* is what pleases immediately by reason of its opposition to the inter-est of sense . . . in *opposition* to sensibility . . . in opposition to our sensible interest" (118–9); "the object of a pure and unconditioned intellectual delight is the moral law in the might which it exerts in us over all *antecedent* motives of the mind. Now, since it is only through sacrifices that this might makes itself known to us aesthetically, (and this involves a deprivation of something—though in the interests of inner free-dom—whilst in turn it reveals in us an unfathomable depth of this supersensible fac-ulty, the consequences of which extend beyond reach of the eye of sense,) it follows that the delight, looked at from the aesthetic side (in reference to sensibility) is neg-ative, i.e. opposed to the interest of sense" (123).

lime experience, which enables or moves him to achieve his own freedom of sublime experience without being afraid of it. Yet in every such case, regarded by him as not intrinsically impossible, his experience of the sublime enables him to recognize his own line of culture, or progression of such presentations, as one to be feared, since it occasions "a momentary check to the vital forces."

As in what is seen to occur in *The Philosopher in His Cave/Lot in the Cave*, Kant pictures the enforcement of God's might through the agency of violent nature. Once this connection among Kant's representations, or suppositions, is made, this and the other visual predicates I have cited from the "Analytic of the Sublime" are seen to form one extended supposition of the sublime experience.

My supposition is that Kant resists (averts his eyes from) Schmidt's etching of Rembrandt's biblical painting (or its double) even as he retraces it (thus fulfilling what Kant himself identifies as the sublime commandment to represent the inadequacy of representation [127]). In this way, the figure in Kant's picture and in Schmidt's etching resists God's commandments yet fulfills them in the representation or experience that is resistance in freedom.[35] The engraver or painter draws each such experience or representation of the sublime with, as it were, one hand tied behind his back. The resulting disposition of mind for each protagonist in this ongoing cultural experiment—"Lot," Rembrandt, Schmidt, Kant—is melancholic or apathetic. There is no full recovery for any individual mind but only what Kant calls the "subjective want of finality" or the "contra-final" mind. Yet we see a symmetry with each representation of the given line of such representations that leads into this picture, threads through it, and points beyond it.

In this momentary check to his vital forces Kant is unable to acknowledge that a historical line of cultural transmission—an endless progression of representations of the inadequacy of representation—has occasioned his freedom of self-deprivation. Yet his own free act of self-deprivation is his casting away of the immediacy, for his own experience, of the immediate representation that provokes his recognition of this line of representations, which he now continues.

35 Much more can be said about the resistance in freedom pictured by Rembrandt in his central figure. I have touched on this matter in the essays cited in note 31. In another essay, now in preparation, I deal with it more systematically.

Ten thousand other pictures contain some, many, or most of the elements that are objects of sublime experiences like the one Kant represents. But to glimpse the moment of freedom in Kant's representation of sublime experience, we must suppose, plausibly, the specific prior representation—and *its* endless progression of prior representations—that "immediately . . . provokes" his resistance, as well as the check to his vital forces. I propose that the picture of effectively endless cultural transmission at which Kant glanced must have provoked him in something very like the guise of Schmidt's etching of Rembrandt's *Philosopher in His Cave/Lot in the Cave*.[36] Yet whether or not this etching of this painting of this biblical scene (and of this philosopher) is the specific identification that we require, my supposition is that the philosopher Kant—simply imagining in thought, withdrawn and resisting in his study in Königsberg—has himself pictured just how particular the cultural provocation to his mind's sublime experience had to have been.

Descartes's freedom and Kant's freedom are both enabled by their experiences of cultural transmission, specifically of a transmission defined by a line of representations, each of which shows us its own inadequacy as representation. With hindsight we may say that there was a certain inevitability to the experiences of Descartes and Kant: two of the greatest European philosophers, while thinking about representation, not least the representation of painters, encountered one of the greatest European painters, representing the philosopher thinking. Yet, however the stage was set for these encounters, the nothingness of

36 Some third-party suggestion of Kant's special attention to Schmidt's and Rembrandt's picture of the philosopher withdrawn to his cave may be available in the four-volume novel *Lebensläufe nach aufsteigender Linie* (Berlin, 1778–81), by Kant's close friend Theodor Gottfried von Hippel. Prior to the publication of Kant's *Critique of Pure Reason* (1781), the first and second volumes of Hippel's novel employed a variety of unmistakably Kantian or pseudo-Kantian views and terms (entries in a "Lexicon der reinen Vernunft" [2:245]). After Hippel's death Kant noted, not disapprovingly, that Hippel had made use of ideas derived from Kant's lectures. (Kant's published letter on the subject, together with the more extensive manuscript draft of the letter, is reproduced in Arthur Warda, "Kants 'Erklärung' wegen der v. Hippelschen Autorschaft," *Altpreußische Monatsschrift* 41 [1904]: 61–93.) It may therefore be of special interest, for example, that Hippel's Kantian philosopher expresses the wish that one of his students might attain to the philosopher's "glance through the crack or opening" [*Blick durchs Ritzchen* (2:246 and passim)] by locating himself in an antique "place of withdrawal into solitude, a place of hiding, a retired spot" [*ein Secessum, Secretum, Angulum* (2:252)].

Descartes's hyperbolic doubt, from which his cogito issued, and the momentary check to Kant's vital forces, from which his sublime freedom for moral feeling issued, were each enabled by this line of representations. Each representation in this line shows us its inadequacy as representation (in addition to its status as supposition), even as each is specifically a representation of the philosopher thinking. For Descartes and Kant, Rembrandt's two paintings—*Le Philosophe en contemplation* and *Le Philosophe dans sa grotte*—are of special consequence.

If we happen to think of ourselves as belonging to Descartes's and Kant's lines of cultural transmission, we too, in glancing at these paintings, may experience anew our own strange condition as free individuals within these transmissions of culture. Whatever other, infinitely varied things we do, each of us may thereby be enabled to think, and to resist freely, the occasion of freedom within cultural transmissions of this sort.

The means of cultural transmission are central to what culture is. In thinking about, and from, a line of cultural transmission—in conceiving the connections among objects in the line of transmission—we divest ourselves of a positivity, or wholly determinate causality. Cultural transmission makes available a field of suppositions, which the individual mind experiences as an infinite potentiality of permutation, as an unlimited unknowability of intended interconnection, and as a certain disposition toward ways of connecting. This disposition emerges from the line of transmission itself, in which the recipient takes part. Lines of cultural transmission do not necessarily become less real because of their counterfactual status. The freedom of association created for the individual mind by this subjunctive cultural transmission in fact renders more urgent the recipient's desire to ground the disposition of connection.

For the literary or art historian describing cultural transmission, the requirement of providing the plausibility of a given supposition is in no way suspended by its being, after all, only a supposition. The plausible force of the supposition is the depth of the historical account itself, and this depth can be achieved only through an awareness of specific objects within the line of transmission.[37]

---

37 There is circularity in this logic, but it is only the circularity of coming to know identity of any kind.

CONTRIBUTORS

NANCY ARMSTRONG is Nancy Duke Lewis Professor of Comparative Literature, English, Modern Culture and Media, and Women's Studies at Brown University. She is the author of *Desire and Domestic Fiction: A Political History of the Novel* (1987) and coauthor, with Leonard Tennenhouse, of *The Imaginary Puritan: Literature, Intellectual Labor, and the Origins of Personal Life* (1992). She has coedited two collections, also with Leonard Tennenhouse, *The Ideology of Conduct: Literature and the History of Sexuality* (1986) and *The Violence of Representation: Literature and the History of Violence* (1989). A new book, *Fiction in the Age of Photography: The Legacy of British Realism*, is forthcoming.

MARSHALL BROWN is Professor of English and Comparative Literature at the University of Washington and editor of *Modern Language Quarterly: A Journal of Literary History*. His most recent books are *Turning Points: Essays in the History of Cultural Expressions* (1997) and, as editor, *The Uses of Literary History* (1995).

SANFORD BUDICK is Professor of English and founding director of the Center for Literary Studies at the Hebrew University of Jerusalem. He has published widely on classical poetry, Milton, Rembrandt, English neoclassical poetry, Hegel, Goethe, Wordsworth, and Freud. *The Translatability of Cultures: Figurations of the Space Between*, coedited with Wolfgang Iser, appeared in 1996.

CATHERINE GALLAGHER is the Eggers Professor of English Literature at the University of California, Berkeley, and the author of *Nobody's Story: The Vanishing Acts of Women Writers in the Marketplace, 1670–1820* (1994).

THOMAS M. KAVANAGH teaches French at the University of California, Berkeley. His recent publications include *Esthetics of the Moment*

(1997) and *Enlightenment and the Shadows of Chance* (1993). He is working on a study of the culture of gambling in early modern Europe.

JON KLANCHER is preparing a study of romanticism and the institutions of cultural transmission. He is the author of *The Making of English Reading Audiences, 1790–1832*, and teaches literary history at Boston University.

JILL ANNE KOWALIK is Associate Professor of German at UCLA and a Clinical Associate at the Los Angeles Psychoanalytic Institute. Her research is primarily concerned with concepts of artistic imitation and representation, psychoanalysis, and the epistemology of the cultural sciences. In addition to a book titled *The Poetics of Historical Perspectivism*, her work includes articles on Kleist, Thomas Mann, Nietzsche, and the psychodynamics of the Enlightenment. At present she is at work on a monograph about pathological grief and secularization in the seventeenth and eighteenth centuries.

JONATHAN BRODY KRAMNICK is Assistant Professor of English at Rutgers University and the author of *The Making of the English Canon: Print-Capitalism and the Cultural Past, 1700–1770* (1998).

CHRISTIE MCDONALD is Professor of Romance Languages and Literatures at Harvard University. She is the author of a number of books, including *The Dialogue of Writing* (1985), *Dispositions* (1986), and *The Proustian Fabric* (1991); editor of *The Ear of the Other: Texts and Discussions with Jacques Derrida: Otobiography, Transference, Translation* (1985); and coeditor of *Transformations in Personhood and Culture after Theory* (1994). McDonald received the 1994–95 Clifford Prize awarded by the American Society for Eighteenth-Century Studies for "The Anxiety of Change: Reconfiguring Family Relations in Beaumarchais."

JEROME MCGANN is the John Stewart Bryan University Professor, University of Virginia. His most recent critical work is *Poetics of Sensibility: A Revolution in Literary Style* (1996); he has also just published *Laetitia Elizabeth Landon: Selected Writings* (1997), which he edited with Daniel Riess.

RUTH PERRY is a Professor of Literature at MIT. She is the author of *Women, Letters, and the Novel* (1980) and *The Celebrated Mary Astell* (1986), and the editor of George Ballard's 1752 *Memoirs of Several Ladies of*

Great Britain (1985) and a volume of essays called *Mothering the Mind* (1984). Her current project is a history of the family in relation to the novel in England, 1750–1810.

MICHAEL B. PRINCE is Associate Professor of English at Boston University. "The Eighteenth-Century Beauty Contest" is part of a longer treatment of eighteenth-century translations and imitations of Plato in *Philosophical Dialogue in the British Enlightenment* (1996). *From Letter to Essay*, a genre-based rhetoric for college composition, derived in part from eighteenth-century educational models, is forthcoming.

LEONARD TENNENHOUSE is Professor of Comparative Literature, English, and Modern Culture and Media at Brown University. He is the author of *Power on Display: The Politics of Shakespeare's Genre* (1986) and (with Nancy Armstrong) *The Imaginary Puritan: Literature, Intellectual Labor, and the Origins of Personal Life* (1992), as well as two collections of essays coedited with Nancy Armstrong.

INDEX

Addison, Joseph, 121
Adventurer, 44
Aesthetics: idea of design and, 212; middle class and, 229; philosophical, 208, 218; theology and, 232–34; universal response and, 220, 225
Agency, 4, 15, 79
Alienation, 154–55
Allegory, 215, 217
Althusser, Louis, 21
Amsterdam, 236, 238–40
Anagram, 240
Analytical Review, 72
Anderson, Benedict, 13–24; *Imagined Communities*, 12–15
Anderson, Michael, 165
Anti-Jacobin Review, 76
Anti-Jacobins, 75, 115
Arnold, Matthew, 21–22
Audience: masculinity of, 206–8, 215, 218; unification of, 208–9
Austen, Jane, 25, 28, 161–62
Authority: maternal, 192; parental, 188, 196–98, 202; paternal, 179, 182
Authorship, 83–84

Baillie, Joanna, 69, 79
Baker, Polly, case of, 189–90
Bakhtin, Mikhail Mikhailovich. *See* Novelization
Barthes, Roland. *See* Detail, contingent
Bastardy, 183, 189–90. *See also* Legitimacy

Beaumarchais, Pierre-Augustin Caron, 173, 175, 183; *Le Barbier de Séville*, 173, 183–87, 196, 202; Countess (character), 193–96; dramatic criticism, 177–81; idea of nature, 197; issue of identity, 192; Marceline (character), 189–93, 198–99, 202; *Le Mariage de Figaro*, 173, 183–84, 187–93, 196, 202; *La Mère coupable*, 173, 183–84, 193–99, 201–2; performance of trilogy, 184
Beaumont, Sir Harry. *See* Spence, Joseph
Beauty: desire and, 219, 224–25; equated with virtue (truth), 222–23, 227; feminine, 209, 223, 225–29; genetics and, 228; ideal (absolute), 206–7, 209, 221–22, 226–27; judgment and, 210; judgment of, affected by climate, 228–29; market pressures on, 233; masculine, 223–24; Neoplatonism and, 217; politics (power) and, 222–23, 227; qualitative, 231; response to, 218–29; science of, 207–10, 227; signification and, 214–16
Behn, Aphra: *Dumb Virgin*, 163
Bentham, Jeremy. *See* Panopticon
Bildung (development), 88, 97, 100. See also *Wilhelm Meisters Lehrjahre*
Blake, William, 129–30
Blood, voice of, 160; confused with romantic love, 161, 163; disregard for, 163–64; natural law and, 161;

Library of Congress Cataloging-in-Publication Data
Eighteenth-century literary history : an MLQ reader / edited by Marshall
Brown.
   p. cm.
Includes index.
ISBN 0-8223-2135-1 (cloth : alk. paper).—ISBN 0-8223-2267-6 (pbk. : alk. paper)
1. European literature—18th century—History and criticism.
2. Europe—Intellectual life—18th century. I. Brown, Marshall.
PN751.E48 1999
809'.894'09033—dc21   98-29562